The World Tea Trade

By the same author:
The Oriental: Life Story of a West End Club
A Hundred Years of Ceylon Tea
Tiger of Mysore: the Life and Death of Tipu Sultan
Tea for the British
The Making of a Manor
Foursome in St James's

The World Tea Trade:
a Survey of the Production, Distribution and Consumption of Tea

Denys Forrest

Woodhead-Faulkner · Cambridge

First published in 1985 by Woodhead-Faulkner Ltd
Fitzwilliam House, 32 Trumpington Street, Cambridge CB2 1QY
and 51 Washington Street, Dover, NH 03820, USA

British Library Cataloguing in Publication Data

Forrest, Denys
 The world tea trade: a survey of the production,
 distribution and consumption of tea.
 1. Tea trade
 I. Title
 338.1'7372   HD9198.A2

 ISBN 0-85941-259-8

Library of Congress Cataloging in Publication Data

Forrest, Denys Mostyn.
 The world tea trade.

 Bibliography: p.
 Includes index.
 1. Tea trade. I. Title.
HD9198.A2F67 1985   338.1'7372   85-13844
ISBN 0-85941-259-8

Designed by Geoff Green
Typeset by Wvvern Typesetting Ltd, Bristol
                ınd in Great Britain by
                y Press, Bury St Edmunds, Suffolk

Contents

Appendices

Preface

The manuscript of this book was put into shape against a somewhat disconcerting background – the explosive rise in the auction price of tea in the opening days of 1984 which, among other things, made newspaper readers and television audiences of several continents familiar with the hitherto esoteric initials 'CTC'. It seemed an awkward moment to be formulating definitive pronouncements about the tea trade of the world, particularly since, looking back, one observes that when the work was commissioned several of the older tea-growing countries were resounding with complaints over rising costs and low returns – the threat of ruin, in fact.

As 1984 proceeded, the situation continued to evolve, and it would be rash to predict when, if at all, stability will be reached. But the whole episode may have left some people curious about this great industry and how it has come to operate in the way it does; if so, perhaps the present work is what they are looking for.

Nobody, of course, can hope to continue on the scale of the late W. H. Ukers (as described in the Prologue). Nevertheless, in a longer perspective, one would like to think of *The World Tea Trade* as completing a useful tetralogy of reference, in which the earlier elements were Sir Percival Griffiths' *History of the Indian Tea Industry* and this writer's own *A Hundred Years of Ceylon Tea* and *Tea for the British*. At any rate, that is the spirit in which it is offered.

As on previous occasions, it seems quite impracticable to name all the companies, still less all the individual men and women, connected in a hundred different ways with the tea trade world-wide, who have helped with information or advice or by constructive criticism of individual chapters or sections. The only alternative is not to name any of them, however reluctantly in the case of friends and colleagues of many years' standing, but simply to assure them of a most heartfelt 'thank you'.

Outside the strictly commercial circle, unstinted help has come from research institutes, Tea Councils (conspicuously that of the UK) and trade associations, many of which find mention in the text or notes; from the international bodies which concern themselves with tea today, including the various segments of the United Nations and of the EEC, established in New York, Geneva or Brussels; from the World Bank and other dispensers of aid; from government departments, in particular the British Ministry of Agriculture, Fisheries and Food; and from more specialised organisations such as the International Tea Promotion Association, the Commonwealth Secretariat and the European Tea Committee.

A debt which needs to be more specifically acknowledged is to the International Tea Committee, seated in London. All statistics, unless otherwise stated, are based on the Committee's *Monthly Statistical Summaries* and *Annual Bulletins of Statistics*. The Committee and its staff have been involved in the project from the start and it could hardly have been brought to fruition without them.

June 1985   D. M. F.

Note on conversions

Imperial measurements in the text can be converted to metric and vice versa, as follows:

1 metre = 3.281 feet	1 hectare = 2.471 acres
1 foot = 0.305 metres	1 acre = 0.405 hectares
1 kilometre = 0.621 miles	1 square kilometre = 0.386 square miles
1 mile = 1.609 kilometres	1 square mile = 2.590 square kilometres
1 kilogram = 2.205 pounds	
1 pound = 0.454 kilograms	

Prologue

The story of tea and tea-drinking, from legendary epochs of Old Cathay to the present time, is one that has often been told – in fact there has been in recent years quite a flood of pleasantly chatty accounts, originating on both sides of the Atlantic. Most writers naturally try to provide a fresh slant on the familiar facts or to dig up a few new ones, but as a rule they achieve only brief excursions from the well-worn path: 'History repeats itself – historians repeat one another.'

In the case of tea, indeed, as often as not they simply repeat William H. Ukers. This very remarkable man had been editor of the American *Tea and Coffee Trade Journal* for many years when, in 1935, he published his two-volume 'block-buster' under the challenging title *All About Tea*.[1] He tells us that it had been planned in a single volume, like his earlier book *All About Coffee*,[2] but that it was found impossible to 'do justice to the subject' within such constricting bounds. Twenty-five years before, he had made his first journey to the Orient and begun to collect materials: for 12 years he sorted and classified them; ten years more were occupied in the actual writing. Apart from chapters on tea in every possible context and dimension, the resulting 600,000 words embrace a chronology with over 500 dates, a dictionary with 500 definitions and a bibliography covering 2,000 authors and titles. Illustrations number over 1,700, including hundreds upon hundreds of thumbnail photographs of personalities, many of whom continued to haunt the *couloirs* of the world's tea trade until fairly recently. No wonder that the index swelled to no fewer than 10,000 entries or that the pay-off line in the 'blurb' to *All About Tea* was a triumphal 'Here is a book which will never need to be written again.'

Agreed, agreed . . . Yet one suspects that that 2,000-entry bibliography could be doubled if brought up to date to cover the past half-century. The present author has no intention of trying to rewrite Ukers – or even himself![3] This book has a narrower objective, to chart the production and distribution of tea in the modern world. But in order to make sense even of that, it is necessary to give a brief account, with or without Mr Ukers' help, of how the trade originated and took the very idiosyncratic form it did, and how all this is still traceable in the way it goes about its business.

Human beings have, for uncounted ages, mitigated the tedium of drinking pure water – and the dangers of the impure variety – by heating it to boiling point and steeping in it the leaves of various plants. Never more so than today, as a glance at the shelves of any delicatessen or health food store in either hemisphere will reveal. There, only too often, are to be found what should be described as 'infusions' or 'tisanes', wrongfully labelled 'tea'. Alas, the abuse of the word is well dug into the vocabulary even of tea-worshipping Britain – one has only to recall the 'camomile tea' with which Peter Rabbit's mother dosed him after his unfortunate safari into Mr MacGregor's garden. So let it be stated at the outset that in Standard ISO 3720 of 1977 the International Organisation of Standardisation laid it unequivocally on the line that Black tea is

derived solely and exclusively, and produced by acceptable processes, notably fermentation and drying, from the leaves, buds and tender stems of varieties of the species *Camellia sinensis* (Linnaeus) O. Kuntze, known to be suitable for making tea for consumption as a beverage.[4]

More will be said later about this Standard and its international status, but at least it is clear that tea, in the title of the present book, relates to the derivatives of *Camellia sinensis* and to them alone.

All the same, there is room for regret that, for highly technical reasons, the word *thea* has been banished from our nomenclature. Linnaeus himself favoured it at first, and even after a botanical congress in Amsterdam (1930) had given *Camellia sinensis* its imprimatur, leading agronomists in India and Indonesia remained for some time loyal to *Camellia thea* and *Camellia theifera* respectively.

However, the Chinese *Camellia* it has got to be, and it was in China, of course, that trading in tea, as an international phenomenon, originated. By the early sixteenth century, when a succession of travellers from Europe began to make mention of the plant, and more rarely to bring back specimens of its leaf, tea-drinking had been an established social habit all over China for at least 1,000 years – and perhaps twice that time. Considering that there had also been centuries of intercourse between the Celestial Empire and the West, on a variety of levels, one's only surprise is that it took so long for news of the wondrous and refreshing beverage to reach the outside world.

Both the Portuguese and the Dutch, but not at first the British, were involved in the beginnings of the trade. It was the Dutch who made up the earliest actual cargoes, and in the second half of the seventeenth century their

East India Company sent home sizeable quantities. At that stage (from about 1660 onwards), the corresponding English Company was picking up only odd parcels, more or less for their curiosity value.

However, our concern here is with the system which finally became established for transferring vast tonnages of tea from China, where it was grown, to the Western world, where it was so eagerly consumed.

Monopoly was the name of the game, and it remained so until less than 150 years ago. Monopoly by China as seller; would-be monopoly by the English East India Company as buyer and distributor. At the Eastern end, the system was a rigid one and quite astonishingly effective in its own terms. It was founded on the conviction, never more firmly held than by the Manchus who came to power in about 1644, that the Emperor of China was the only civilised ruler in the universe and that if the barbarian powers outside desired to approach him they must do so as suppliants. It followed that merchants, too, would be allowed in strictly on sufferance. What the Chinese government did was simply to designate Canton as the sole port which foreigners might use and then only under regulations which assured that no property could be acquired except on lease, that no individual should make more than seasonal visits and that no business should be done except through channels officially laid down. These channels eventually solidified into the celebrated consortium of China's authorised merchants, the 'Co-Hong'.

The English East India Company was only one of several companies whose 'factories' can be detected, lining the Canton waterfront, in many an old topographical print. At first the Company was, like the others, mainly interested in silk, with gold and spices as supplementary items, but by the second decade of the eighteenth century the people of Britain were rapidly developing their taste – their mania – for tea. From then onwards, to grab as much of this valuable crop as possible, at anyone else's expense, and to convey it to Europe in British bottoms, was the Company's overpowering preoccupation.

This tendency to regard other traders at Canton as interlopers was fuelled by the fact that much of the leaf being bought by Dutch, German or Scandinavian interests was, in fact, intended to compete, by fair means or foul, for the lucrative British market. An extreme case was the 'Ostend' Company, established for the supposed benefit of the Emperor's subjects in the Low Countries. It turned out that many of its ships were owned by London merchants and from about 1720 onwards there was a running battle between the English Company and the 'Ostenders', the former stopping at nothing to thwart the latter of their cargoes. The fight went on well into the middle of the century and was exacerbated as competition to smuggle tea into Britain rose to its peak, with the London men – disguised as Ostenders – cheerfully joining in!

This episode of the Ostend Company is well worth recording as an early instance of that 'undying resentment of the City of London merchants against monopoly, which has left a permanent mark on the character of the British tea trade'.[5]

However, once the company had got its tea home, monopoly triumphed once more and was not seriously undermined until 1836. The rule was that every chest must be auctioned at East India House, and one may wonder why it should have been so, when most other traders seemed able to operate quite happily through the normal machinery of commerce. But, of course, the East India Company was a quasi-government body – the oldest and grandest 'quango' of them all – and no doubt felt it was more prudent to dispose of its cargoes by 'public outcry' in the auction room than by private deals, with the rich scope for corruption which they afforded.

In fact, long before tea had become significant, auctions were regularly being held for the company's imports which, up to the end of the seventeenth century, consisted mainly of Oriental textiles, with spices and tea and miscellaneous bric-à-brac occupying just a day here and there. As tea gradually took over, the sale of other products in this way became obsolete and the famous quarterly tea auctions, with all their tedium and acrimony, continued as a unique phenomenon.

One reason for their staying power was that from very early days it was recognised that tea was not just *tea*, as nutmegs were nutmegs or cloves cloves, but an infinitely varied product, which needed to be sampled, graded and catalogued, almost literally chest by chest. The obvious way of establishing a satisfactory scale of values was in the auction room, where the 'outcry' was sometimes so vehement as to create panic among passers-by in Leadenhall Street. It should be mentioned that London was not the only place where it was found convenient to dispose of tea in this way; there was a parallel institution from very early times in Amsterdam.

As fully developed by about 1750, the East India Company's auction system closely resembled that still obtaining, though in a shrunken state, in the City of London and, subject to some modifications, in several of the most important countries of origin. At the end of a round voyage, which might last as long as four years and never less than two, the East Indiamen unshipped their cargoes along Thames-side. The tea chests were transferred to the 'Company's warehouses', at first attached or adjacent to East India House, but later proliferating until they reached their apogee in Cutler Street (the 5-acre complex off Bishopsgate, now partially dismantled). Samples were taken from each chest and submitted to the Company's 'tasters and smellers', who graded them according to a classification which grew ever more elaborate. Huge, fat catalogues were then issued and on the appointed date the brokers[6] and their clients, the tea merchants, would turn up at East India House and for four gruelling days the bidding for the countless lots continued. As usual, monopoly was under fire, and the trade (headed as a rule by the Mr Twining of the day) missed no opportunity of arraigning the Company for alleged sharp practice.

Bids were 'by the candle'. This did not mean that the disposal of every single lot had to wait until an inch (or whatever) of candle had burned down; a successful bidder could take up subsequent lots until there was a significant variation in type or quality. A relic of this is the convention whereby the purchaser of a lot is still invited to bid first for the next one, if comparable.

So the great caravan rolled on, and to many it must have seemed that the East India Company had a heaven-bestowed right to sell 'all the tea in China' to British consumers – and to foreigners as well – in perpetuity. The Company even survived the trauma of losing most of its North American market following the Boston Tea Party (1773), itself precipitated by the choice of the American colonies as a dumping ground for a temporary glut of leaf.

But other events were incubating which would change the face of the world's tea trade for ever. That second great monopoly, the Chinese, was beginning to crumble at the edges. Opium, not tea, was the cause. The East India Company's finances had always been embarrassed by the need, forced on it by the Manchu government, of paying for its tea in silver bullion. The directors felt, rightly or wrongly, that if they had been allowed normal commercial access to the ports and trading stations of China, they could have earned this quite easily. As it was, they looked around for some other means of meeting their tea bills. Unfortunately, the opium poppy was already being extensively grown in eastern India and the product even being auctioned there by the Company, which then turned a blind eye when the opium was smuggled into China with the connivance of corrupt mandarins. By the 1830s, all this was generating an impossible tension *vis-à-vis* the Chinese authorities, who were perfectly aware that the Company was giving countenance to activities by British shippers which were deeply injurious to the health and morale of the people of China.

It happened that in 1834 a renewal of the Company's Charter was due. Among other things, its tea monopoly came under close scrutiny and, though the directors put up a stout defence, the spirit of the age was all against them and the opposing merchants (especially in the 'out-ports' – Glasgow, Liverpool, Bristol – always jealous of London) took full advantage of the fact. A bill providing that the Company should cease to trade was introduced into Parliament and received the Royal Assent on 28 August 1833.

The immediate, visible result was the end of the auctions at East India House and their prompt resurrection under the tea trade's own management in the ambience of Mincing Lane and even, for a time, in the out-ports.

But by then, monopoly was receiving its second quietus, further east. Parenthetically, tea-growing had never, since very remote times, been unique to China. Its origins in Japan are lost in much the same mists of antiquity, but long before the Co-Hong system was established at Canton the Japanese had been trading in tea. It was, in fact, from their island of Hirado that the Dutch East India Company sent home its very first shipment in 1610. Japan was again the source of the seeds used in experimental plantings some 74 years later in Java, though without permanent results at the time. But for political barriers, the West might well have turned to Japan when seeking to break the Chinese stranglehold.

As it happened, the drama followed a different course. The crucial initiative was taken by the British government. In default of Japan, anyone wishing to grow tea – and by the late eighteenth century a lot of people were thinking about it – had to envisage obtaining seeds and plants (openly or by stealth) from China. In a remarkable report to the East India Company in 1788 the great botanist, Sir Joseph Banks, even suggested that tea-growers from the Province of Honan might be persuaded to embark 'their shrubs, their tools of culture and themselves' at Canton and come to work in a nursery in the Calcutta Botanical Gardens. The mandarins would surely have had a word to say about that!

More practically, Banks identified North-east India as a region whose soil might well be congenial to the tea plant. This was recalled when, with the Company's monopoly extinct in 1834, the British government decided, as a matter of policy, to reduce the home country's dependence on China by setting up a tea industry within its own territories. The location chosen was Assam: it was in the zone indicated by Sir Joseph and had problems which the Governor-General, Lord William Bentinck, thought tea might help to solve. Assam had been acquired, reluctantly, ten years before as a result of the Second Burma War; it was turbulent and very poor and there was a chance that the new industry might stabilise it.

Inevitably, plots were hatched to acquire Chinese planting material, and in spite of all obstacles sufficient batches of seed were obtained for nurseries to be set up in Assam, and in South India as well.

The fact that the tea plant (or, rather, tree) had already been found growing happily in the depths of the Upper Assamese forest somehow escaped official notice. But since then the story of the discoveries between 1823 and 1831 by C. A. Bruce and his brother Robert, the independent sightings by Lieutenant Andrew Charlton and the claims and counter-claims to which the whole episode gave rise, have become perhaps the most familiar of tea sagas – barring the Boston Tea Party and the Clipper Race of 1866 – and will not be rehashed here. Two points only call for emphasis: most agronomists do not now believe that the extensive 'tea tracts' found represented genuine 'wild tea', but were more likely the remains of ancient tribal plantings; and the leaves they yielded were of a variety far better suited to the Black tea market of the future than the old China sorts.[7] It took time – and some desperate merchant-venturing – for their claims to be asserted, but as the century advanced 'China or Indian?' became a well-understood choice around the tea tables of Britain.

Reverting to the 1830s, it is to be regretted that at a moment when the Kingdom of Tea (as Ukers liked to call it) was so rapidly extending its borders no corresponding 'tea tracts' were found elsewhere in India or, for that matter, beyond the seas. The China *jat*, kept more or less under subjection in Assam, got a head start in South India, having a considerable influence on the earliest plantings in Travancore and the Nilgiris, though by the time production was fully established there in the 1860s it was mainly from Assam seed.

Java and Sumatra were also 'colonised' by the China *jat*, with some possible dilution from Japan. The story is complex, not to say confused, but it can be said that from about 1830 until as late as 1878, when a British teaman, John Peet, promoted the importation of Assam seed, the then 'Netherlands East Indies' were producers of a somewhat 'down-market' version of 'China tea'.

In Ceylon (now Sri Lanka), when the fungus disease *Hemileia vastatrix* began to undermine her great coffee industry in the 1860s and a new crop was sought, it was for a short time neck-and-neck between China and Assam as the favoured source for seeds and plants. A complicating factor was that during the coffee era the tea sold in the shops came from China, not India, and it was something 'as like China tea as possible' that the famous pioneer, James Taylor, aimed to produce on his estate of Loolecondera. However, as in Java and Sumatra, the requirements of the European, and particularly the British, market ensured that in Ceylon, too, Assam would eventually come out on top.

As to less familiar territories, China seedlings were imported into the southern United States from 1795 onwards, 'shrubs' – and even skilled workers – from China are said to have reached Brazil as early as 1812 and, generally speaking, most of the very numerous experimental plantings in the first half of the nineteenth century were China-orientated.

The world-wide progress and prospects of *Camellia sinensis* will be charted in subsequent chapters. But first, a more detailed look at the plant in its modern setting and at the interrelation between the way it is grown and processed and the ever-increasing demand for 'a nice cup of tea'.

Part one
Growers and Exporters

1 New Ways in Field and Factory

As the Prologue suggests, the tea-planter today is the inheritor of a most ancient tradition; his task is to adapt it to the needs of a market which is changing more rapidly and drastically than in any previous epoch.

It is both an advantage and a drawback that his basic material is so tough, enduring and weather-resistant. There will be no table in this book equivalent to the memorable one in Mr C. F. Marshall's *The World Coffee Trade*, where he lists all the 'registered' frosts in Brazil since 1882 and grades them for intensity.[1] Nor, with one possible exception (see page 13), has tea in general ever been seriously threatened by disease or by an insect pest.

The tea plant

What the planter has under his care is not a mere bush (though it will be convenient to use that term), but a forest tree with an exceedingly sturdy stem and – if grown from seed, as it always was until recently – a deep tap-root. So long-lived is it that much of the original tea planted in Sri Lanka about 100 years ago is believed to be still in bearing. An article on the somewhat parlous condition of gardens in the Nazira Circle, Assam, goes further, stating that 'most of the mature trees . . . which contribute a major portion of the total yield, were planted about 130–145 years ago'.[2] That is an extreme case, but a count made in India in 1978 showed that the number of bushes over 50 years old varied from 31.6% in Assam up to 53.7% in West Bengal and 55.2% in Kerala. Bushes approaching 100 years old are common in Darjeeling.

Such longevity at least implies an assured investment, and looking over a well-kept carpet of tea it is easy to imagine it continuing to yield its harvest for ever. Given a careful routine of soil conservation and nutrition, a percentage of diseased or superannuated bushes replaced every year, generations of managers and workers can pass by without the smallest visible change becoming apparent in that particular field. The same is likely to apply, broadly, to the layout of the entire estate or garden. (*Estate* is the term in widest use today, though India still likes to talk of *gardens*.) The layout may have been far from ideal in the first place and may have become increasingly uneconomic by today's stern standards, but the cost of any major replanning and replanting – including an inevitable break in production – would be astronomical. So what happens if, for example, conventional plucking should become so expensive or labour for it so scarce that mechanisation (see page 17) is the only solution? It is hard to imagine any old estate, as traditionally planned, being able to meet that challenge.

But to start with, the tea bush (or tree) itself. We saw in the Prologue how *Camellia sinensis* has at last been accepted as a single species, but comprising two main varieties, the China and the Assam. To these is usually added a third, the Indo-China or Cambodia form. Planters have sub-divided the Assam itself into several *jats*, but the essential difference is between them and the China variety, characterised by its divided stem and small frost-resistant leaves. There has been much hybridisation and in Sri Lanka, for example, it is often possible to detect numerous variations, and consequent uneven bush yields, within an individual field.[3]

Cultivation and harvesting

Left to itself, as is well known, the tea tree will soar to a height approaching 12–14 m. Its original habitat was almost certainly sub-tropical forest, subject to heavy monsoon rains. Where it meets such conditions, it tends to go dormant in the comparatively cool, dry winters, with their shorter hours of sunshine, then to produce a rich 'flush' of shoots and leaves. Where there is little seasonal variation of temperature – Sri Lanka and parts of Africa are examples – plucking can and does go on throughout the year.

All this, of course, depends on pruning. Pruning has three objectives: to keep the bush in a vegetative (as distinct from a reproductive) phase – no flowers or seeds allowed; to form a 'frame' on which the flush will rapidly regenerate; and to maintain the upper surface, or 'plucking table', at a convenient level. As Dr Eden remarks:

Pruning is still more of an art than a science, because the physiology of the tea bush is still very imperfectly understood . . . There is no single aspect of tea cultivation that is so controversial as that of pruning.[4]

Not a subject, in other words, to generalise upon in a brief summary like the present!

Given that under most estate conditions plucking has to be carried out every seven days or so (at longer intervals, of course, in cooler regions of comparatively slow growth), it is obvious that here lies the most serious element of cost. With the number of pluckers averaging perhaps 1.5 per hectare, they can represent up to 70% of the whole labour force and their wages amount to 60% of cultivation costs or 40% of estate expenses as a whole.[5]

Everywhere in the plantation industries wages will continue to rise (as often as not, well in advance of the legal minima); in India they have increased more than twice as fast as output over the past decade. And, since hand-plucking represents a more or less irreducible element of expense, there is a constant need to economise elsewhere. An example is 'cultivation' – the hacking up of the soil around the bushes by men armed with hoes or similar implements. This used to be a regular part of estate routine. It was meant to keep down the weeds as well as to 'aerate the soil' – what it mainly did, in fact, was to damage the roots of the tea bush, which tends to be a topsoil feeder. It is now realised that it is far better to provide *Camellia sinensis* with something approaching its natural 'forest floor' by letting prunings (even quite heavy branches) and leaf-fall lie and leaving soil and roots undisturbed. This in itself tends to discourage weeds, at least a hundred species of which make themselves at home on tea estates. Even though, as Dr Eden sadly remarks, 'their ecology is such that, almost always, they have the advantage in proliferation over the crop in which they grow',[6] modern herbicides can effectively complete the job of control. The new methods have had a dramatic effect on yields in recent times.

The 'forest floor' technique also discourages the leaching-away of the fertilisers which are so essential to keep production at a high level, especially on old tea land. Nitrogen, with phosphates and potassium in support, is still the stand-by, and applications of the 'NPK' mix may rise to the equivalent of 200 kg of nitrogen per hectare in some areas. The idea that manuring stimulates flush at the expense of the rest of the bush is a fallacy.

Another element in keeping the tea bush in good productive heart is, of course, to protect it from pests and diseases. Fortunately, few of the former can be regarded as lethal and perhaps the worst of them, such as Red Spider in Assam and the Shot-hole Borer beetle[7] in Sri Lanka, can be kept fairly well at bay by prophylactic measures; sudden plagues like the wholesale descent of Looper Caterpillars of some luckless Assam estate, which can threaten a complete stripping on the crop, have to be dealt with as they arise. One estimate is that in spite of all precautions these various pests account for a loss of up to 10% of production in the older tea countries. Africa, on the whole, is comparatively free from them.

Among the diseases of the tea bush, the most difficult to contend with is perhaps Blister Blight (*Exobasidium vexans*). Of spasmodic occurrence almost everywhere, the dense monoculture of central Sri Lanka has given it particular encouragement and soon after World War II there were those who feared it might do to tea what *Hemileia vastatrix* did to Sri Lankan coffee; however, copper sprays and other fungicides now provide an effective control.

Increasing the yield – clonal tea

Reasons of cost, and more particularly the pressure of demand on land for other purposes, make it unlikely that in most parts of the tea world (excluding perhaps China) there will be any further significant increase in the area devoted to the crop. Somewhat ambitious 'projections' for India, and the problems concerning these projections, are discussed in the following chapter: East Africa may also see some limited extensions of hectarage. But the need to make maximum use of every existing hectare is paramount. When an individual bush is beginning to show its age it can either be dealt with summarily by eradication and replacement or it can be given a rest. This can be done by pruning it severely and letting it lie fallow, so to speak, for up to 12 months, at the end of which its yield should more than compensate for what has been lost in the meantime.

However, the main emphasis today is on in-filling and replanting with the best available material. For more than a quarter of a century teamen have been familiar with the principle of *clonal propagation*, that is, the use of leaf cuttings instead of seed, and with the advantages of uniformity and high yield which this method offers. The actual statistics of the operation are not yet imposing. To give one example, according to the International Tea Committee,[8] cumulative replacements and replantings in North and South India between 1970 and 1980 covered some 15,000 ha out of a planted area which grew from 356,000 to 380,000 ha over the same period. Yet the fact that India as a whole managed to increase her annual production from 418,000 tonnes per annum to 569,000 during the decade must be attributed in part at least to the higher yield of clonal tea. Another contributory factor has been closer planting – as much as 12,000 bushes per hectare is an acceptable modern standard and this in itself helps to discourage weed growth.

Everywhere, research institutes are developing new clones and releasing them, when proven, to the industry. Nevertheless, notes of caution have been sounded. Much clonal tea is more sensitive to drought than tea from seed, because it lacks a tap-root, so that there is a tendency today to establish seed nurseries from clonal stocks, thereby obtaining – hopefully – the best of both worlds. There are also warnings against 'excessive uniformity' in the use of clones, since this might eliminate genetic material which could be of great value.

Trends in manufacture

For obvious reasons, it has been easier for the spirit of innovation to make progress in the factory than in the field and it is there that the interplay with the demands of the market is most sharply visible. Some results of that interplay must now be noted.

Traditional processes

From the earliest times, tea manufacture consisted essentially of five processes, pursued with stately deliberation. The green leaf, when weighed and brought into the factory, was spread by hand on hessian shelves or 'tats' and left there to *wither* for anything up to 20 hours. After that it was gathered up again in baskets and given a series of *rolls* on circular, flat-bed machines, designed not only to 'rupture the leaf-cells and release the juices and enzymes' (in the time-honoured phrase), but also to reproduce mechanically the 'twist' imparted by hand-rolling in Old Cathay.

Next the leaf was spread out, again by hand, to *ferment*, or more accurately to oxidise slightly, in rooms of appropriate humidity and temperature. It was then gathered up once more for insertion into the *drier*, where trays mounted on an endless chain carried it over hot air from the furnace. And so at last it emerged as the crisp, black, aromatic substance beloved of every tea-drinker, and was ready to be *sifted* and *graded* into sizes, the names of which mostly derived from, though bearing little relation to, the ancient Chinese nomenclature.

Modern processing methods

The aim today is to convert what has always been essentially a batch process into, as nearly as possible, a continuous or conveyor-belt one. Changes have been made at every stage. Hessian withering tats are out; various alternatives have been tried, but the *trough* has come out on top. In this, air is blown through the leaf from a fan at one end and the withering process is reduced from 20 to 16 or to as little as 12 hours. Incidentally, this speeding up of the wither is held to account for a marked lessening of the traditional loss of quality in what North India, for obvious reasons, calls 'rains teas'.

It is at the next stage, rolling, that the influence of the market is felt most strongly. Throughout the Western world (much less, so far, in the Middle East) there has been a trend towards quicker-brewing, small-leaf blends. It can be charted in the increasing popularity – and price – of the Fannings grades, which at one time were the poor relations, and recently of the Dusts. More potent, if anything, has been the influence of the teabag. Here, appearance counts for little and the smaller the leaf the better, so long as it does not seep through the perforations, where that type of teabag paper is used. The smallest Dusts are therefore unsuitable.

So the modern rolling objective has been a small leaf and an accelerated process. The first step was the creation, as far back as 1930, of McKercher's CTC ('cutting, tearing, curling') machine, in which ridged, cylindrical rollers revolve at different speeds. It made a slow start and one remembers the shocked disapproval which demonstrations sometimes evoked, even after World War II. But CTC swept on and today it can be said to dominate production in India, Bangladesh and most of the African and other 'new' territories in various parts of the world. Only in Sri Lanka, Indonesia and China, among major producers, does the out-turn remain overwhelmingly Orthodox (see Table 1.1).

CTC itself now has a rival in LTP (Lawrie tea processor), which, in fact, pulverises the leaf with a hammer, amid considerable uproar, and is both simple and space-saving. Both machines can be operated in conjunction with the Rotorvane, which may best be described as a 'preconditioner' with a mincing-machine action. It was developed by Ian McTair in the 1950s, in conjunction with Assam's great Tocklai Research Institute.

Table 1.1 CTC and Orthodox manufacture ('000 tonnes)

	1977		1982		1983	
	CTC	OTH	CTC	OTH	CTC	OTC
North India	301	122	337	92	375	93
South India	49	80	63	60	60	55
Total	350	202	400	152	435	148
Bangladesh	17	21	29	11	31	12
Sri Lanka	–	209	–	188	–	179
Indonesia	–	63	–	74	–	93
China (Mainland)	–	63	–	69	–	68
Taiwan	–	1	–	3	–	4
Iran	–	24	–	23	–	23
Japan	–	–	–	–	–	–
Malaya	–	4	–	3	–	3
Turkey	–	78	–	68	–	70
Total Asia	367	665	429	591	466	600
Burundi	1	–	2	–	2	–
Cameroon	1	–	2	–	2	–
Kenya	82	4	95	1	119	1
Malawi	32	–	38	–	32	–
Mauritius	5	–	5	–	6	–
Mozambique	–	17	–	21	–	15
Rwanda	5	–	7	–	7	–
South Africa	4	–	7	–	7	–
Tanzania	17	–	16	–	16	–
Uganda	15	–	2	–	3	–
Zaïre	6	1	5	–	5	–
Zimbabwe	7	–	11	–	11	–
Total Africa	175	22	190	22	210	16
USSR	–	106	–	140	–	143
Argentina	–	22	–	37	–	37
Brazil	8	–	10	–	10	–
Ecuador	1	–	2	–	2	–
Peru	–	3	–	3	–	3
Total South America	9	25	12	40	12	40
Papua New Guinea	5	–	8	–	8	–
Grand total	556	818	639	793	696	799

Note: Estimated figures are in italics.
Source: International Tea Committee.

At the present time, one may find all three machines being used in varying combinations. It should be added, however, that even in India, where CTC represented over 75% of output in 1983, Orthodox leaf still finds a lively market and, in fact, some factories have had to reinstate their conventional rollers for a dual manufacture process – perhaps 25% Orthodox, 75% CTC.

CTC has, of course, had a drastic effect on grading. As Appendix 1 shows, it produces a severely limited range, in which Pekoe Fannings and Pekoe Dust predominate.

Driers have not been exempt from change. The continuous tray drier has already had quite a run and is being largely replaced by the fluid bed drier, in which the fermented leaf particles are desiccated in a suspension of hot air, and which is reported to give a made tea output more than twice that of the old-time apparatus.

One result of the summary treatment to which the leaf is now subjected is that extra care has to be taken to keep it free from fibrous and other extraneous material. This can only too easily clog the incredibly high-speed teabag machinery of the present day. Thus the stalk-extractor plays an increasingly important role; in fact, one hears of an African factory, recently rebuilt after a fire, where the machinery section consists simply of a couple of LTPs, a continuous fermenting unit, a fluid bed drier and a positive battery of stalk-extractors.

Mechanical harvesting

The substitution of some form of mechanism for the human finger and thumb in plucking tea goes back more than half a century. Specially designed shears with a bag attachment were in widespread use in Japan between the wars, while Ukers noted (1935) that 'the world's first plucking machine, constructed by Sadovsky' had recently been tested in Georgian Russia and had shown excellent results.[9]

The objective, of course, has always been to speed up plucking and to economise in labour. It was estimated that whereas a Japanese hand-plucker could bring in no more than 25 kg of green leaf per day, a woman with shears could pluck 100–125 kg and a man 150 kg. One pioneer Russian machine (not Sadovsky's, apparently) could cover $3\frac{3}{4}$ acres in 10 hours, as against 30 hours for hand labour.

Mechanisation has gone far since those days, but the objectives remain the same. It follows that there is no particular incentive to mechanise where labour is plentiful, and there is a positive disincentive where jobs are scarce and governments look to the tea estates to provide employment.

So, apart from the special case of the USSR (where the original impulse may have come from post-revolutionary tractor-worship), we find the main thrust towards mechanisation almost entirely in certain comparatively minor producing territories in which tea has to compete for workers with other more important crops and/or high-wage industries. Such territories include South

Africa, Nigeria, Mauritius, Malaysia, Papua New Guinea, Australia and (on a larger scale) Argentina. There is limited mechanisation on individual estates in Kenya and Mozambique and another 'special case' is Uganda, where it seems that machines will have to take the place of the pluckers who have disappeared (see page 86).

The field is one where experiment continues to be rife, but the fundamental division is still between the hand-held apparatus and the wheeled or tracked vehicle. Dr Ellis has recently given an interesting description of the hand-held apparatus, as operated on Bois Cheri Estate, Mauritius.[10] Here Japanese Kawasaki machines are used, 'motorised, with reciprocating cutter bar and air blast, which takes the cut leaf into the receiving sack', the width of the cut being about 39 in. Three persons work as a team, of whom one supports each end of the machine as they move along the row. The team reckons to cover 2 acres in about 4½ hours and to harvest 500 kg in a day. Machines of this type are in fairly widespread use; at Mambilla in Nigeria the present target is 300 kg per day, against 36 kg by hand-plucking.

It happens, however, that the same Mauritius estate provided Dr Ellis with an example of fully mechanised plucking. For this, use is made of the tractor designed for vineyards by the Bobard Company of Beaune in France, but already making a notable impact in the tea world. This is essentially a straddling machine with half-tracks and a diesel engine; the details of the reciprocating cutter mechanism, conveyors, leaf hoppers, etc., are a matter for the individual user. Not unlike the 'Bobard' is the Australian 'Teahawk', while another straddling machine is the Japanese 'Valiant', reported to be doing very well in Papua New Guinea.

Finally, there are the real heavyweights – giant machines such as those used in the USSR, and the 'Tea Harvester', developed by the British firm of Cab-Craft and operated by Messrs Mitchell-Cotts, first at Nandi in Kenya and now on their rehabilitated Ugandan estates. This machine has a variable track width, can cover two rows of bushes at a time and can carry out a number of ancillary tasks such as manuring and spraying. It is reckoned to pluck at a rate of 10 ha per day, a task which would normally require 150 men, and one machine can take care of more than 100 ha on a 15 to 20-day plucking cycle. Output of green leaf is about three times the 220 kg per hour claimed for a typical Russian machine.

Two points inevitably arise: can mechanical harvesting be applied to tea fields not specifically planted for it and what sort of quality results? As to the former, the hand-held machine is obviously more versatile than the tractor, though the Cab-Craft machine can apparently cope with some fairly unpromising layouts. To operate with maximum efficiency, however, most tractors really require hedge-type planting and no more than a gently undulating surface. A further limitation is that the rows should run up and down the contours (which is against anti-erosion doctrine), as any marked lateral gradient may cause instability.

As to quality, it is obvious that no mechanical harvester can be truly selective, though the Russian machines apparently have rubber 'fingers' which on the first pluck snap off the shoots instead of cutting the leaves. It is argued, however, that any bush mechanically plucked soon develops a good, even 'table' from which the shoots spring and, provided the cutter operates cleanly,the leaf gets to the factory in creditable condition and well suited to modern manufacturing methods.

What happens next? Well, we owe to Australia (see page 175) the example of an estate where 140 ha are in bearing and all the field and factory work is done by just 23 men.

2 The Indian Sub-continent

India

The world today is humming with 'plans', 'targets' and 'projections'. Tea is particularly subject to them. Perhaps it is just as well, since they at least set the various sectors of a somewhat fragmented industry thinking about its future – for example, the likely long-term demand for the product and ways of meeting competition from other beverages.

Prospects for expansion

One plan/target/projection which has been widely publicised in recent years relates to production levels in India. When it first became current about 1977, it envisaged output rising from a then 556,000 tonnes approximately, to 1,400,000 tonnes by the year 2000 and exports to at least 400,000 tonnes; the balance would be absorbed by the country's ever-growing domestic market.

This figure of 1,400,000 tonnes emerged as a sequel to the National Tea Seminar held in 1976, at which a rather less ambitious target of 1,000 million tonnes had been adumbrated. The higher aim was later endorsed by the 1978 Tandon Committee,[1] and has now attained a certain authority.

The Indian industry up to the present day has certainly shown remarkable powers of expansion, often in adverse circumstances. During the decade 1970–80, while the area under tea increased by less than 5% (356,000 ha to 380,000 ha), production rose by more than one-third (418,000 tonnes to 569,000 tonnes). Subsequent crop figures were well below that peak and the 1983 yield of 589,000 tonnes still fell short of the 650,000 which Tandon envisaged for 1982. With the stimulus of high prices, however, that target was virtually reached in 1984, when the all-India figure was 645,300 tonnes.

This was mainly due to South India boosting its output from an exceptionally low 115,225 tonnes in 1983 to a record 148,600.

So what chance is there for any sustainable rise from now on? Looking at the possible options, one thinks first of additional tea fields being set out where *Camellia sinensis* already abounds and where the labour and the skills to cultivate it are already mobilised. But up until now, prospects for that have been poor. The authorities have given little encouragement to more land being taken over in the existing tea zones; in fact, the reverse, since several State governments, in the interests of land reform, have appropriated peripheral tracts which could have been used for extensions. So far, there has been no indication of these being returned and though various official statements during 1983 and 1984 showed a much more understanding attitude to this and other practical problems of increasing production, it has to be remembered that once land has been given to others to inhabit and develop, it is extremely difficult to recover it.

However, thought is also being given to possible new developments in non-traditional locations. For this, the target is 25,000 ha during the current plan period. One such project is in the Keonjhar district of Orissa where, it is reported, 1,000 ha of land have been identified as having a 'hospitable soil and climate for tea'. Orissa is, of course, one of the regions from which the tea garden labour of India was originally drawn. The scheme would include extensive tree-planting, which, in addition to its function as shade, would benefit a district denuded of its natural forest growth.

It is somewhat relevant that Keonjhar, as a location, was only a second choice; the environmentalists – as vocal in India as anywhere else – had already chased the project out of another area where it was regarded as a threat to the local wildlife. Exactly the same problem has arisen in Tamil Nadu (see page 28). Just one indication that to start growing tea *de novo* may not be such a simple solution as it sounds.[2] Ironically, the tea industry can claim, and with justice, that, 'far from causing any pollution or environmental hazard, tea plantations have actually helped in preventing soil erosion and maintaining an ecological balance'.[3]

Such projects as these have another purpose – to provide employment. It was estimated that the Orissa enterprise would ensure all-the-year-round jobs for nearly 3,000 workers and the full 25,000 ha national programme would provide jobs for some 70,000. Here again one is reminded that a little-publicised service rendered to India by the existing industry is, in fact, the provision of stable employment, much of it in otherwise underdeveloped regions of the country. It has been estimated that up to a million jobs are directly dependent on tea and countless others indirectly; still more workers benefit from the industry's over Rs4,000 million annual earnings in foreign exchange.[4]

Reverting to targets, one falls back on the 'yield per hectare' factor as the most hopeful in promoting growth. India ranks well below some of the

African countries in that particular league; nevertheless, an overall rise from about 1,100 kg per hectare to an average of 1,500 kg between 1968 and 1978 was an impressive feat. The crucial element in all this has been the programme of in-filling, replanting and (in the 1950s and 1960s) some extension with clonal material, though according to official figures it has not involved 10% of India's tea lands (36,600 ha out of 380,000 ha) during the past decade. The government's Seventh Plan, covering the years 1985–89, envisages a rapid speeding up of this programme. If it could be achieved the Indian crop would rise spectacularly, since like other traditional tea countries India does not lack areas of worn-out soil and superannuated bushes. Until recently, apart from a useful planting subsidy, the incentives for such an 'explosion' hardly existed, but there is already evidence that profits from the recent price rise are being channelled into vigorous modernisation on many gardens.

It is not proposed to enter here into the hotly contested argument about what has been called the 'irrational and capricious' taxation of the Indian tea industry, though it obviously has a crucial bearing on the climate for future expansion. There has been some relief from excise duties, but national and state taxes totalling as much as 67%, against only 56% for other enterprises, are claimed to be inequitable and in a good year the surcharge on profits can push the average rate up still further. Add the steadily rising price of labour and of such essential inputs as fertilisers and pesticides, and it can be understood why tea costs more per kilogram to produce in India than anywhere else in the world.

Producing regions
Assam

Before exploring further the current situation we ought at least to take a glance at the geographical layout of the great Indian tea industry. As we saw in the Prologue, Assam was identified very early as an ideal location for the new enterprise, and Assam today still stands supreme for the quantity and quality of its Black tea. Geographically, what we mean by 'Assam' is in essence the broad, almost flat valley through which the Brahmaputra river makes it slow way from the Himalayas towards the Bay of Bengal. In the seven districts – Darrang, Goalpara, Kamrup, Lakhimpur, Dibrugarh, Now-gong and Sibsagar – some 168,000 ha are under tea on about 655 estates (many of them grouped) and the yield per hectare is well above the national average. Here is one of tea's mightiest heartlands, and though in this chapter space has had to be found for certain less celebrated territories, one must never forget for a moment that in an average year close on half of India's total production comes from this single source. No wonder that for millions of people in the outside world 'Indian tea' and 'Assam tea' are often synonymous terms.

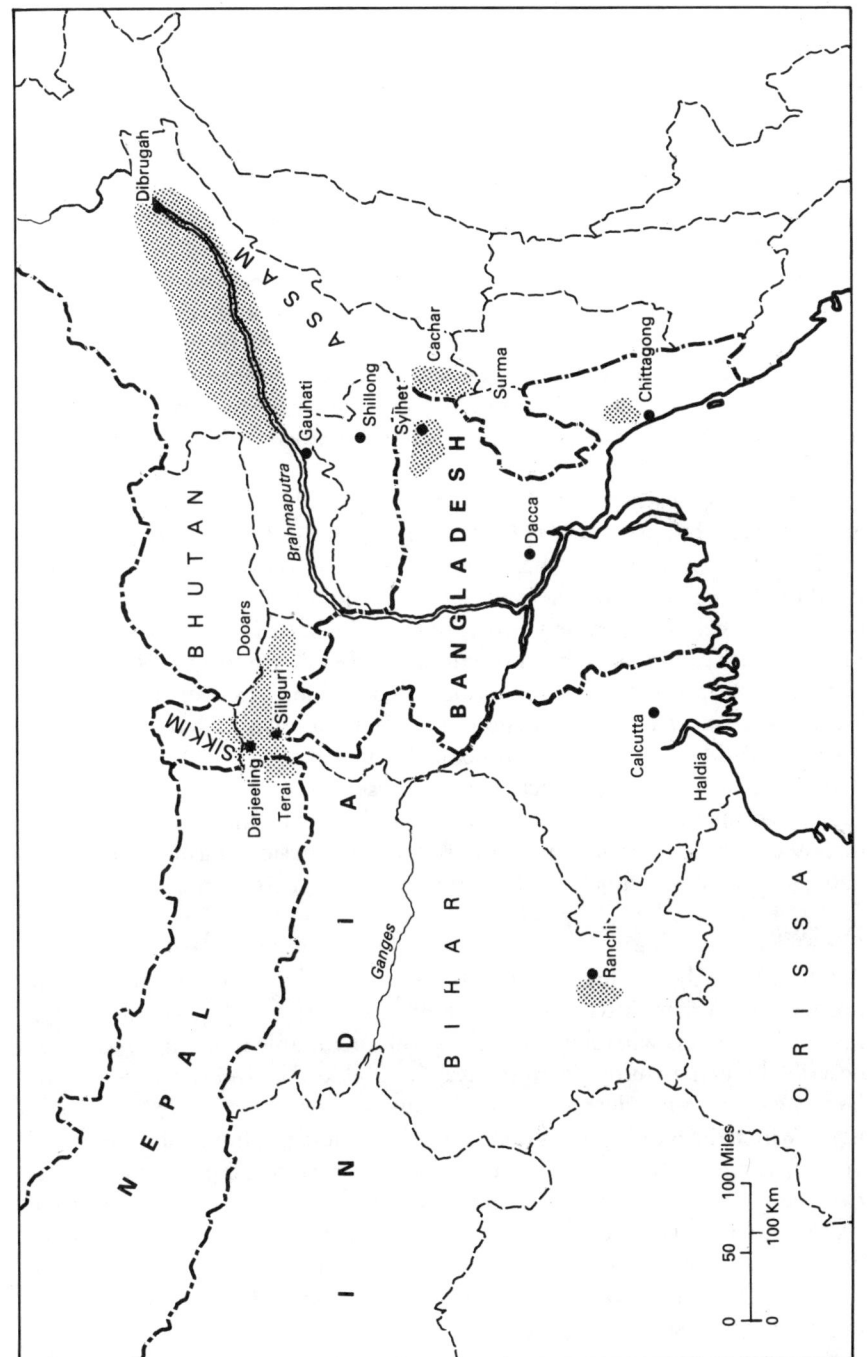

Tea-planting districts of North-east India

Cachar

Linked to the Brahmaputra's basin is that of the Surma, further to the south-east, with its two tea districts of Cachar and Sylhet. While the former remains in India, the latter (along with a smaller area near Chittagong) in 1947 became part of East Pakistan, now Bangladesh. The separation of these long-time 'twins' is symbolic of what has happened to tea, as to so much else in the Indian sub-continent, as the result of partition.

The rise of the Assam tea industry is part of history (see the Prologue) and need not be enlarged upon here; Cachar's is less well known. As in certain parts of South India, and, of course, in Sri Lanka, the planting enterprise began with coffee, which in the 1840s was reported to be luxuriant and of high quality. However, it was shouldered aside when 'indigenous' tea was found growing quite extensively on Cachar's characteristic *teelas*, or jungle hillocks.

From 1855 onwards, land was taken up with an enthusiasm which amounted to a boom and today Cachar has about 31,700 ha under tea – 10% of the area in all North India, though providing only 7% of the output. Neither the climate nor the soil was ever quite as ideal as those early enthusiasts believed; among other things, the *teelas* are an obstacle to replanting on economic lines. A recent Indian Tea Board survey found a level of vacancies approaching 60% on many gardens and 43% of the surviving bushes were more than 50 years old. Rehabilitation would have to take the form of subsidised replanting with clonal material.

It is not surprising that Cachar tea (almost all CTC) fetches lower prices than its competitors at auction, though in point of fact three-quarters of it is disposed of by ex-factory (what the British or American farmer calls 'farm gate') sales, giving a quicker return and sometimes better prices.

Darjeeling

A tally of North-east Indian tea will not be complete without crossing the border from Assam into adjacent West Bengal. Darjeeling! It needs a book in itself. The process whereby a 'worthless, uninhabitable mountain', as it was described when acquired from the Rajah of Sikkim in 1835, was converted into one of the tea industry's most precious assets is an epic story. The only use to which the Indian government thought it could put this chilly, damp and virtually unpopulated patch of Himalayan forest, some 20 miles square, was to serve as a 'sanatorium' for refugees from the hot weather plains. Yet within six years, China *jat* seedlings were being set out at a height of over 7,000 ft, with more to follow lower down. Immigrant labour poured in from Nepal, Sikkim and Bhutan, roads and bazaars were built and a 'simple system of administering justice' was set up.

By about 1870 the classic North-east Indian seasonal pattern of the Darjeeling crop was recognisable – the 'first flush' in March when the bushes woke from their long winter dormancy, the still more prestigious 'second flush' in May–June and, after the less distinguished interlude of the 'rains', the choice 'autumnal flush' in October.

The inevitable question is: what gives Darjeeling tea, at its best, its unique flavour and aroma, compared by some to that of muscatel grapes? Slow growth at high elevations is universally associated with flavour in tea, but, for the late Dr Harler and others who have studied the subject, the particular type of China/Assam hybrid with which Darjeeling was originally planted is mainly responsible.[5]

It seems hard to believe that anything so choice and even revered as Darjeeling tea should have fallen on evil times. But so it has, and its problems are worse than Cachar's. The 18,000 ha which Darjeeling's 100 or so estates comprise have never been easy to work; the yield per hectare (and per worker) is the lowest in North India and continues to decline, and a large proportion of the bushes have seen their best days. The weather, too, can be infinitely disobliging – witness the hail storms which ruined the first flush in 1980 and caused considerable damage to the second flush the following year. Some 16 estates are said to have been closed down for various reasons and many others are reported 'sick'.

To show a profit, the average Darjeeling garden must get at least Rs37 per kilogram for its tea, roughly double that required in Assam, and seldom is that achieved except during the first and second flush periods or when the market is in euphoria (for example, during 1983/84). For Darjeeling as a whole to pay its way – so the experts believe – it will need by the turn of the century to double its annual output of about 12 million kg, and that, assuming no substantial extensions, would represent at least 1,200 kg per hectare, against 600–700 kg today.

The problem has been mulled over again and again, but it does seem that help is at hand in the form of a programme of 'soft' loans to finance some 9,500 ha of extensions, replantings and in-fillings over the next few years. Factory modernisation is also to be covered and a Tea Board subsidy will help with the interest on the loans.

What of the world market for this legendary product? A curious statistic has been much bandied about recently, though nobody seems to know exactly where it came from. According to this, while Darjeeling sends only about 12 million kg of leaf abroad, 40 million kg of alleged 'Darjeeling blends' are sold every year around the world. There is probably no final answer to the question – which goes back nearly a century – of what content justifies a local or national tag being attached to a particular blend. From the fact that the USSR is by far the biggest purchaser of Darjeelings – indeed, it is sometimes their sole prop in the auctions – it does seem that the Darjeeling element in some of the packs labelled as such in the West must be fairly low and not all of the finest quality.

As a further rather desperate measure, it is being suggested that Darjeeling estates should set up units to undertake authentic packet or teabag production on a 'value added' basis, and that a concession should be given on West Bengal State taxation to encourage this. We shall be returning to the 'value added' question, but one wonders whether, with all the other problems on their hands, the time is ripe for the Darjeeling planters to enter this highly technical field. An alternative plan for co-operative or 'unified' sales seems to hold out more promise.

Dooars and Terai

Situated further south at the foot of the Himalayas is the long strip of land known as the Dooars. As a tea area, it is much more extensive than Darjeeling (61,000 ha, against only 18,000). When annexed from Bhutan in 1865 it presented a frowning face of dense jungle and torrential rivers and did not even offer the attractions of a 'sanatorium', since blackwater fever and malaria were rife.

However, the climate seemed congenial to *Camellia sinensis* and by the 1880s development was well under way. As usual, the pioneers were mainly British, but there were also Indian planters there from a very early date and in spite of setbacks they maintained a substantial presence.

Today, the Dooars represents a superbly productive tract of tea land and its 150 estates send over 100,000 tonnes of leaf to market every year. The average yield per hectare – 1,600 kg – is as high as any in North India. Dooars teas are now overwhelmingly CTC and while, unlike Darjeelings, they may not qualify as 'self-drinkers', their full-bodied, 'coloury' liquors are invaluable to the blender and are generally available at prices below the Assams.

As with leaf from the small, adjacent territory of the Terai (46 estates, 11,000 ha, output per hectare 1,268 kg), the Dooars has found an important outlet in the auctions begun at Siliguri in 1976. The big move forward was in 1981, when some 45,000 tonnes of Dooars tea passed through this centre.

Central and North-west India

Before proceeding southwards, a word about some minor, but interesting, pockets of production strung out across Central and North-west India. At Ranchi, in the State of Bihar, tea has been grown for over 150 years, though when Harler was writing in the 1960s he was pessimistic about its chances of survival, mainly because of the incidence of drought.[6]

Nevertheless, there are still over 12,000 ha under the crop in the Ranchi area; the bushes are of China origin and, in fact, make a conspicuous contribution to India's output of Green tea.

Moving up again towards the Himalayas, the grand old cantonment zone of Dehra Dun in Uttar Pradesh State (formerly the United Provinces) is also quite venerable in tea. Some 30 estates (most of them under 50 ha) now produce Green or orthodox Black leaf.

A little further to the north-west is the more important area of the Kangra

Valley in Himachal Pradesh. This is the only region in North India where tea-growing is pursued on a smallholding scale by Indian successors to the British officers who operated there in the days before the 1905 earthquake. The result is that Kangra Valley has more than 1,200 gardens of just a few hectares each, and Green tea predominates. Topographically, in fact, the Valley is nearer to the tea-growing countries of Caucasia – Iran and Turkey – than to Assam and it had the distinction of providing the seed on which the Iranian industry was founded (see page 98).

South India

And so to South India, second only to Assam as a 'powerhouse' for the production of Indian Black tea. It was also not far behind Assam as the scene for pioneer experiments in the 1830s, though commercial exploitation came much later and had a quite different provenance.

Historically, there is an affinity with South India's neighbour Sri Lanka, since over much of the area tea only 'took off' when coffee began to decline under the onslaughts of the fungus disease *Hemileia vastatrix*. Even today, tea is not a monoculture in South India, as in parts of Assam and central Sri Lanka, but comes third to coffee and rubber in a whole array of plantation crops.

Production is widely dispersed through the States of Tamil Nadu and Kerala, with a small enclave in Karnataka. Almost everywhere – again in contrast with Assam – it is a matter of hill planting, with few of the vast, flat sheets of tea characteristic of the Brahmaputra valley. Indeed, in the famous Kanan Devan Range in Kerala, some of the 'highest-grown' tea in the world flourishes at up to 3,000 m.

To sort out the main divisions, in Tamil Nadu (formerly Madras Province) are the important areas of the Nilgiris, the Wynaad and the Anamallai Hills, comprising in all some 37,000 ha under tea. The Nilgiris, forming a high plateau, where South India's two mountain systems of the Eastern and Western Ghats converge, long shared Darjeeling's character as a 'sanatorium', focused on the famous hill-station of Ootacamund. Tea-growing in the Nilgiris has a history of participation by small farmers, dating from a time when coffee and cinchona were still preoccupying the British planting community, and nowadays there are said to be as many as 20,000 smallholders, each with a hectare or two of tea, scattered through the region. Most of them sell their crop to 'bought leaf' factories and in 1983 there was controversy over this. Press stories alleged that smallholders were getting a worse deal from the commercial factories than from the dozen or so government-sponsored co-operatives ('INCOs') to which about a third of them belong. Needless to say, such accusations were vigorously denied, but the mere existence of the dispute underlines the special character of Nilgiris tea-growing.

This area has also been the setting for an interesting development known as

TANTEA, begun in the late 1960s to give employment to Tamil repatriates from Sri Lanka. The original intention was to plant out some 4,000 ha of forest land, but opposition by the environmentalist lobby reduced the target to a little over 2,800 ha and all new planting is now on grassland. Great drive has been put behind the scheme and a yield of up to 2,800 kg per hectare was expected from the 1982/83 crop. Both CTC and Orthodox teas are produced from these new plantings.

In addition to all this smallholding activity, there are, of course, excellent major estates in the Nilgiris, but not on anything like the North Indian scale.

Less 'high-grown' than the Nilgiris teas are those of the Wynaad on the

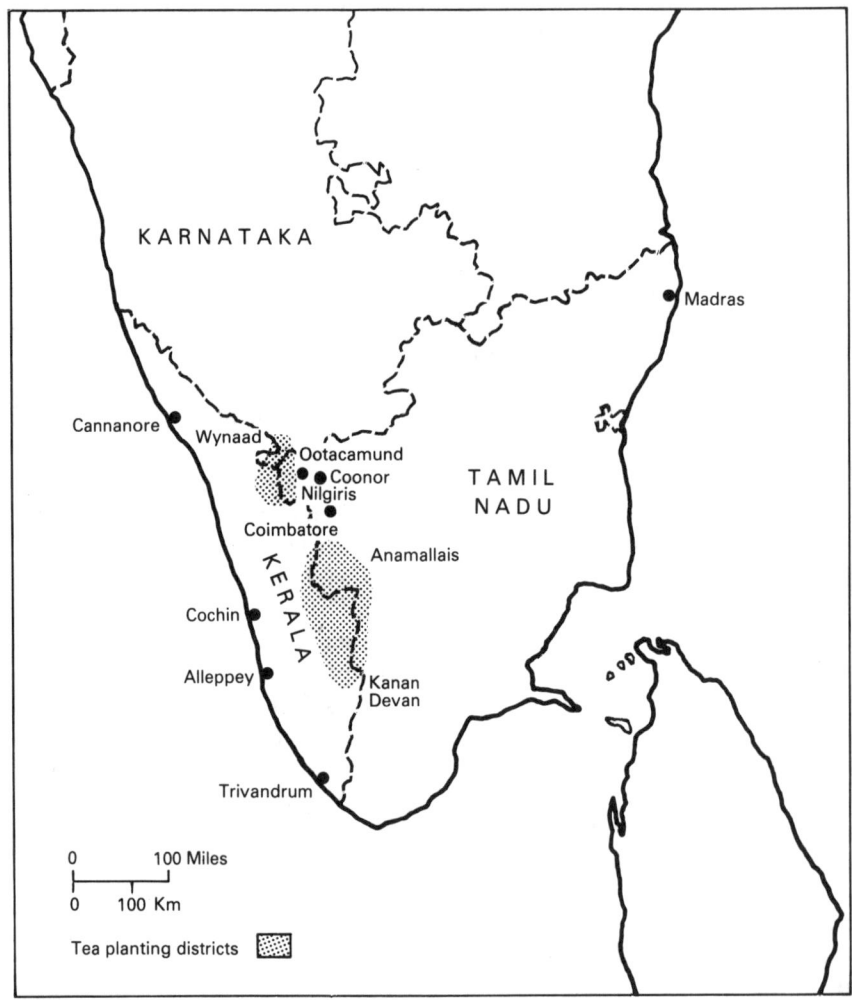

Tea-planting districts of Southern India

slopes of the Western Ghats. Britain's great adversary, Tipu Sultan of Mysore, was trenchantly dismissive of the Wynaad – 'nothing there except forests and heaps of stones' – when the Indian government conceded his right to it in 1798, but eventually coffee gained quite an impressive hold, with tea only making its appearance as an alternative crop at the end of the nineteenth century. Sir Percival Griffiths tells us that at that period many coffee planters sold their estates and took to gold-mining: 'When the gold venture ended in disaster, they planted tea, and to this day there are estates on which horizontal shafts are found among the tea.'[7] The growing area in the Wynaad and what is called the Nilgiri-Wynaad is almost exactly equal to that in the Nilgiris proper – that is, some 12,000 ha.

Closely similar again in extent is the somewhat isolated region of the Anamallais, occupying a basin in the Cardomon Hills, themselves in turn a sort of extension of the Ghats, south of the Palghaut Gap. Not far away, but in the State of Kerala, is the High Range area of the Kanan Devan hills, perhaps the cream of all South Indian tea-growing. Cinchona rather than coffee was the pioneer crop in the High Range, but that was only a brief boom and from the moment when Messrs James Finlay began to take an interest in the region in the early 1890s, tea land was opened up with characteristic *élan*. The High Range has indeed always been identified with the Scottish energy and enterprise of this concern, though it has now withdrawn from tea-growing in India. In 1983 the Finlay interests, extending to 11,000 highly productive hectares in South India and 12,000 in the north, were transferred to the great conglomerate, Messrs Tata, with whom there had already been a working partnership for some years.

In contrast to the High Range, Kerala also has its 'low-grown' tea in the central and southern regions of the State. Altogether, Kerala's tea covers 36,000 ha, about the same as Tamil Nadu's, but output is much lower – 47,648 tonnes in Kerala, against 71,564 in Tamil Nadu in 1981. The area under tea in the State actually fell by over 7% between 1968 and 1978 and Kerala is expected to be made the subject of a rehabilitation programme not unlike Darjeeling's.

Transporting and marketing of Indian tea

So far we have surveyed summarily the wide panorama of India's tea lands, from great estates to tiny smallholdings, an area of 380,000 ha in extent.

We have seen something of the obstacles which the pioneer planters overcame. When eventually they had cleared away the jungle, set out their seedlings, collected labour (often from distant states) and got their primitive factories into motion, they were still faced with the hardly less frightening problem of conveying their manufactured tea to market. There were no railways, of course, in the earliest days, and though the second half of the nineteenth century was a great period of railway construction in India, Assam was not reached by the network until well into the 1880s. Roads were wretched or non-existent and one chest of tea carried by two 'coolies' or six by an elephant were the normal transport units. It would, in fact, have been impossible to develop Assam as tea country at all but for that unique asset the Brahmaputra river and its subsidiary streams. However primitive the 'country boats' or unreliable the first steamers, it did mean that once the chests had reached the river bank (at Gauhati for example), by whatever painful means, they had a reasonable chance of safe delivery to Calcutta and the ocean-going ships.

The tale of how all this developed forms an absorbing chapter in Sir Percival Griffiths' *History of the Indian Tea Industry*.[8] Two rival concerns, the Indian General Steam Navigation Company and the Rivers Steam Navigation Company, competed for the trade.

Even when the railways had appeared and the road network improved, the river route linking Assam and Calcutta continued to command a major share of the traffic until the border between West and East Bengal was closed following the India–Pakistan conflict in 1964.

The first crisis in communication had come with Partition in August 1947. As we have seen, East Pakistan received Sylhet, while Cachar remained in India, and both it and Assam found themselves cut off geographically from their natural outlets on the Bay of Bengal. The transport situation in North-east India, especially on the railways, was already pretty chaotic in the wake of World War II disruption and the Calcutta dock strike of January 1947. Though the direct route down the Brahmaputra valley was not for the time being closed, the introduction of Customs on the border between the two Bengals caused much friction and delay and auguries for the future were not good.

In these circumstances, India felt it imperative to create an Assam–Calcutta rail link upon its own soil. This could only be done 'round the top' of East Pakistan, through the very narrow gap between the latter and Nepal, at Siliguri. The decision to create the 'Assam Link' was taken on 27 January 1948 and the project was completed by Republic Day, 26 January 1950. Even in a less formidable terrain, this would have been an extraordinary feat of speedy construction.

The need for the link was only too sadly vindicated when war broke out between India and Pakistan in 1964. All passage down the Brahmaputra was, of course, debarred and in practical terms has not so far been restored, despite the reopening of the frontiers since the creation of the Republic of Bangladesh.

Strictly in relation to tea movements, the link did not turn out to be all that significant, since the greater part of the Assam–Calcutta deliveries are now made by road. This is bound largely to continue, even when the container 'port' planned for Gauhati is fully in action. River transport would be ideal for this particular traffic, but – politics apart – the former great fleets of river steamers have mostly rotted away and it would be a mammoth task to recreate them, to say nothing of the vast back-up organisation of pilotage, workshops and berthing facilities.

All the early tea lands of India shared the communications problem to a greater or lesser extent and in the south it was compounded by the lack of inland waterways. Human and four-footed humping of chests along primitive bridle-paths slowly gave way to reasonable cart-roads and a resourceful use of aerial ropeways. One area, the Nilgiris, eventually benefited from the excellent road and rail communications provided for the Madras government's summer headquarters at Ootacamund.

South Indian teas have always found their outlet to the west, being routed at first to a miscellany of ports along the Malabar Coast, from Cannanore to Aleppy. But in the present century Cochin, with its deep-water facilities, asserted its leadership, culminating in the establishment of auctions there in 1948.

Auction centres
Calcutta

It is almost absurd to start talking about Cochin – or any other Indian auction centre – before due tribute has been paid to Calcutta.

The enormous city, for so long the capital of British India, has many another claim to fame (and even to notoriety), but only Canton, Colombo and – in its palmiest days – London have ever matched it as a centre for trading in tea.

Over the years, Calcutta has had three main functions, two of which will be discussed in this section. The first has to do with the agency system. Most of the capital to develop the Indian industry, starting with the original Assam Company in 1839, was raised in the City of London and the problem was how, given the then sluggish state of communications across the world, the promoters were going to look after their investment. In the case of the Assam Company itself, the difficulty was eased by amalgamation with an Indian-based concern called the Bengal Tea Association and the appointment of twin boards in London and Calcutta. In general, however, agency houses were the answer, established in the East, but having intimate links with London and capable of handling an immense range of responsibilities, including the supervision of estates and the disposal of their crop. The oldest of the houses, in fact, predated Indian tea – the doyen among them, Messrs Gillanders Arbuthnot, was founded as long ago as 1819 – and took it all in their stride when the new product came along. The agency house (or managing agent) system has always had its critics and certainly in these days of airliner and telex its original *raison d'être* has largely vanished. Yet it still provides invaluable local 'know-how' in an increasingly complex trading situation. Names like Balmer Lawrie, Begg Dunlop, Duncan Brothers, Macneills, Octavius Steel, Shaw Wallace, Williamson Magor, and Andrew Yule are the very stuff from which the greatness of Calcutta as a trading capital was built up. Even where they still operate under their old titles, they are for the most part wholly or partially Indian-owned.

And so to the auctions. As we saw in the Prologue, the East India Company never contemplated selling its tea otherwise than by auction and in 1840 the 'privatised' trade went on from there – just when Indian leaf began to make its appearance in Mincing Lane. The idea of auctioning tea in Calcutta was slower off the mark. The received version is that it all began on 27 December 1861, though an isolated sale had, in fact, been held as far back as 26 May 1841. The interesting thing is that the auctioneers on that occasion, Messrs Mackenzie Lyall, were acting for the East India Company, which had a residual interest in certain Assam estates and stuck to its traditional method of getting rid of the product. The Assam Company also tried to dispose of some inferior leaf by the same means two years later.

However, the December 1861 sale certainly marked the birth of the Calcutta auctions on a regular basis. In control was the broking firm of J. Thomas & Co.,[9] still leading the field in Calcutta, and the scene was the saleroom at 8 Mission Row. Fannings went cheap, as might be expected in those far-off days, but Pekoes fetched up to Rs1.56 per pound.

The motive behind this development at the Eastern end of the pipeline was no doubt the one that has become so potent in our own day – the producer's desire to see the colour of his money in the shortest possible time. In fact, even before the auctions started, small parcels of leaf were being sold by private treaty in Calcutta instead of being shipped off to Mincing Lane.

Nevertheless, the build up of the catalogues in the Calcutta saleroom was slow and very much under the shadow of London, where the world price was established. Even by the end of the nineteenth century, less than 25,000 tonnes annually were coming under the hammer in Mission Row – and much of this leaf found its way to Mincing Lane to be reauctioned! The cash motive mentioned above did not, of course, weigh with the big London-based plantation companies, which had now taken the lead, but there were other reasons why, much nearer our own time, Calcutta became a powerful rival to London.

One was straightforward nationalism – the feeling that, to put it crudely, India would never be mistress in her own house as long as the fate of her most valuable crop was being settled by bids and deals thousands of miles away and out of her control. This is not strictly logical, of course, since the commercial forces governing the public sale of tea in a free market remain exactly the same wherever that sale happens to be taking place. There may be very good reasons why a particular tea will fetch a better price at a particular moment in Calcutta than in London, or vice versa, but that has nothing to do with any 'working' of the price level by buyers to the disadvantage of producers – the age-long suspicion (more perhaps in political than mercantile circles) against the London market.

This lingers on even today, when the UK auctions have shrunk to a shadow of their former predominance. A broker commented recently, with reference to a similar feeling in Colombo, that the current annual offerings of Sri Lanka tea at Sir John Lyon House[10] were the equivalent of one day's sale in Colombo; for India, the discrepancy is not quite so extreme, but the proportion is still nearly 20 to 1 in favour of the six Indian auction centres.

Nationalism apart, many Indian officials and economists argued that their country had lost out heavily over the years both in terms of employment and in foreign exchange through so much of her tea being sold in London instead of in its native country. The idea, floated long ago, that the *whole* of the Indian crop should be auctioned in Calcutta gained its first big stimulus after World War II, when the British government showed what seemed like undue timidity in freeing tea from wartime controls. Not only did the bureaucrats retain rationing until 1952, but they insisted on continuing direct contracts with producers, by-passing Calcutta. The London auctions, of course, were still closed; nevertheless, the Indian Tea Association was able to convince its government that to give the Calcutta auctions a monopoly of North Indian tea sales was impracticable.

Other centres

In 1985 any such idea of monopoly would seem fanciful indeed. Not because of London competition, but because of the recent decentralisation of India's own auctions and the growth of ex-garden and other direct sales. The first of Calcutta's rivals in North India was Gauhati on the Brahmaputra, long a centre for the shipping of Assam tea down river. The decision, taken in 1970, to start auctions there arose from the government of Assam's resentment at West Bengal's 'entry tax' on teas for Calcutta. The beginning was modest, but by 1978 the tonnage sold had risen to 76,737. All this movement in turn created a bottleneck at Siliguri, so that the tea interests of Northern Bengal decided to have auctions there as well (first sale, 29 October 1976). Both Gauhati and Siliguri have flourished, the former mainly handling Assam tea, of course, but including a quantity from Cachar, while Siliguri is now the main outlet for the Dooars. The build-up of the Siliguri auctions in recent years has been quite a success story (only 16,748 tonnes in 1980, 55,483 in 1981, then 79,945 in 1982, thus moving ahead of Gauhati's 75,342). Meanwhile the percentage of Indian tea passing through the Calcutta auctions (58% 20 years ago) had shrunk to 38% in 1981, 27% in 1982 and only 24% a year later.

Decentralisation has also invaded the south, where Cochin had reigned alone since 1947. In 1963 Coonor started up, specialising in the sale of Dust grades, and much more recently Coimbatore, that thriving city in the Palghaut Gap between the Nilgiris and the Anamallais, has become more important. It is a welcome outlet for small lots not conveniently dealt with elsewhere. About two-thirds of the Coimbatore tea is shipped through the port of Tuticorin.

All this sent Cochin, like Calcutta, into something of a decline as an auction centre, though not as an exit port. In 1982, only 55,000 tonnes of tea came under the hammer there, against 58,000 the previous year, 79,000 in 1980 and 86,000 in 1979. By 1983 the total had sunk to 47,000 tonnes.

Internal consumption

There is a wider question here. Gauhati and the other new auction centres (including the 'mini-auctions' which a few firms – notably Duncan Brothers – conduct on an almost *ad hoc* basis in various territories) tend to be identified with the home market; Calcutta and Cochin with exports. A wider question? *The* question so far as the future shape of the Indian tea industry and even of the world market is concerned. The simple mathematics are that in 1982 India produced some 565,000 tonnes of tea and exported 190,000 tonnes, leaving 375,000 tonnes for the home market. 1983's margin was somewhat better; as already mentioned, provisional figures showed production up to 589,000 tonnes and estimated exports up to 208,000 tonnes. 1984 was expected to reveal a further advance, allowing perhaps 425,000 tonnes for the Indian consumer, and some 215,000 tonnes to go abroad. In questions of consumption per head, it is usually best to follow the International Tea Committee's triennial average, and it shows that during 1980–82, India's 684 million people were drinking a mere 0.54 of a kilogram in a year. Though this is one of the lowest figures for any producer country (Sri Lanka, 1.41 kg; Japan, 0.97; Kenya, 0.82), it is rising all the time.

So what are the implications? Fifty years ago, the Indian home market hardly entered anyone's thoughts, since it represented no more than a residual quarter of the crop – all the rest went for export. But after World War II the alarm bells faintly rang, the graph crept up and by the 1950s people were beginning to say, 'Here are the people of India, millions of them, drinking ½lb of tea per head. If they ever have the means and the inclination to absorb even 1 lb – against the UK's 9 lb – there wouldn't be a drop of Indian tea left for the rest of the world!'

Well, that supposedly fatal 1 lb (or 0.5 kg) has been reached and the only reason why, despite the January 1984 'crisis' (more about that in a moment), the world is still waiting for the remainder of the forecast to come true is because of the expansion in the total Indian crop. Looking to the future, no wonder bodies like the Tandon Committee commit themselves to the idea of that expansion continuing indefinitely – or at least until it reaches 1,400,000 tonnes by the end of the century. But reasons have already been given for doubting this concept.

No clear consensus emerged over the years on what, if anything, ought to be 'done about' the growth of the internal market. Tea-drinking in India did not take off spontaneously but was actively promoted over a long period, both in a general (or 'generic') sense and brand-wise. In each case the year 1901 was, rather precisely, the starting point. It was then that an Indian Tea

Market Expansion Commission, with Messrs Andrew Yule as its agent, began to 'push' tea as vigorously as a modest grant of Rs40,000 for three years would permit. Special attention was given to sales in mills, factories, railway stations and mines, and this was also the moment when the famous 'pice packet' (96 packets to the pound) first put the beverage within reach of the least affluent classes.

At the end of the three years, however, the Indian Tea Association reported that 'it cannot be said that the results . . . indicate the existence of a proper tea market in India' and the grant was not renewed. Further attempts were made in a somewhat dispirited way up to 1914, but when work was renewed after World War I, under the auspices of what was now called the Indian Tea Cess Committee, it was in a much more dynamic spirit. By 1936 the sale of pice packets had reached 8 million and no fewer than 26 million cups of liquid tea were distributed in that year. The good work went forward until it was suspended once more by the impact of war.

Meanwhile, brand promotion had followed a parallel course. In *Brooke Bond – a Hundred Years*,[11] David Wainwright gives a remarkable account of how, ever since the opening of the firm's Calcutta branch (now Brooke Bond India Pte) in that seminal year 1901, the expansion of its Indian sales has been pursued through good times and bad, until today India stands first among the firm's world-wide markets. Another great name in internal distribution is also of British provenance – Messrs Lipton, who appear to have been active in India even before Brooke Bond. Now that they have come together (see page 131) they represent a mighty force indeed in the packet trade, with perhaps a 30% combined share. However, it should be borne in mind that in spite of packet promotion India remains predominantly a loose tea market,[12] with perhaps a third to a half dispensed in liquid form in a countless number of tea-shops. Nor are these an outlet for 'rubbish tea', since many of the tea-shop folk are keenly aware of the relation between reasonable quality and 'cups per kilo'. The spread of tea-drinking in the Indian sub-continent from a small urban base out into the multitudinous villages is another of those subjects about which a whole book could be written.

The alarm bells of the 1950s resounded most loudly in the offices of the Indian Tea Board, which in 1954 had become responsible for promotion. India's need for foreign exchange was pressing and there was optimism that exports could be greatly increased. In these circumstances generic promotion was put into cold storage (in 1961), where it has largely remained to the present day.

Government intervention

One was left with the query: if tea production in India did not expand as hoped, would the government be driven – long before the year 2000 perhaps – to take drastic measures, going beyond mere fiscal restraints, to ration the internal market? The political consequences might be serious. Distribution of tea in India is a free-wheeling affair, with thousands of 'little people' involved in various ways, in addition to the giants of the packet trade. To put them under any form of restraint would be a difficult and unpopular departure from the hitherto fairly easy-going relationship between the government, the private sector and the consuming public.

However, government intervention, when it came, was in exactly the opposite direction. The reasons for the accelerating rise in world tea prices towards the end of 1983, culminating in near panic in the first week of 1984, are analysed elsewhere (see page 199). The Indian authorities, thoroughly alarmed by what they saw as a shattering increase in the cost of tea on the home market, coupled with a fear of shortfalls before plucking resumed in North India in March/April, placed a ban on the export of all CTC teas. The official rationale of this choice was that a 'shortage of Orthodox teas which are mainly exported' had led to a 'greater export demand for CTCs which are largely used by the domestic consumer'. The ban was indefinite, but was expected to last at least three months; the only exemptions were for teas which had already received an export licence and for teabags.

In the event, the ban was lifted in May, only to be reimposed in September. This was because the limit for 1984 exports, which had been fixed at 215,000 tonnes, had nearly been reached already. By the end of August licences had been issued for 145,000 tonnes, but forward contracts for another 54,000 tonnes had been registered. That still left 16,000 tonnes for export, but, since under the new regulations only one-third of exports could be CTC teas, this was to all intents and purposes a complete ban. Further regulations issued in late 1984 and early 1985 showed that the Indian government intended to continue to keep a firm control on all exports, in the interests of the internal market. Its measures would include export quotas and separate 'floor' prices for auction and direct-sale export teas.

In another context, the role of the state has so far been carefully limited. Compared with what has happened in certain other territories, including Sri Lanka, national policy has dealt lightly with the production side of the industry, in spite of its still strong expatriate element. There has been no sweeping nationalisation, though all companies are 'rupeeised', and under the Foreign Exchange Regulation Act (FERA) at least 26% of the equity has to be held by Indian investors. Quite apart from speculators, who tend to appear in some number during periods of optimism (for example in 1974–77) and to buy up small tea gardens and distributive concerns, opportunities for gaining a solid stake in the industry are keenly sought by Indian capital. The Tata take-over of the Finlay empires in South and North India has already been mentioned, and later the extensive estates of the Assam Frontier Tea Co. and the North Indian planting interests of Messrs Warren passed into Indian hands.

The trend towards Indian investment will no doubt continue. Much of it has been by members of the enterprising Marwari community from Rajasthan in Western India; it is fascinating to read that as far back as 1888 the *Annual Report on Tea Culture in Assam* described the Marwaris as having entered the tea business 'not indeed as producers but purchasers of tea from small village growers for sale to local tribal people'.[13] Today they are growers and merchants alike.

It may be noted that the figures given for British investment in UNCTAD Secretariat's widely circulated 1982 paper, 'The Marketing and Processing of Tea',[14] were out of date almost as soon as published.[15] They sought to prove that through interlocking shareholdings and boards the 'concentration of ownership' by some ten British companies had increased in recent years. In fact (omitting Finlay and Warren) expatriate companies have, on UNCTAD's own showing, been responsible in recent years for annual production totalling only some 111,000 tonnes out of the all-India figure of 560,000 tonnes. This puts the whole matter in perspective; it can surely be claimed, in any event, that India has benefited, and is continuing to benefit, from the long-time commitment to efficient tea-growing and manufacture by the surviving British firms. Their staffs on the ground are now entirely Indian and this applies as much in Calcutta and the other commercial centres as on the estates.

Export

Earlier in this chapter, Calcutta was viewed in two of its three important aspects – as the mercantile capital of Indian tea and as a great auction centre. It is appropriate to finish with its third aspect – as the principal exit port for the North Indian crop.

The nature of the country's export trade has changed considerably in recent years. For example, a landmark was reached when in 1980, for the first time, the USSR replaced the United Kingdom as the principal market for Indian tea (see Table 2.1).

Table 2.1   Indian tea exports to UK and USSR (tonnes)

	1979	1980	1981
UK	53,266	45,509	40,971
USSR	40,388	63,838	77,807

Full figures for 1982 were expected to show an even more pronounced tilt but, in fact, the Russian offtake (dependent on barter deals) fell back rather sharply to 56,602 tonnes, while the United Kingdom's share recovered somewhat ●o 47,963 tonnes. Since then, absorption by the two countries has continued in roughly the same proportions.

No other country imports Indian tea on anything like the same scale as these two voracious consumers. Next in importance in 1983 came Iran (17,028 tonnes), Egypt (14,936 tonnes), Iraq (12,859 tonnes), Poland (11,715 tonnes) and Afghanistan (5,613 tonnes).

It will be perceived that all this left only a comparatively minor role for the countries of the West (the United Kingdom apart) on the Indian export scene. The presence or absence of Polish interest at, say, Cochin can be decisive in setting the price averages for that particular day. The USSR, like Poland, buys its Indian tea in open competition at the auctions, with purchases ranging over the whole spectrum, including CTC as well as Orthodox leaf; we have already noted the Russian appetite for Darjeelings.

Thus, in spite of the growth in ex-garden sales and much talk of big buyers intending to 'by-pass the auctions', the traditional mechanism for disposing of India's tea harvest continues to 'chug along', though somewhat creakily in the case of the port of Calcutta. A reputation for unhappy labour relations has in particular undermined its prestige. As recently as December and January 1982/83 – at the height of the export season – the auctions came to a standstill and no tea was shipped for six weeks owing to a strike in the warehouses.

Unsettling in a different sense has been the sensational rise of the container (see Chapter 8) as a means of speeding the movement of tea and providing an additional measure of security. Calcutta was a little late in bending to this wind of change, but by early 1980 about 45% of Indian tea was containerised and in June 1982 it was reported that a site had been chosen for a new container terminal where space could be allotted to the three main lines now involved in the trade – Overseas Containers Ltd, Indian Container Lines and the Russian Line.

Though Calcutta, of course, sends tea to a lot of places unable to handle containers, by 1982 the containerised percentage had risen to nearly 60%; in the case of important destinations like the United Kingdom and the USSR the proportion is well over 90%.

Subsidiary to Calcutta so far is the port of Haldia, on the west side of the Hooghly estuary and much nearer the sea. In spite of its lack of commercial infrastructure and still somewhat sketchy equipment, Haldia is thought to have considerable potential, especially as a terminal if and when the stage is reached of containers being shipped down from inland depots. However, in 1983 Haldia handled only 150,000 chests against Calcutta's 2,400,000.

The pattern of movement 'on the water' has equally had to conform to containerisation, in contrast with the old procession of freighters – mostly under famous UK flags and each loading its thousands of chests. By 1983 Indian Container Lines was running a fortnightly service from Calcutta and Haldia to UK and Continental ports, with a transit time of 23 to 24 days (given a full ship and no intermediate stops), while one of the Overseas Containers' COBRA (Continental British-Asia Container Service) was calling at Madras, Colombo, Cochin, Bombay and Karachi. However, the OCL also provides a 'feeder' service by which considerable quantities of North Indian tea are ferried to Colombo, where there is a choice of shipping to all destinations.

Promotion

The promotion of Indian, as of other teas, will be a theme of Chapter 17, but it may be noted here that in recent years the Indian Tea Board has reckoned to spend about Rs25 million (US$2.6 million at 1982 rates) on campaigns outside the country. Some 40% of this goes on generic promotion ('tea as tea'), including support for the Tea Councils of the United Kingdom, Ireland, West Germany, France, the United States, Canada, Australia and New Zealand, by far the largest recipients as a rule being the United Kingdom and West Germany.

On the uninational side, the emphasis has been on the promotion of 'pure Indian tea', whether exported in packet or in teabag form or processed locally, and successes have been reported in a number of countries. The spearhead of this particular drive has been the government-sponsored Tea Trade Corporation of India (TTCI). India maintains Tea Board offices in London, Brussels, New York, Sydney, Cairo and Kuwait, but the three Tea Centres operating for a number of years in London, Sydney and Cairo have been handed over to a new body, controlled jointly by the Tea Board and the Hotel Corporation of India, and will no doubt be run in the future on more commercial lines.

An overall increase in India's promotional budget was forecast during 1984.

Bangladesh

Ninety million people live in an area of about 143,000 square km – 630 for every square kilometre. Island communities apart, this represents the greatest population density on the face of the globe, and when one adds that Bangladesh is 90% agricultural, with much of its farming hardly above subsistence level, it is obvious how vital to the country's economy are the few industries which can help to raise the gross national product (only US$130 per head at the latest estimate) and to earn foreign exchange.

Results of Partition

Chief among Bangladesh's industries is jute, of which the country produces 90% of the world's total supplies, but tea comes a useful second. Under the 1947 Partition, which almost severed Assam from the rest of India, the State of Pakistan fell heir to only two tea-growing districts – Sylhet, on the border of East Pakistan and Assam, and a much smaller zone near Chittagong. Painful adjustments were needed – in communications, for example, and from the loss of access to the Calcutta auctions. Hardly had the dust settled on all this when 'East Pakistan' gave place to 'Bangladesh' (1971). Only a handful of the experienced British planters remained and virtually all the Pakistani estate staff vanished. With this loss of expertise in every aspect of estate management, the number of properties damaged during hostilities and the difficult financial circumstances facing the new nation, there was not only a catastrophic fall in output (from 34,400 tonnes to 12,400 tonnes between 1970 and 1971), but a widespread deterioration in the quality of made tea.

Current production

Since then, there have been brave efforts to increase tea's contribution to the young country's wealth; output figures have mounted steadily, if slowly, and, at just over 44,000 tonnes per annum, now easily exceed the pre-independence figure. Sylhet contributes about 38,000 tonnes of this, the rest coming from the Chittagong area. Out of 152 estates, some 25 are still in non-Bangladesh ownership (including Finlay, Duncan and Shaw Wallace interests) and these produce more than half the crop. Bangladesh companies cover 17,800 ha and proprietary estates 6,000 ha.

Tea Rehabilitation Project

Some of these smaller holdings were abandoned altogether in 1971 and measures have been taken by successive Bangladesh governments to help those capable of rescue. During the 1970s studies of the industry were undertaken by a variety of international agencies, culminating in 1979 in the setting up of the Bangladesh Tea Rehabilitation Project. In this the Bangladesh Tea Board has the co-operation of the UK's Overseas Development Administration (ODA), with local assistance from the British consultants, Duncan Macneill & Co. The British government is putting £22 million into the Project and there is EEC support as well. All but about 20 of the country's estates, which were considered to be beyond redemption, are eligible to benefit.

Working with Bangladesh counterparts, the consultants now have in each district or 'valley' of the Bangladesh tea lands a development officer advising on all aspects of day-to-day estate management and on improvements in the field (helped by a generous planting subsidy), in the factory and in labour welfare. One target is to build some 6,000 houses for the workers during the next few years and some £2.17 million of ODA money has been earmarked for the purpose.

The Project is also concerned with a number of ancillary subjects such as marketing, the electrification of factories, natural gas as a heat source, irrigation, local road improvements, forestry for fuel and plywood timbers, crop diversification, research, and so on. Advice to the Project on health and hospital matters and on setting up an appropriate medical structure has been sub-contracted to the Ross Institute of Tropical Hygiene.

In addition to the British aid, Bangladesh estate owners have in recent years imported a quantity of new machinery from India under a credit scheme operated by the Industrial Development Bank of India.

Geographical factors

Formed as it is out of the vast delta of the Brahmaputra and allied river systems, most of Bangladesh is extremely flat and subject to regular flooding during the monsoon season – not too bad for paddy and even jute – but it means that, on the 20% of land above flood level, tea must compete for space with numerous other crops, to say nothing of forestry, livestock and housing. Thus, expansion of the industry, as elsewhere in Asia, has to come mainly from higher yields rather than from extended plantings. Increasing use is being made of the clones – few in number as yet – produced by the Tea Research Institute at Sri Mangal.

Although climate and soil are unlikely to permit yields comparable to those of neighbouring Assam, Bangladesh now compares closely with Indonesia in the 'yield per hectare' table and is well above Sri Lanka. Both drought and torrential rain affected output and quality in 1984.

In the factories, Orthodox manufacture is largely giving place to CTC, which represents more than two-thirds of total production today. Virtually all this leaf is railed down to Chittagong, where, although some private sales are permitted, three-quarters of it passes through the auction centre, usually for export.

Export

Some 25 countries take a share in Bangladesh tea, but such a figure can be misleading, since as a rule half the total goes to now tealess Pakistan; of the rest, the only four-figure exports in 1984 were to the United Kingdom, Egypt, Poland and the USSR. As to prices, there are in this case few useful yardsticks other than the London auctions, where the modest total of 2,019 tonnes of Bangladesh tea brought forward in 1984 (less than in several recent years, and mainly representing the better estates) averaged 229.32p per kilogram, against an 'all teas' figure of 262.85p.

In the years between Partition and the break away from Pakistan a large part of the crop was consumed in what was then West Pakistan. Not surprisingly, that market virtually disappeared in the aftermath of the 1971 war. However,by the mid-1970s the old pattern had begun to re-emerge, with sales to Pakistan of 4,123 tonnes in 1976, rising to 11,000 tonnes two years later and 15,268 tonnes in 1983. But a question mark remains. What might happen should any *rapprochement* between India and Pakistan have as one of its symbols a renewed trade in tea? Signs of this were not altogether wanting in 1983. Starting with an order for Green tea, destined eventually for Afghanistan, the Trading Corporation of Pakistan appears to have struck several bargains with the Indian government, and private Indian exporters were even authorised to open negotiations with Pakistani customers. Against this is the pressure of India's internal demand which may eventually make it difficult for her to satisfy even her traditional overseas customers.

In general, Bangladesh leaf has to take its chance in a free and competitive market, though more or less complicated bilateral agreements are set up with such countries as the USSR, Poland and Egypt. The last two both increased their orders in 1983.

Bangladesh is, however, actively seeking further outlets, notably in Africa, so there are a number of reasons why the long-term prospects for her exports are by no means gloomy.

The fact that at least one of the inter-governmental deals referred to above was for Indian Green tea is a reminder that in Bangladesh, too, the production and export of this variety is an aspect of the industry which receives little notice. Pakistanis drink a lot of it, especially up on the North-west Frontier, and no doubt the arrival of thousands of Afghan refugees in that quarter provided a further stimulus. At any rate, demand is so brisk that one Green tea factory which was out of commission has been reactivated and a new one erected at Jagcherra, making three in all.

Internal consumption

Export activity leaves a mere 10 million kg or so of tea – Black or Green – to fill the teacups of the 90 million of Bangladesh's own people. As in India, much of this is sold loose, but the packet trade is on the march with the British firms of Brooke Bond and Lipton prominent. Clearly, the internal offtake could be enormously increased if the need to sell abroad were not so dominant.

Reverting to exports, movement of tea through the port of Chittagong was greatly speeded up by the establishment, early in 1982, of a regular container terminal primarily for use by COBRA, referred to already. The fact that the government did all it could to ease the intricate logistics of getting this terminal established is just one example of the genuine concern in Bangladesh for the health and prosperity of the tea industry. Apart from the foreign exchange earnings referred to earlier, it is estimated that tea gives employment to about 90,000 permanent workers plus seasonal reinforcements of 13,000. Behind this workforce stand anything up to 200,000 dependants, so that tea's 'family' in Bangladesh adds up to quite a formidable group.

Pakistan

The politics of Partition have caused many a trauma in the Indian sub-continent, and tea has not been exempt. From the time that the British found *Camellia sinensis* growing wild in the jungles of Assam down to the creation of Pakistan in 1947, the tea industry in that part of the globe represented a huge and seamless web of activity spreading from the foothills of the Himalayas to the Bay of Bengal. East Pakistan, incorporating most of the Brahmaputra delta and Assam–Calcutta rail system, tore a great rent in this logical pattern, even though, as we have seen, only two comparatively small tea-growing districts fell within the new State's boundaries. But even these ceased to be Pakistan territory when Bangladesh was born in 1971. The Republic of Pakistan now consisted only of its former western limb and, since this had never had an indigenous tea-planting industry, its 85 million people, most of them keen and discriminating tea-drinkers, were left entirely dependent on imports.

Internal consumption

Disruption, however, went further than that. Year after year, in the absence of any trade treaty covering the product, virtually no tea reached Pakistan from the nearest of its 'natural' suppliers, the Republic of India. Thus the Pakistan market became the focus of ardent and world-wide competition, with Bangladesh, Sri Lanka, Indonesia and Kenya setting the pace. Some way behind, though seeming likely at one stage to close the gap, came China, while a dozen other minor exporting countries bobbed about in the rear. The endless romance of trading in tea could hardly be better illustrated than by the fact that in 1982 Pakistan's top supplier was Kenya. Who, in the days of the Raj or even as recently as 1972, could have predicted the time when an East African country would be sending 17,000 tonnes of tea per annum to one in the Indian sub-continent?[15]

The lead has changed hands several times between the 'big four'. However, to one of them – Bangladesh – Pakistan is not just *a* market, it is *the* market, and we have already seen sales steadily built up until Bangladesh now directs more than half her 30,000 tonnes of exports there. We have also taken a peep into the future, when a resumption of trade links between Pakistan and India might or might not put the 'Bangladesh connection' at risk.

Pakistan's 1983 imports, amounting to over 80,000 tonnes, put her second only to the United Kingdom, and, for the first time, ahead of the United States. In addition, more Green tea (popular especially in the tribal areas) crosses the border than ever gets into the official statistics.

The strain which this vast intake places on Pakistan's foreign exchange resources hardly needs to be stressed and it is not surprising that the government shows no disposition to increase the quota of imports, which at present cost well over US$100 million per annum. Left to itself, it is probable that consumption would continue to mount almost indefinitely at the rate of 5% every year. Quality tea is particularly in demand and this extends to the liquid market – so important in that parched land; visitors bold enough to drink tea in the bazaars of Karachi report that they get an excellent cup.

An unusual factor which has recently been putting pressure on tea supplies is that shortages of milk in country districts have encouraged a switch to tea. Internal prices are strictly controlled by the government and there is tension – not unknown elsewhere – between the political need to keep down the cost of living and the temptation to raise extra revenue through import duties. To compensate packers for their losses on price-controlled tea, import duties were actually reduced from 32.5% *ad valorem* to 25% in 1982.

Tea-growing experiments

This section on Pakistan began with tea-growing, and there it should perhaps end. There is no indigenous tea industry, but that may change. Several times since Partition – in 1959, 1964 and 1977 – attempts have been made to establish plantations, but without success. However, for the latest experiment, under Chinese auspices, prospects seem distinctly brighter. The likely locations are in Hazra and Swat, way up in the North-west Frontier Province, where conditions are not unlike those in the Tibetan foothills of China. *Jats* of tea analogous to the ones which resist cold and drought in those bleak regions will be introduced, and, if the first experimental plantings succeed, Pakistan looks forward to producing at least 12 million kg of tea per annum by the end of the 1980s. All eyes, therefore, are on the 40-acre research plot near Manshera.

3 Sri Lanka

Development of tea-growing

The history of Sri Lankan tea has one element which marks it off from every other producing country and still has influence today.

Its tea estates were not originally planned and planted as such. They were coffee estates, crudely converted to meet an agricultural and financial crisis. The beautiful small island, until then only famous commercially for cinnamon and pearls, had become in the late 1830s the scene of a feverish coffee boom, comparable to the 'gold rushes' of Australia and the Klondike. Crown land was alienated on an enormous scale, much of it to public servants. In the central highlands splendid forests were cleared and coffee was planted out, with fanatical thoroughness, wherever human foot or coffee bush root could find a purchase. In contrast with tea, there was no question of 'plucking rounds' to be considered. Coffee was, of course, an annual crop, which could be harvested in a scrambling one-off operation and the layout of the estate meant nothing to the rugged types who were put in charge.

Moreover, the factory or 'store' was usually built on a somewhat cramped site, down by a stream, in order to take advantage of water power. So that when tea took over, with its essential requirement of spacious and airy withering facilities, the solution was to build upwards – hence the characteristic Sri Lankan factory with its two or three tiers of lofts, instead of the separate 'leaf houses' familiar in Assam. Even when the factory, as often happened, was moved to a more suitable position the multi-storey plan was retained. Nowadays, with the new withering techniques described in earlier pages, the upper floors of factories have been largely abandoned.

The reason why Sri Lanka, after some 40 years as one of the world's leading coffee-suppliers, turned over to tea is one of the classic case histories of tropical agriculture. *Hemileia vastatrix*, the dreaded Coffee Rust fungus, seems to have made its first appearance in the island early in 1869 but, contrary to much traditional belief, did not bring immediate ruin to the coffee fields; the area under coffee actually increased by 75% between 1869 and 1879, mainly through planters leaving devastated areas and seeking what they thought might be disease-free locations higher up. As late as 1890 some of them were still making optimistic noises about 'recovery' on their estates. That was about the last of many false dawns; coffee had already been uprooted and tea popped in at a rising tempo for over a decade and even today a substantial proportion of the country's tea crop comes from bushes planted in that hectic time, still yielding a good flush.

The centenary of Sri Lanka's tea industry was celebrated in 1967, however, and this is accounted for by the fact that, long before *Hemileia vastatrix* loomed up, coffee planters and scientists had been experimenting with tea, among other alternative crops; 1867 was the year when one of these visionaries (a pretty solid Scots one), James Taylor of Loolecondera Estate,[1] set out the country's first commercial field. China *jat* had been his earliest love, but the surviving 1867 bushes, as seen by the writer on No. 7 field at Loolecondera 98 years later, were definitely of Assam origin.

Considering all the improvisations which had to be made in the early days – and on a shoestring – Sri Lanka's swift emergence as second only to India among sources of Black tea, much of it of the finest quality, was a startling achievement. She still holds that position today.

Current production
Geographical factors

Geographically, the compact shape of the island (the 'Pearl of the East') is reflected in the layout of its tea lands. Traditionally they are classified by height – low-grown (sea-level up to 2,000 ft (610 m)), mid-grown (2,000 to 4,000 ft (610 m to 1,220 m)), high-grown (over 4,000 ft (1,220 m)). There are approximately 2,100 low-grown estates (representing 24.6% of the area under estate tea; this excludes some 135,000 smallholdings), 1,378 (38%) mid-grown and 525 (37%) high-grown. It will be perceived that the high-grown properties are on average much greater in area than those lower down. In fact, the high-grown zone of central Sri Lanka, with Dimbula, Dickoya and Nuwara Eliya as representative districts, has justly been described as perhaps 'the densest monoculture in the world'. In terms of output, too, it remains comfortably ahead, producing 67,761 tonnes of made tea in 1983, against 48,458 tonnes of mid-grown and 63,068 low-grown.

The significance of *elevation* in the production of quality tea has already been touched on and when the three height categories became recognised in Sri Lanka they tended to be equated rather crudely in much the same way – *high-grown* tea, high grade; *mid-grown*, medium grade; *low-grown*, low grade. Average prices in the Colombo auctions provided a lingering confirmation of this until about 20 years ago (see Table 3.1).

Table 3.1 Average prices – Colombo auctions (Rs per kilogram)

	1962	1972	1982	1983
High-grown	4.96	4.72	23.05	35.79
Mid-grown	3.68	4.08	21.53	35.39
Low-grown	3.51	4.39	22.77	39.34

This latter-day prosperity of low-grown tea stems from the fact that the type of leaf produced is particularly suitable to the booming markets of Iraq and neighbouring territories.

Elevation apart, the compactness of Sri Lanka's tea lands has meant very little differentation by district, in contrast with India's far-flung diversity. With the exception of Uva and Uda Pussellawa, east of the central massif, practically all the tea country expects its main rainfall from the south-west

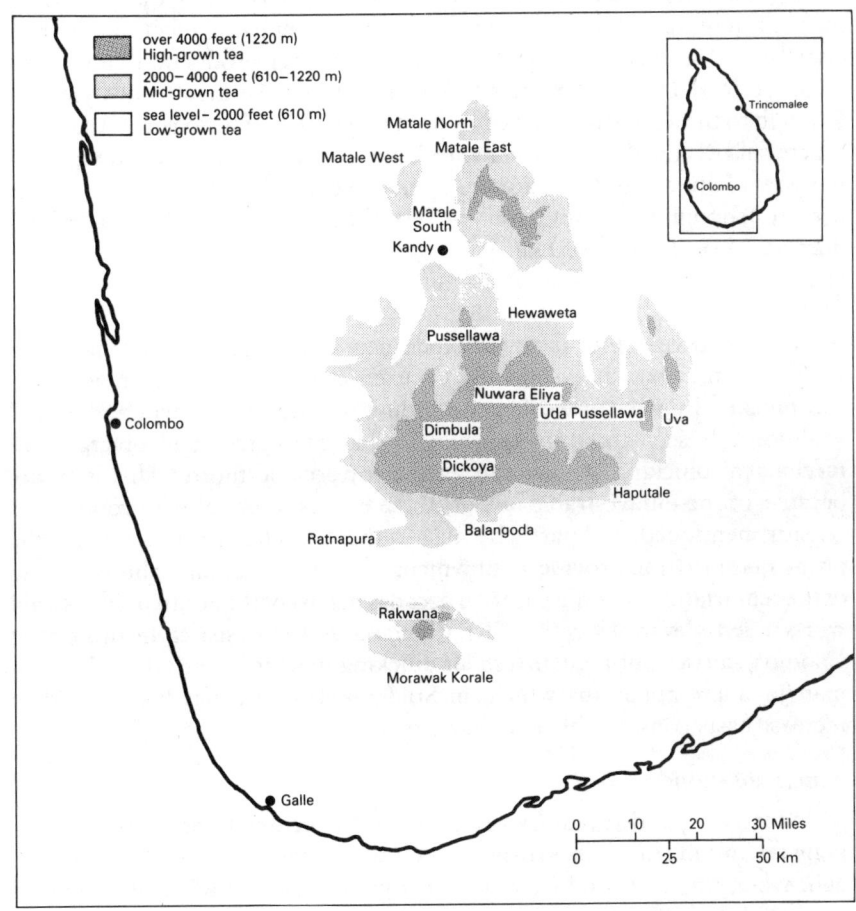

Tea-planting districts of Sri Lanka
Source: *A Hundred Years of Ceylon Tea* (Chatto & Windus, 1967)

monsoon, sweeping in between May and September, though its operation has become notoriously erratic in recent years, causing frequent drought conditions in East Africa as well as Southern Asia. Uva and Uda Pussellawa rely on the normally less copious north-east monsoon (October–January) and during the dry season produce tea of uniquely mellow flavour. Plucking goes on all the year round in Sri Lanka, since it is virtually frost-free.

The only thing lacking, in fact, is a truly congenial soil, even though by good fortune its structure is fairly resistant to erosion. Eden recalls that when, during World War II, estates were required by food shortages to devote their underdeveloped land to subsistence crops, the mediocre agricultural quality of the soil was strikingly revealed.[2] A moral for today, when diversification is again in fashion!

Eden goes on to say that because the soils of the Sri Lankan tea lands are among the oldest and least fertile on which the crop is raised, the 'pattern of nutrient requirements' is thrown into more emphatic relief there than elsewhere. Nitrogen is, as usual, the clue to higher production and it was recorded in *A Hundred Years of Ceylon Tea* that the then record yield of 8,000 lb to the acre was achieved by applying 480 lb of nitrogen to a selected 1-acre field of clonal tea at Millakande in the Low Country.[3] In contemporary terms, Sri Lankan estates reckon to apply the equivalent of up to 115 kg per hectare. Though yields of tea vary widely, the average throughout the island does not exceed about 860 kg.

Manufacture

Apart from three or four factories experimenting on a commercial scale with CTC, Sri Lanka remains essentially a source of Orthodox grades, made from leaf plucked by women workers according to strict 'two leaves and a bud' traditions. It seems extremely unlikely that Sri Lanka will diverge into mechanical plucking, at any rate in the foreseeable future. This is partly because of the unfavourable layout of the estates, especially up country, as already mentioned, and partly because in the Asian tea lands as a whole the problem is rather to provide employment than to save labour. This is in spite of the repatriation over the past two decades of part of the South Indian Tamil workforce.[4] Nevertheless the 'TRI' (the famous Tea Research Institute at St Coombs) carries out regular tests of plucking machines, including the two-man Japanese apparatus which, in Sri Lankan terms, has been found to increase costs considerably over hand-plucking.

Nationalisation

As industry expanded year by year, the country ceased to be so overwhelmingly reliant on tea for its prosperity as it was in the days, less than 20 years ago, when this one product yielded between 60% and 65% of all export revenue. But the figure remained at about 35% and in terms of taxation, too, tea was still the biggest single contributor. The 1983/84 price boom caused a positive 'explosion' in revenue. November 1983 alone saw a record Rs165,400 million being collected from the *ad valorem* sales tax (35% on any excess over Rs26 per kilogram); in the first six months of 1984 the figure was Rs1,800 million, against only 365 million in the same period in 1983.

Thus, it can be understood, historically, that everyone with the country's well-being at heart keeps anxious watch on anything that may affect the great enterprise. Such an event, of course, was the nationalisation in 1975 of all tea estates over 20 ha in extent.

Up until that time, the pattern of ownership was very much as it had been in colonial days. Apart from indigenous proprietary planters (always a numerous class, especially in the Low Country), there were about 80 companies with sterling finance and 70 with rupee which had interests in Sri Lankan tea. Many of them owned only a single estate or group, but there had long been a few giants which accounted for more than half the capital invested. The smaller companies were naturally in no position to give adequate supervision to their estates or to handle the crop. For all this they relied on the Colombo agency houses and the corresponding firms in London, with which the former were in close alliance.

Though they came under fire at intervals, from the very start, as unproductive – even 'parasitic' – middlemen, Sri Lankan tea owes a very great deal to the agency houses, as can be seen from the remarkable, even romantic, history of such firms as George Steuart, Mackwoods, Whittall Boustead, Bosanquet & Skrine, Carson Cumberbatch, Bois Bros and Colombo Commercial Company.[5] Not least they provided that long succession of visiting agents, whose creative advice helped to keep the coffee and then the tea estates of old Ceylon on progressive paths long before research institutes were thought of.

From being mere valuers, whose main concern was with the financing of the coffee crop, the visiting agents came to be chosen from among the island's most experienced planters and it was natural that they should often graduate to a partnership in their particular agency and thence to a directorship or two at home.

Nationalisation disrupted all such links stretching from the tea estate to the London boardroom. The main feature of the system set up in 1975 was the formation of two huge state organisations which became responsible for most of the more important estates. In the high-grown zone, the Janatha Estates Development Board has 154, covering 40,000 ha, and the Sri Lanka State Plantations Corporation, 103 (24,000 ha). Lower down, the JEDB looks after 155 estates (36,000 ha) in the mid-grown and low-grown categories and the SLSPC 248 (39,000 ha). A variety of other public bodies – the Land Reform Commission, co-operative societies and so on – own or manage some 236 estates, mostly small and aggregating no more than 10,000 ha.

Below nationalisation level, 2,887 estates with less than 20 ha are recorded as remaining in the possession of Sri Lankan families or individuals, and the smallholders (for whose welfare and expansion successive governments have shown zealous care) have about 53,000 ha between them.

It was the emergence of the giants, the JEDB and the SLSPC, which gave rise to the most concern in post-nationalisation days. Their mere size called for entrepreneurial skills on a scale hardly matched anywhere else in the tea world. It is not surprising that management problems arose and have been only gradually overcome. For several seasons, too, the corporations had cash-flow difficulties, though these were eased when prices began to rise so spectacularly in 1983/84.

Most of the estates themselves remain in reasonably good heart and where there has been a drop in yield per hectare this has more often than not been due to the recent vagaries of the climate.

On the other hand, many feel that the new era has had a somewhat depressive effect on estate superintendents, almost invariably, of course, Sri Lankans. The old-time planter was a rampant individualist, so intensely proud of 'his' estate that one almost forgot that in 99 out of 100 cases he did not actually own it! His successor today feels the familiar lack of incentive which is nationalisation's bane the world over.[6]

In the longer perspective, Sri Lanka hardly has the characteristics of a tea country 'on the way up'. In terms of sheer output, the high-growns had their best cropping year as long ago as 1965 (91,361 tonnes, against 67,761 in 1983) and the mid-growns had theirs three years later (80,927 tonnes, against 48,458); only the low-growns have more or less held their own – 1981 was their top year with 70,311 tonnes, 1983 showing a decline to 63,068. (In 1984, however, with climate conditions 'just right' for once, plus the incentive of higher prices, output figures began to climb again.[7]) The estates, especially in the mid-country, have suffered from the alienation of land for settlement and other purposes and now cover only about 189,000 ha, against over 200,000 in the 1960s.

To counterbalance such losses, Sri Lanka has been energetic in the uprooting of old tea and replacing it with modern clonal material, mostly developed at the TRI. However, it is estimated that the area so treated in the past two decades has amounted to no more than 30,000 out of a total 245,000 ha of tea lands. If the programme were to continue at its present tempo of about 2,000 ha per annum, it is plain that, as in India, obsolescence would continue to run ahead of rehabilitation!

Development and aid

Plans were therefore afoot in 1983 for a 'great leap forward' – or at least for a substantial stride. With the help of a US$20 million credit from the World Bank, it was proposed to carry out block replanting or in-filling of some 4,600 ha over and above the normal programme and soil conservation over a further 5,000 ha. A total of 84 factories (out of some 660) were to be brought up to date and substantial sums spent (notably by the JEDB) on improving workers' houses. This scheme is only part of a much wider plan which is intended to place the tea, rubber and coconut plantations of Sri Lanka on the same level of priority as, for example, the great hydro-electric and irrigation project in the Mahaweli river basin.

It should be noted that quite apart from foreign aid on this scale, the industry benefits by a variety of government incentives. As revised under the 1983 Budget, private sector estates and smallholdings could claim replanting subsidies of Rs36,000 per hectare in the low-grown areas and Rs43,000 in the mid- and high-grown areas. Corresponding figures for the state sector were Rs30,000 (low-grown) and Rs36,000 (mid- and high-grown areas), but under the 1985 Budget the state sector was excluded from this scheme and will in future be sustained by funds from the World Bank and other donors. There are also subsidies to promote the planting of clonal tea on virgin land and yet other subsidies and tax concessions for the improvement of factories. The total expenditure on factory development projects (including new construction) between 1966 and 1980 was nearly Rs157 million.

The high cost of electricity and liquid fuels has led to the reactivation of many 'mini-hydro' units, which supplied power to tea factories before they went over to the national grid, and there is a big programme of reafforestation in uneconomic or heavily eroded tea areas, so that more wood can be used to fuel driers. It was recently reported that 6,000 ha of timber had already been planted and that there would be something like another 7,000 by 1986.

Colombo auctions

If Sri Lanka's tea-growing is highly concentrated geographically, so is her marketing and export. It can in fact be summed up in one word – Colombo. Such was the case in the pioneer age and so it is today. Yet we have only just emerged from a phase when the honours were shared, at least on the shipping side, with the rather unlikely north-eastern port of Trincomalee. Unlikely because, despite the grandeur of its natural harbour, 'Trinco's' renown up to 1958 had been almost exclusively as a naval base. In that year, labour troubles and the consequent accumulation of tea at Colombo sent exporters urgently seeking an alternative and the Trincomalee Tea Administration was born. The whole thing was sheer improvisation, yet by the end of 1958 all tea for the UK market, and much more, was going out by that route.

Trinco continued in the lead throughout the 1960s and 1970s. However, conditions at Colombo gradually improved and then came the 'container revolution' which made it the inevitable port of call for container ships on their Eastern circuit. Since February 1980 Trincomalee has ceased to be a tea port and its main commercial function now is the landing of materials for the Mahaweli scheme.

So far as the warehousing or auctioning of tea in Sri Lanka is concerned, Colombo has never had to surrender its monopoly, which in fact is doubly strong: government policy firmly supports it and Colombo has nothing to fear from the sort of competition Calcutta now experiences from new centres. The consequence is that today incomparably more tea is auctioned in Colombo than anywhere else – in 1982, 180,000 tonnes, against Calcutta's 120,000, Siliguri's 80,000, Gauhati's 75,000 and London's 60,000 tonnes. Various causes (mainly climatic) reduced the figure to 167,000 tonnes in 1983, but 1984 more than redressed the balance with a total of 202,000 tonnes. For the record, the largest quantity ever offered at a Colombo auction was 6,524,000 kg (sale No. 12, 7–8 June 1982).

Thus, the Colombo trade felt it had something to celebrate as it approached another centenary – that of the first sale of tea by auction in Sri Lanka on 30 July 1883. The story of that event, held in the offices of Somerville & Co., first emerged in any detail in *A Hundred Years of Ceylon Tea*[8] and was given a fresh lease of life in the handsome volume, *Centennial Year of the Colombo Tea Auction*, which appeared in 1983. The intention had been to mark the occasion with a ceremonial auction to be held on 26 July, but alas this coincided with the first tragic outburst of communal violence and the celebration had to be postponed until 3 December.[9] It then went off with *éclat*, 30 silver caskets being sold for charity at prices between Rs62,000 and Rs101,000, and no less than Rs1,210,000 (US$58,000) being given by the Janatha Estates Development Board for the most important lot, a sterling silver teapot.

In addition to Messrs Somerville, who appropriately sold the first lots on this occasion, five firms of selling brokers handle the vast throughput of Sri Lanka's auction tea. They are Forbes & Walker, who celebrated their own centenary in 1981; John Keells (the former name of which, John, Keell, Thompson, White Ltd, encapsulated two very old Colombo concerns, E. John and Keell & Waldock, plus two London brokers); Bartlett & Co., founded in 1904; De Silva Abeywardena & Pieris, successors to the much older Pieris & Abeywardena; and the newcomers, Eastern Brokers, who obtained a share of state business in 1980 and took the rostrum for the first time at the 3–4 March sale of that year. A sixth firm, Mercantile Brokers Ltd, opened for business on 1 January 1984.

Export

What is the destination of all of these thousands of lots? In a country whose population rose from 12.5 million in 1971 to 15 million ten years later, one might expect the internal market to be buoyant, but so far as published statistics are comprehensive it has remained stagnant at about 21,000 tonnes, so that the 'per head' figure has slipped gently downhill from 1.55 kg to 1.43.

Thus, tea sold in the Colombo auctions is to all intents and purposes tea sold for export, though with vast changes of destination since the 'old days'. It can be said that, from the first plantings in the island until the early 1960s, the producers' prime target was the United Kingdom. Up to the eve of World War

II, indeed, more than half the tea shipped out of Colombo was consigned to London and though the proportion declined with Sri Lanka's expanding production and new customers, the peak tonnage was reached in 1967 – 83,724 tonnes out of a total export of 216,537. This 83,724 tonnes represented 44,074 tonnes sold in London and only 38,650 in Colombo. The year 1974 was the last time that the United Kingdom appeared to be holding its own as Sri Lanka's best customer (30,393 tonnes, with Pakistan runner-up at 22,621) and after that for several years Pakistan took first place or was a close second, though it has now been overtaken by Iraq and Egypt. Table 3.2, showing the 'top five' for 1979–83, gives a more recent picture.

Table 3.2   Exports of Sri Lanka tea (tonnes)

	1979	1980	1981	1982	1983
UK	21,491	20,671	17,772	19,071	9,376*
Pakistan	18,575	12,834	21,657	16,113	8,669
Iraq	16,667	21,806	16,004	28,291	21,711
Egypt	14,819	16,401	17,343	24,217	31,018
USA	14,510	13,255	13,647	10,138	7,311

*Only 1,706 tonnes of this were for the London auctions. Clearly, the most significant current fact of life for the Colombo trade is Sri Lanka's huge and ever increasing stake in the Gulf and contiguous regions; this was emphasised further in 1984, when exports to Iraq reached a record 33,900 tonnes – just ahead of Egypt. In that year the United Kingdom assumed third place at 15,000 tonnes, while Pakistan's share shrank still further to 6,933 tonnes.

As long ago as 1967 it was noted that 'a great stretch starting with Libya and the UAR (Egypt), swinging through the Levant and down across Arabia to the Persian Gulf' was absorbing a tremendous total of over 80 million lb of tea and could have taken vastly more but for foreign exchange difficulties.[10] Tremendous it may have seemed then. Yet ten years later the metric tonnage reaching that wide zone had risen from 40,000 to 57,000 tonnes and in 1982 to over 80,000 tonnes.

Each territory has its own character as consumer, as we shall see later (Chapter 13), but from Sri Lanka's point of view the most potent are, and have been for many years, Iraq and Egypt, especially the former. There is no 'Iraqi buyer', such as represents the USSR in the auction room, but tea is very much a state concern. When Iraq has a requirement for Low-country Broken Orange Pekoes, which that market favours, the price soars; when she holds off, it visibly wilts.[11]

Egypt's taste for Ceylon tea goes back a very long way, but though there have been problems from time to time in financing the trade it seems now to be on a stable basis, embracing both the subsidised 'ration shops' and private retailers and including increasing quantities of prepacked tea.

Elsewhere in the Gulf and beyond, Saudi Arabia is an excellent customer, taking up an average of 10,000 tonnes of Sri Lankan tea in recent years, with a special penchant for long-leaved Orange Pekoes. Two state-controlled markets (in contrast with free-wheeling Saudi Arabia) are Syria, now also close to the 10,000 tonnes mark, and Libya, distinguished from all neighbouring territories by bringing in its 3,000 tonnes or so of Sri Lankan tea (this figure doubled in 1983) almost exclusively in packets and on a government-to-government basis. This is a reminder that nowadays nearly a quarter of the tea going out from Colombo is in 'value-added' form – packets and teabags; the point will be taken up again in Chapter 18.

All this has more than made up for Sri Lanka's loss of ground, not only in the United Kingdom, but in other traditional 'white' markets such as Australia (exports were halved to less than 5,000 tonnes by 1982 and were down to 2,104 tonnes in 1983) and the United States, where Sri Lankan leadership is now strongly challenged by Indonesia and Argentina.[12]

Compared with the handful of selling brokers the bidders who confront them are quite a numerous host, reflecting Sri Lanka's global export commitments. Heading the list in terms of tonnage handled are the familiar multinationals such as Lipton (buying extensively for Pakistan and the United States, but, of course, with wider interests), their new associate Brooke Bond (again a broad spectrum, including Iraq, Iran, Australia and much else), Harrisons & Crosfield, Finlay and Van Rees.

A comparative newcomer handling a significant tonnage of tea among other products, especially where government-to-government deals are involved, is the officially sponsored CONSOLEXPO or Sri Lanka State Trading (Consolidated Exports) Corporation, to give it its full title. Also to be seen are the present-day representatives of several of the once British-owned agency houses mentioned earlier; active buying agents such as Heath & Co.; and, perhaps the most significant in the current context, firms of indigenous origin like the Jafferjee Brothers, Akbar Brothers and M. S. Habtulabhoy, each with powerful connections in West Asia and the Gulf.

Links with the past

In spite of all changes, the Colombo scene is linked with the past in more ways than is sometimes realised. Witness the recent suggestions (endorsed by the Sri Lanka Cabinet in 1980) that teas should be brought in from other countries to be blended and packeted or teabagged for export, and even that Colombo might become a 'world centre for the auctioning of international teas'. This goes back 80 years and more! In 1901 Colombo was apparently acting as a 'blending centre' and there were complaints that 'already some tea of Indian origin is being exported in circumstances which unquestionably lead purchasers to suppose that it is the product of Ceylon'. Forward to 1935 and Ukers was commenting that

There has been periodic agitation in favour of permitting tea to be imported and blended in bond. According to its protagonists, this scheme would make Colombo a great blending and distributing centre for India, Java and possibly China tea, in addition to the Ceylon product.[13]

Whatever may have been happening in 1901, nothing came of the idea in the 1930s and, though it has obvious attractions as a boost for 'value-added' exports, it has hardly got off the ground this time either. According to the centennial volume, 20 July 1981 was the date 'when the first shipment of imported tea in Sri Lanka's history' arrived from India by the SS *General Eisenhower*, to be blended by Messrs Lipton, but neither they nor anyone else has so far put real steam behind the idea. 'Exports of Imported Foreign Tea' in the 1982 customs returns amounted to no more than 3,000 kg. Stringent labelling regulations are applied.

There were more echoes from the past when small parcels of 'Golden Tips' and 'Silver Tips' provided a mild furore in the Colombo auctions late in 1980. These highly specialised teas, consisting largely of leaf buds sorted out by hand, have a particular appeal in some Middle East countries and are bought by exporters with contacts there. Bearing in mind that the record price fetched by a conventional Sri Lankan tea up to that time was Rs215 per kilogram,[14] the Rs1,275 per kilogram given for a 25 kg invoice from Oodoowerre Estate on 2 September was fairly spectacular, but was eclipsed by Rs1,600 (Berubeula) on 26 November, Rs2,000 (Halgalla) a few days later and Rs2,200 (Walahanduwa Estate, near Galle) on 10 December – the equivalent of US$137 or £58 per kilogram, as the exchanges were then.

It all takes us straight back to the Golden Tips madness in London in 1891, when, amid hysterical scenes, the price of these same fancy Ceylons went zooming up from £4 15s. per pound to £17, to £25 10s., to £36 15s. – and then, collapse!

Promotion

The promotion of Ceylon tea has a long and colourful history, going back over 100 years (see Chapter 17), and perhaps it is partly for that reason that the name 'Ceylon' is still preferred to the more up-to-date 'Sri Lanka' on packets of the island's most important product.

Today, the work is carried out by the Ceylon Tea Promotion Bureau under the general umbrella of the Sri Lanka Tea Board. In 1982 the Bureau had overseas offices in Cairo (for North Africa, Iraq, Syria and Jordan), Dubai (for the Gulf States), at the Ceylon Tea Centre, London (for the United Kingdom and Europe)[15] and in Tokyo, Sydney, Johannesburg, and Auckland.

Out of its advertising and publicity budget of Rs27.5 million for 1982, the Sri Lanka Tea Board took its proportionate share in financing the generic campaigns already mentioned (see page 39). The report for that year also summarised uninational activity in some score of countries. Funds, however, did not permit large-scale advertising, and the word was spread mainly through support for individual brands of Ceylon tea and in the trade fair and educational fields.

Promotion in Sri Lanka itself, which also goes back a very long way, is the responsibility of the head office of the Ceylon Tea Promotion Bureau.

4 China and
her Neighbours

China

As soon as it became clear in the late 1940s that China's victorious Communist regime was buckling down to a programme of modernisation in every sphere – agricultural, industrial and administrative – the more far-sighted importers of the West realised that it could not be long before 'China tea', in a sense long since obsolete, would become a potent element in the world trade once more.

Development of tea-growing

Until Ceylon joined with India, a century ago, in 'steam-rollering' the mass market, China leaf had everywhere formed the basis of popular as well as speciality blends. Then came a silent and surprisingly swift reversal of fortune. After a brief transitional period, ending about 1890, in which Chinas met and mingled somewhat confusedly with Assams and Ceylons, 'China tea' dwindled to hardly more than a minority cult. But at least it was drunk as a distinctive and distinguished beverage, with such names as Keemun, Lapsang Souchong and Jasmine to keep the memory of the great days alive.

In his interesting compilation, *Tea and Coffee*, Mr Edward Bramah pinpointed 1950 as the year when the first shipments of China tea for over a decade reached the London market.[1] There was not much of it and, being large-leaved tea of indifferent quality, it appealed neither to connoisseurs nor to the modern packet trade. Mr Bramah urged the Chinese Trade Mission in London that the future lay with the production of Black teas to a European standard. By 1958, the Chinese were, in fact, offering a 'low-priced, low-grade, not unacceptable tea'[2] and on 22 October, '300 years after China had been first drunk in this country and twenty years after its last appearance in the auction',[3] the product came under the hammer before a crowded auditorium in Mincing Lane.

Though the contemporary Market Report records that the 709 chests offered ('on producers' account') met good competition and 'sold readily', the prices fetched were modest – about 25.4*d*. per lb against an overall average on the day of 45.6½*d*. Thereafter, 25*d*. was seldom reached but the importers pressed on and between October and the following February over 10,000 chests were sold. One packer after another began to use the new China Blacks for blending, but then, according to Mr Bramah, there was a scare about lead contamination (involving, in fact, a consignment from Taiwan) and the demand for China tea in London temporarily collapsed.

However, the Chinese authorities continued methodically to build up their foreign trade and during the 1970s, when for the first time the International Tea Committee was able to publish official figures, exports doubled from 50,000 to over 100,000 tonnes, divided more or less equally between the Black and Green categories.

Current production
Geographical factors

How has this happened and what does trading in tea mean in the China context of today? Quite apart from the question of exports, we are, of course, contemplating the largest (as well as the oldest) tea producer by far – by *how* far is still and is likely to remain a question. *Camellia sinensis* has a foothold, and usually a substantial one, in at least 16 Chinese provinces. It is essentially a South China crop, though the myth that it will not flourish north of the Yangtze-Kiang river is disproved in the important tea areas of Hubei (Hupeh), Jiangsu (Kiangsu) and western Anhui (Anhwei).[4] These three provinces form part of what Tregear defines as the 'Rice-Wheat Region' of the lower Yangtze Basin, as distinguished from the 'Tea-Rice Region' somewhat further south, where tea provides the main economic element of Hunan, Jiangxi (Kiangsi) and Zhejiang (Chekiang) Provinces.[5] Other regions mighty in tea include Guizhou (Kweichow) and Yunnan in the comparatively remote south-west; their sprawling neighbour Sichuan (Szechuan); along the sub-tropical south-east coast, Fujian (Fukien) and Guangdong (Kwangtung); and, way down on the Vietnam border, what is called the Autonomous Region of Guangxi (Kwangsi).

China Standards

In a country so vast, embracing almost the whole gamut of climates and soils and until recently so fragmented administratively, it is not surprising that the national drink, tea, should have become diversified to an extreme degree; the old-time merchants are supposed to have recognised 8,000 different origins, types, grades and qualities. Local variations will always persist, of course, but it was obvious by the 1950s that if China was to regain a foothold in the mass markets of the world some degree of uniformity would have to be achieved. And so emerged the 'China Standards' which are such a dynamic and, to some, a disturbing influence in the tea scene of today.

Traders who deal in them may have, in fact, a list of several hundreds and drawers upon drawers crammed with samples, identified with the various provinces. The latter in turn are organised as branches of what is generally referred to as the Tea Corporation, though its full, resounding title is the China National Native Produce and Animal By-Products Import and Export Corporation. The Standards, which correspond to the internationally recognised grades of Black tea, are kept remarkably consistent, so that overseas importers, ordering them by numbers, seldom find their expectations misplaced. For closer contacts between buyer and seller the most important arenas are: in the north, Shanghai, which is not itself in a tea-growing district but which is an important collecting and blending centre;

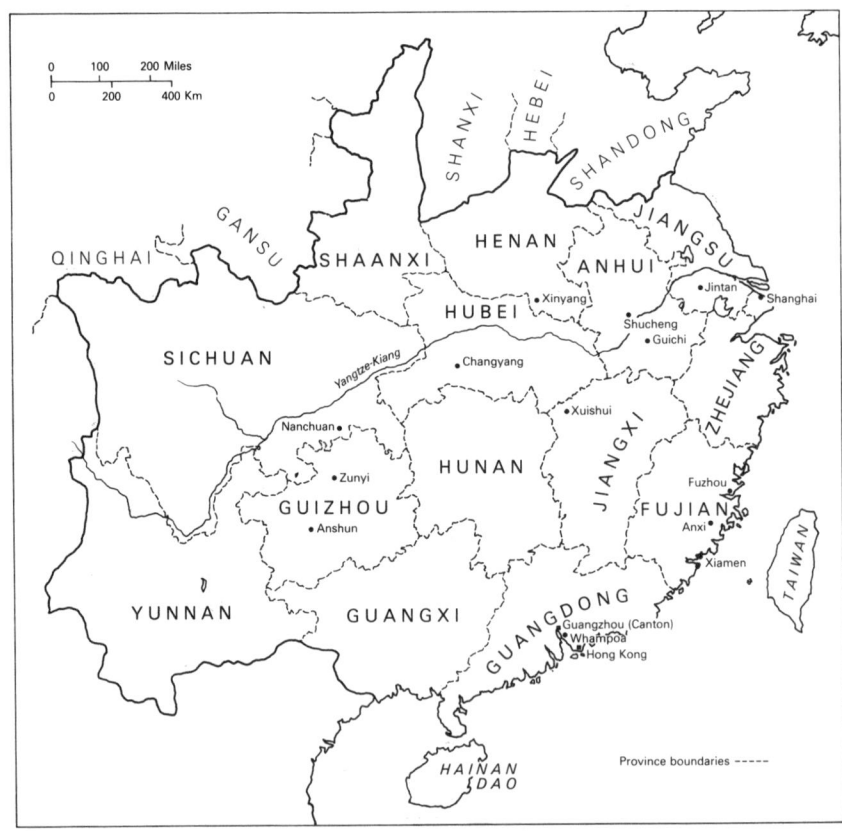

Tea-planting districts of China
Source: China National Native Produce and Animal By-Products Import and Export
Corporation and the Woodhouse, Drake & Carey Group

and in the south, Guangzhou (Canton), where the great commodity and export fairs are held in April and October. Here the teamen from the West will find representatives of all the Corporation branches; here too, tasting can take place in a fairly rough-and-ready fashion and bargains can be struck.

The teas which provide today's China Standards derive mainly from two sources, communes and state farms. Both represent a rationalisation of what was originally a gigantic, but piecemeal, peasant industry, seldom rising above smallholding level. Many of the new units are predictably vast – one foreign visitor, invited to tour a particular 'tea garden', found that it covered an area of 40 square miles! He was also, however, surprised to see only a comparatively few pluckers dotted about in any particular section – no sign of that ant-like communal activity with which a thousand films and photographs of the 'new China' have familiarised us. It seems that in some districts, at least, individual responsibility for a group of bushes is the rule, thereby anticipating the most recent trend in one or two other tea countries. The leaf thus produced goes to factories which, while often far from modern in layout, are in general well equipped, with a wide range of indigenous machinery for both CTC/LTP and Orthodox production.

Standardisation does not prevent the buyer from identifying the various provinces with distinctive leaf. The warm, dry winter days and ample summer rains of Yunnan produce high-grown teas of marked character and the province was among the first to show improved quality in our own day. Yunnan's Standards include some ten basic Broken Orange Pekoes. From the uplands of Hunan, by contrast, comes leaf mainly of 'filler' status. The quantity is enormous, second only to the output of its neighbour in the Yangtze Basin, Zhejiang, which is believed to furnish one-fifth of the national crop. Hunan, along with misty Sichuan ('when the sun shines the dogs bark'), is also the source of some of the coarser growths destined to be pressed into the legendary 'brick tea' still in demand in Central Asia, though now transported by lorry and not on the backs of human beings. (According to W. H. Ukers, 'coolies' carrying 300–400 lb each would cover 140 miles in 20 days.)

Along the borders of Jiangsu and Anhui in the lower Yangtze Basin, new state plantations for the export trade in Black tea are being developed and some reliable Standards will doubtless emerge.

Among the most interesting tea areas in China are those in the hill country of Fujian, more or less contiguous to the old southern tea ports of Fuzhou (Foochow) and Xiamen (Amoy). Here is a climate comparable to that of Southern Asia, with a consequent long plucking period of up to ten months. Not far away, on the Fujian–Guangxi border, are to be found the fabled Bohea Mountains, from which the West's generic term for China Black tea was derived. Guangxi itself has been as forward as Yunnan in improving its teas and close behind has been its off-shore island of Hainan Dao (Hainan), almost as large as Taiwan, but a much later arrival in the world of high-class tea production.

Specialities

Reverting to Fujian, it is also famous as a source of the traditional large-leaf sorts which still mean 'China tea' to connoisseurs of good living – the Panyongs and Jasmines and the smoky Lapsang Souchongs. The equally celebrated Keemuns, on the other hand, derive from Anhui Province, though no particular location appears to account for the name. Today, of course, these specialities form only a small sub-division of the China trade – maybe 5% to 10% of total exports, though much higher than that in one or two choosy European markets such as West Germany. Elitist they are, no doubt, but may their homeland continue to cherish and promote them!

Internal consumption

The Black teas, whether Standard or speciality, which we have so far been discussing do not, in fact, make up the major part of China's output and exports. It was estimated in 1983 that out of a total recorded crop of 430,000 tonnes only 80,000 tonnes was Black tea, the rest being the unfermented Green which has been the staple drink of the Celestial Empire throughout the ages. Members of a recent delegation to the United States were quoted as saying that 90% of China's 1 billion people drink tea daily. An adult male is likely to consume six to 12 cups a day, his female counterpart three to eight – perhaps reversing the Western ratio! Tea, said one speaker, was consumed on an almost cultural basis, being present in the home, the office, the factory, the school and even on the street corner.

Such universal consumption – however weak the brew – would seem to throw doubt on the crop estimate just quoted, since the residue after export would leave a mere 0.3 kg per head per annum for those 1,000 million souls. There is every indication that even in well-regimented China a vast proportion of the tea grown and drunk in and around her countless villages never finds its way into the official statistics at all.

Export

However that may be, the *export* of China tea is beyond doubt carefully organised and punctually performed. The chief ports involved in the trade are Shanghai, Fuzhou and Whampoa in the Guangzhou estuary. All are equipped for containerisation, though it was from Shanghai only that container vessels began sailing direct to the West; cargoes from the other ports were trans-shipped at Hong Kong.

This British colony, giant entrepôt centre for so much of China's agricultural and industrial products, also plays a more direct role in the movement of tea. Something like 7,000 tonnes a year is delivered there by rail and about half of this is re-exported to over 60 countries, representing every part of the habitable globe. Naturally, some of the quantities are minute, but most of the South-east Asian countries get their main supplies of China Green tea by this route.

For the China Blacks, the United Kingdom is the principal market in terms of tonnage. The years 1982 and 1983 indeed showed a remarkable stride forward – 11,800 tonnes and 15,045 tonnes respectively, against 1981's 6,000 and the previous 'high' of 7,967 in 1976. The main grades shipped in container loads to British ports are Fannings and Dusts – in other words, their target is the teabag trade, and in this the China Blacks are decidedly competitive. The 1982 surge put China into fourth place among the UK's suppliers, behind Kenya, India and Malawi. In 1984, with 15,354 tonnes, she came fifth after Sri Lanka.

China's traditional links with the United States were severed after the Communist revolution and were not renewed until 1972/73. Then the tea started to move, the graph crept upwards and today hovers about the 7,000 tonnes mark. Australia exhibits much the same pattern – only a few hundred tonnes up to 1979, now over 2,000.

On the Continent of Europe, as has been said, increased interest in China Black Standards is tempered by a continued strong taste for the traditional specialities. In the United Kingdom, incidentally, that banner is upheld by the much enhanced cult of 'Earl Grey' (see page 132).

But the China Greens are also on the march. Apart from their natural habitat, South-east Asia, they are making a very big impact in North Africa. Outstanding is the case of Morocco, which, after a see-saw relationship with China and Taiwan, seems to have chosen the former as principal partner, from whom she currently takes a formidable 12,000 tonnes per annum.[6] Egypt and the Sudan are other countries where China imports have see-sawed. There is often a good deal of politics in all this – a shifting labyrinth into which it is hardly necessary to enter.

On the strictly economic front, many people in the West believe that within a very few years China Blacks will have flooded the market, thereby severely upsetting the Indian, Sri Lankan and African applecarts. The Chinese are sensitive on this issue and deny any intention of destabilising a world market in whose orderly development they have as strong an interest as anyone else. The fact is that their dilemma is very similar to the Indians'. If the latter are feeling the relentless pressure of home demand, how much more are the former! It is true that China is beyond doubt better placed to increase her overall output and is actually doing so at an impressive rate today.[7] Yet, for the foreseeable future, it looks as though she would have to impose severe and even dangerous restrictions on her multitudinous tea-drinkers before she could build up her exports to menacing proportions.

Taiwan

In 1949 General Chiang Kai-shek withdrew from the Chinese mainland to the island of Formosa and there set up what he called 'the Government of the Republic of China'. It may not have made good that grandiose title, but Formosa, under its modern name of Taiwan, has certainly carved a niche for itself in the world of textiles and other consumer goods. It has also done its best to improve its competitiveness as an exporter of tea.

Traditionally, Taiwan was famous for three sorts of leaf, none of which are now in the mainstream of world demand – unfermented Green, semi-fermented Oolong and scented Pouchong. It was expected that as part of its modernisation programme Taiwan would step up its production of commercial Blacks, into which considerable effort had been put during the Japanese occupation before World War II. But this has not exactly happened. After a peak of some 13,065 tonnes of Black out of 20,120 tonnes exported in 1965 the proportion of Black to Green and other teas began to fluctuate at much lower levels, bottoming out at 386 tonnes out of 21,112 in 1976. Since then there has been a slow recovery.

A determined assault has been made on the more limited market for Green tea, of which, next to China, Taiwan has long been the chief exporter. Japan, South-east Asia, North Africa and North America are the main objectives, and Morocco has been the great 'plum' until recently – 11,006 tonnes in 1978 dwindling to hardly more than 1,000 tonnes per annum at the latest count. Mainland China has always been a close competitor here and may well exert a strong grip in future, especially as her experts are now *growing* tea in Morocco (see page 162).

The United States, with its large Chinese and Japanese communities, finds a ready use for Taiwan Greens, though here again the link seems to be weakening.

Mention of the United States reminds us that that is one country where a 'connoisseur-ish' taste for 'Formosa Oolongs' still lingers. Mr James Pratt is quite lyrical on the subject of a certain US$70 a pound Fancy Formosa Oolong – 'certainly one of the most beautiful teas I have ever seen or tasted'.[8] One suspects, nevertheless, that not all the quite considerable weight of Oolong which flows across the Pacific (1,048 tonnes in 1983) is in the US$70 category.

Tea-growing in Taiwan is mainly concentrated in broken hilly country at the extreme northern end of the great island, with a few scattered areas of cultivation in the centre. There is a long growing season from April to November. Formosa Oolong, says Mr Pratt, may be 'the last tea grown in commercial quantities in the old Chinese way, by families on family farms'[9] and he adds that, though there are 120-odd factories on the island, a number of those families process the tea themselves.

A recent comment from a private source is that production is bound to decline as more and more plantation land is taken over for industrial use. This has already happened in several traditional tea-growing districts, although so far statistics show only a modest decrease in the total area under tea – 29,000 ha, against a peak of over 34,000 in the early 1970s. Overall production remains steady at about 24,000 tonnes.

Japan

Geography and history unite in laying Japan, like Taiwan, alongside China in the map of the tea world and that is where we are placing her, even though one suspects that for most users of this book her significant role is as an importer of Black and Green tea rather than as a producer of the latter. In the export field, her share has never been more than modest and would appear to be dwindling.

Current production

The Japanese Green tea story can be quickly told. Today it represents virtually the whole national output, amounting to some 102,000 tonnes annually. There was a time, between the wars, when Japan sought to step up Black tea production, with the idea of challenging India and Sri Lanka in world markets. But the results were not spectacular and what seems to be a natural affinity between the Japanese and the manufacture of Green is now in full control.

Suitably enough, the most important growing region is Shizuoka Province at the foot of Mount Fuji, in the Japanese heartland, though the most prized variety, Gyokuro, comes from Kyoto, further west. This is a real connoisseur's tea, carefully hand-plucked and hand-rolled – cosseted, in fact, at every stage. Meticulous care, too, is given to the production of the powdered leaf destined for the tea ceremony (Cha-no-Yu), that peculiar, almost neurotic, but long-enduring expression of Japanese sensibility. The variety used is called Tencha and it is a measure of the refinement of Cha-no-Yu that its ritual extends far back into the tea-field itself: leaves from bushes at least 20 years old must be used for the frothed-up 'thick tea' served first, whereas the 'thin tea' which follows is supposed to derive from bushes between three and 15 years of age.

One must be forgiven for quoting at least one foreign observer's verdict on Tencha. He says that he cannot honestly recommend anyone to drink it, ceremonially or otherwise, but that it makes 'a strangely delicious ice cream'.[10]

Run-of-the-mill Green tea, however, is apt to have a cruder start in life than these exotic brews. For at least half a century much of it has been harvested with *shears*[11] instead of finger and thumb. This incessant clipping of the bush, so that it becomes part of a smooth, dome-topped hedge, at least gives a pleasing sense of elegance and order to the best Japanese estates. Much of the tea, however, is grown on tiny family plots, of which there are said to be as many as 90,000.

Internal consumption

Green tea is the country's social and complimentary drink, served free and as a matter of course in hotels and restaurants and offered as a courtesy to business visitors. There is evidence, however, that especially perhaps in the home Green tea does not quite occupy the position it once did as a 'national' beverage. Graphs and diagrams published in the American *Tea and Coffee Trade Journal* (July 1982) showed a slow but continuous decline over the past decade. Why? Mainly because of a growing taste for coffee, which has been strongly promoted and has achieved a decided social vogue.

Importation and distribution

All this has also affected for the worse the smaller but prestigious trade in imported Black tea, much of it of British origin. It has always had its distinctive place on the food store shelves. Attractively packaged in tins of traditional design and being sold at very high prices, it is in special demand at the twice-yearly seasons of family and business 'present-giving'. Names like Lipton, Twining, Jackson and Melrose have a natural lure in this context and the British connection – or snob appeal if you like – is fortified by packs christened 'Queen Mary', 'Prince of Wales', 'Lady Londonderry' and so on; names like 'High Forest Uva' and 'Teesta Valley' hint at authentically Asian origins.

Long-time importers, such as the firms mentioned above, know their way through the Japanese commercial maze, but anyone who might contemplate breaking into it it would find himself faced by a singularly cumbersome chain of distribution. Bulk tea is usually brought in by one of about five general importers or trading companies. It next passes through the hands of at least two and probably more wholesalers (there are said to be 80,000 of them) and thence to a multitudinous host of retail food stores – one for every 155 inhabitants of Japan![12] On top of that are some quarter of a million coffee shops, many of which stock tea, and a much smaller number of which sell tea only, while for liquid consumption there are the countless 'tea houses' which pervade Japanese life.

Statistically, apart from the 102,000 tonnes of home-grown leaf already mentioned, Japan needs to bring in about 12,000 tonnes annually. In 1983, the total of 11,984 tonnes could be broken down into 6,886 tonnes Black, 2,422 Green and 2,675 'other kinds' (for example, Taiwan Oolongs and Pouchongs). After losing out for a couple of years to Sri Lanka, Taiwan was once again the biggest supplier (2,708 tonnes), Sri Lanka's share being 2,579. Mainland China came third with 2,264 tonnes, while the UK's 'value-added' contribution amounted to 1,117 tonnes, worth US$4,583,000 or just over US$4 a kilogram. This suggests a sharp decline in tonnage since the mid-

1970s, when UK shares of 4,000 tonnes were recorded, but the figure is distorted – from 1979 onwards the Lipton contribution has been credited to their base in Singapore.

It is estimated that 78% of retail trade is now in the form of teabags.

5 The South-east Asian Complex

'India, Ceylon and the Netherlands East Indies' – such was the simple trinity of Black tea producing countries which dominated the market up to World War II. Dominated it, in fact, to such a point that agreement between them was all that was required to put into effect a far-reaching regulation of exports. As we shall see in Chapter 16, they had to make concessions to the nascent industries of Africa (and even, to a minor extent, of the Malay Peninsula), but in every practical sense the world tea scenario had a cast of three.

None of the participants survived the shocks of war unchanged. Ceylon gained independence and in due course a new name – Sri Lanka – but for the time being was the least affected 'tea-wise', India was rent by Partition, and the whole structure of the Netherlands East Indies was gradually pounded to pieces and rebuilt as something dramatically different.

Indonesia
Development of tea-growing

The Indonesia of today, in fact, had a difficult conception and birth. Taking all products into account, the Dutch had built up in Java, Sumatra and the rest of the archipelago what one writer has called 'the apogee of tropical export agriculture' and another 'the largest and most scientifically-based estate economy in the world'. They had also taken the initiative – unusual a century ago – of encouraging smallholders to grow tea as a cash crop and to sell it to the factories on a 'bought-leaf' basis.

The estate system was almost shattered by the impact of war and of the Japanese occupation. The planters, returning to be confronted by their wrecked factories and the tea 'growing up to the sky', believed they could rebuild, and set about it. One important phenomenon emerged, however:

The harsh treatment of collar-pruning and long years of neglect killed low-grown tea, while medium- and high-grown survived. This . . . resulted in a greater proportion of effort in all tea expansion and rehabilitation programmes thereafter being applied to the medium- and high-grown teas.[1]

By 1948 the exports were almost miraculously flowing again. But nationalism proved too strong; in 1957/58, on the insistence of President Sukarno, the Dutch-owned estates were expropriated and most of their technicians went home. Estates owned by other foreign firms were left undisturbed at first, but they could not make up for the vast Dutch plantation system having been thrown once more into confusion. It was only in the mid-1960s that reorganisation on a new basis began to pay off in terms of a higher output and exports.

Current production

This basis has no parallel in any other country. Some 28,000 ha of foreign-owned estates[2] continue to produce both Black and Green tea, while 42,000 ha of smallholdings are the main source for Green, but in the competitive world of commercial Black tea, the pace is set today by what are known as the PTPs. Twenty-nine in number, they are, in fact, great government-owned conglomerates, mostly of ex-Dutch estates and each responsible for growing a selection of the main plantation crops – rubber, coffee, coconut, cinchona, tobacco and, of course, tea. The last is to be found on 23 of them and adds up to over 40,000 ha, but just three PTPs – numbers XII and XIII in Java and number VIII in Sumatra – reckon normally to produce some 65,000 tonnes of Black leaf out of the total crop, which in 1983 reached 92,000 tonnes.

One says 'normally' because early in 1982 the much-tried industry suffered a severe blow from a series of volcanic eruptions centred on Mount Galunggung in the Bandung area of West Java. This is at the heart of the Javanese tea-growing enterprise; some estates are laid out on the very slopes of volcanoes and soil conditions are measured by the age and depth of the volcanic detritus which forms the greater part of the topsoil. PTPs XII and XIII both suffered badly. It is estimated that some 15 tonnes of ash were deposited on every hectare of tea, all plucking was suspended until the rains came to clean off the bushes and large quantities of made tea, destined for the Jakarta auctions during May 1982, had to be destroyed or used for fertiliser. The result of all this, coupled with a subsequent spell of drought, was that the 1982 crop was reduced by 11,000 tonnes to 74,000 tonnes.

Government intervention

Given no more eruptions this was no doubt only a passing phase, but it seems unlikely, in the longer term, that the prospects are for an expanding tea industry in Indonesia. In this, government policy is a more potent factor than the rumbling menace of Mount Galunggung. Until recently, at any rate, the view had apparently been taken that, in spite of periodical 'tightness' of supply, a world surplus was going to be the general rule, and that tea could not be relied upon as a foreign exchange earner. So, while other crops such as rubber, coconut and coffee were due to be boosted under an ambitious ten-year expansion plan, proposals for tea so far have been comparatively modest.

On the other hand, much has been done to improve the output of the existing estates, to modernise their factories and to better the workers' lot. It is estimated that between 15% and 20% of all production costs come under the heading of 'welfare expenses' – the provision, lavish by plantation industry standards, of free housing, education, medical care and religious centres. This reflects the government's philosophy that the workers ought to benefit materially from the wealth their labour generates.

Foreign aid

Foreign aid has played its part in the development and progress of the PTPs. It is estimated that in recent years some US$25 million has been channelled into them – not all for the benefit of tea, of course, but it has had its share. In 1971 a credit of over US$15 million was made available by the International Development Association (a World Bank affiliate) for the rehabilitation and replanting of estate tea, and World Bank funds have also helped to improve the productivity of the Java smallholdings. As a result, their average yield, at 1,600 kg per hectare, now almost equals that of the estates. Again, the Commonwealth Development Corporation has joined with the Anglo-Indonesian Corporation and the government to finance three tea and two rubber estates in an area of high unemployment in Central and West Java (PT Tatar Anya).

Auctions

Some 90% of Indonesia's Black tea is exported, and nearly half of it passes through the auctions established at Jakarta at the end of 1972 to take the place of those in Amsterdam and other European centres. Held every Wednesday and dealing solely with export teas, they are strongly supported by the government and by the PTPs, which thrive on vigorous competition between themselves; some private tea is now offered, too.

As at other auction centres, a few big buyers tend to dominate the proceedings – they represent British, American, Australian, Dutch and Singaporean interests. During 1980 the PTPs were getting a price equivalent to US$1.33 per kilogram, against all-in production costs of about US$1.22. That modest margin of 11 cents increased, of course, considerably in 1982, when the average for the year was US$1.45 and by early 1983, US$1.73. Since then, Jakarta has fully reflected the general worldwide tea price boom.

In view of the effort which has been put into getting Jakarta off the ground, the Indonesian government discouraged any idea of sending tea to the new Singapore auctions (see page 72).

Internal consumption

Internally, Indonesia is a land of Green tea. Though scarcely figuring in export statistics, it is produced in large quantities, mainly by the smallholders of Western Java, and 90% of it is processed into the 'Jasmine' or 'scented' product which is the characteristic drink of the country. A cup of this beverage, we are assured, is to be seen 'on almost every desk in government and commercial offices'. Consuming tea in business hours is not exclusively a British disease!

That having been said, total production of Green tea in Indonesia (unaffected by volcano trouble) was quoted as 22,000 tonnes – 22 million kg – in 1982, which does not appear to provide an awful lot of cups of tea, however weakly brewed, among the 150 million inhabitants of the archipelago, whether in their offices or homes. It may be suspected that, as in China, Green tea in statistics and Green tea quietly dispersed about the countryside are two different things. Up to 8 or 9 million kg of Black tea may also go into the home market.

Green tea has recently found a new and fairly demanding outlet. This is as a base for the non-carbonated soft drink known as Tee Botel. With its always popular jasmine flavour and with a good deal of sugar and a spot of Black tea (for colour) as its other main ingredients, it just suits the Indonesian palate and has made notable inroads into, among other things, the cola market. Over half a million bottles a day were being sold in 1983 and, needless to say, the success of Tee Botel has attracted rivals and imitators.

Export

Most of the tea is shipped from the Jakarta port of Tanjung Priok, but smaller quantities go from Sumatra. Rates by the Conference (long-established groupings of the traditional lines) appear slightly to favour the Continent of Europe and consignments for London have tended to move in non-Conference bottoms. A 20-ft container is the almost universal rule.

There have been great changes since World War II in the main destinations of Indonesian export teas. Up to 1939, the Netherlands East Indies sent about a third of its crop to London, where it became an important element in the popular blends, the remainder being divided more or less equally between the Netherlands, Australasia and 'other destinations'. How different today! It is now to the United States that Indonesia dispatches nearly a third of its tea, having usurped Sri Lanka's proud position as the number one supplier until Argentina in turn took over, with 15,122 tonnes, in 1983. The figures are striking as can be seen from Table 5.1.

Close behind the United States as a customer comes Pakistan – inconceivable in this context even a decade ago, but now absorbing nearly 12,000 tonnes of Indonesia's leaf. Two traditional markets regained are Australia and Egypt. Like the United States, Australia represents progress at the expense of Sri Lanka, which has found it difficult to match Indonesia's offerings at a competitive price. As to Egypt, Indonesia was dominant there before World War I and then had a long eclipse, but in recent years she has re-established her foothold. Absorption by the United Kingdom, having had its ups and downs, is now in an 'up' phase (6,924 tonnes in 1983, with a big jump to 13,784 in 1984). When the Dutch appear at Jakarta it is no longer as 'colonialists', but as keen buyers in the auctions.

Table 5.1   Imports of tea into the United States (tonnes)

	1970	1980	1983
Sri Lanka	20,634	12,649	8,672
Indonesia	10,071	14,137	13,793

One way or another, it seems that Black tea production is likely to mark time in the immediate future; it is a somewhat striking fact that while almost every other country has increased its production enormously over the past half-century, the output of Indonesian Black in 1982 was almost exactly as in 1930 – 74,000 tonnes, against 72,000 tonnes. Even this, of course, has been achieved only by strenuous efforts at rehabilitation, which were rewarded by somewhat better figures in 1983 and 1984. Green, on the other hand, may well progress, especially since a thriving home market and prosperous peasantry are just what the government would like to see.

Malaysia

When Malaysia is mentioned among teamen, the automatic mental reaction is – 'Boh Plantations'! And indeed this quite venerable enclave of tea-growing in a territory dominated by rubber, coconut and tin is a good example of the penetrative power of *Camellia sinensis*.

The Cameron Highlands were beloved by generations of expatriates as providing a 'hill-station' climate some 1,500–1,800 m above the steamy plains. Soil sampling thereabouts began as far back as 1914, but the first nurseries for imported Assam seed were not established until 1925, and it soon became apparent that here were almost ideal conditions for the production of good quality high-grown leaf. Progress, in fact, was sufficient for 'Malaya' to be given specific exemption under the restriction scheme of 1934 (see page 179).

A recent visitor to Malaysia provided an enjoyable, as well as technically informative, account both of the Boh Estate and the various plantations hemmed in by rubber in the Low Country.[3] Boh now has 747 ha under tea, with a yield of over 2,000 kg per hectare. While the original plantings were, as already mentioned, from Assam seed, there has recently been extensive use of clonal material and 'Sri Lanka 20 series of clones look particularly vigorous and attractive'.

On Low Country estates like Bukut Reedam and Bukut Cheeding, the most persistent problem was found to be the scarcity and high cost of labour. Peasant communities from which there has been a wholesale migration to the booming towns are familiar even in Europe, but the phenomenon has hit Malaysia tea hard. The only solution, in all but the most precipitous tracts, is, of course, mechanical plucking; the Malaysian version of this is being achieved with the help of Japanese 'knapsack' motorised units.

The Boh Estate is a little unusual in that its compound incorporates a packing plant from which it supplies the tea-drinkers of Malaysia with their favourite blend. However, the country's total production (3,500 tonnes in 1983, excluding smallholdings) is not enough to meet demand and in most years an equal amount, at least, has to be brought in. By far the greater part of it is in the form of Dust from China and Indonesia, plus a quaint variety of other sources. Against this, up to 1,000 tonnes are sent abroad, if exports to Singapore, Sarawak and Sabah can be so described. Some Boh tea is, in fact, packed in Singapore and does well there.

All in all, one gets the impression of Malaysia's indigenous tea-growing enterprise as a useful and well-balanced, if small, contribution to a prosperous nation's economy.

Vietnam

'French Indo-China', like 'Dutch East Indies', was a concept which, among other things, superimposed modern and ambitious plantation industries on a much older native culture. In both Tonkin (later part of North Vietnam) and in Annam in the South very fine estates, planted after the Java style, were established between the wars, while alongside them smallholders continued to produce both Black and Green tea by methods which owed little to twentieth-century science.[4]

Exports from the undivided Indo-China reached their peak during the restriction period of the late 1930s, when the 'big three' producers were pledged to cut back; exports, which before 1930 had been no more than 1,000 tonnes, reached double that figure in 1937–41. About 60% of the tea then went to France and her various territories. After that came chaos, but with the eventual partition of the country, South Vietnam emerged as a more or less regular exporter of Black tea to the West. By then the United Kingdom was its chief market, rising to 1,887 tonnes out of 2,341 tonnes in 1966.

The latest estimate for exports from both territories combined is about 10,000 tonnes, the greater part of it probably from the North, which always had a bigger area under tea (mainly around Hanoi). As might be expected, neither France nor the United Kingdom receives any measurable quantities of Vietnam tea today; apart from the considerable amount which has always been drunk locally, most of it now goes to the Eastern European bloc. In

1980, the USSR took 4,758 tonnes, Poland 558 and Czechoslovakia 269, which did not leave much more to be disposed of. In 1981, the Russian import declined slightly to 3,636 tonnes, but recovered to a record 5,341 tonnes in 1983.

Laos, Kampuchea and Burma

Indo-China, along with adjacent Laos and Kampuchea (Cambodia), has always been identified as one of the indigenous homes of the tea tree. 'Wild tea' has been found in all three and also in Eastern Burma. The latter country has a small Black tea industry which supplies local needs.

Thailand

Thailand is a grower and an importer of tea – in each case on a very modest scale in relation to her big and rapidly increasing population (46.5 million people in 1980 and a growth rate of 2.5% per annum).

Black tea is produced in the Chiang Mai region of the north, where it has a certain social significance as one of the cash crops being encouraged as alternatives to the opium poppy. No doubt because of this, the 1,000 tonnes or so which the factories turn out are heavily protected by import duties and by a requirement that packers using imported growths must buy proportionate amounts of the local product – 60% in the case of leaf, 50% of Dust.

The two main suppliers from abroad are China and Taiwan, the former sending about two-thirds and the latter a quarter of the total imports of 700 tonnes – mostly in the form of China Greens. Sri Lanka, Indonesia, India and the United Kingdom gather up the fragments of the market which remain, including very small quantities of packeted tea and teabags.

It seems just possible that if the encouragement of local production is pressed home, Thailand might eventually become a net exporter of Black tea, though probably not of high quality.

Singapore

Singapore is not a tea-growing area, but claims a place here because of its importance in the distribution network for teas of many origins. The great port has long fulfilled that function. Way back in the nineteenth century Ceylon producers found it cheaper to have teas for Russia reshipped from Singapore rather than consigning them direct, and today this applies equally to Sri Lankan teas for Japan. There is also a good deal of packing activity in which several multinationals, as well as Indian and local interests, take a hand.

Recently, however, Singapore really made the headlines by setting up as an auction centre. Here again the *rationale* lay in Singapore's 'cross-roads' character; it seemed just the place to provide a spot market for a diversity of teas – the Eastern equivalent of London, in fact. With Lipton as the moving spirit and two leading firms of brokers, J. Thomas of Calcutta and (in the earlier stages) George White of London, lending their expertise, a Tea Auction Association of Singapore was formed and the first auction was held, amid gratifying publicity, on 2 December 1981.

The target was fortnightly sales, with something like 4,000 chests on offer. Quite a good start was made; the teas coming forward were mainly from North India, with some Kenyas and much smaller consignments from South India, Bangladesh and Papua New Guinea. Altogether, the throughput up to the end of 1982 was just over 1,700 tonnes. But support from Sri Lanka and the nearest neighbour, Indonesia, failed to materialise and in 1983 the impetus was hardly kept up, with sales totalling only 475 tonnes. The early months of 1984 showed some buoyancy, but the year's total was down again at 368 tonnes.

One of the problems is that though Singapore has a first-class infrastructure, it is, among other things, an expensive place to maintain an office and it will need a much bigger turnover than anyone has shown so far for a worthwhile rate of profit to be shown. Nevertheless, prices remained good enough to attract a certain flow of tea from Assam and even though Kenya seemed to feel that a couple of containers at a time was about as much as the traffic could stand, the backers of the experiment were evidently prepared to give it a further period in which to prove itself.

Papua New Guinea

Here is one of tea's more curious and individual case-histories. There are a few other instances in which the destination of much of a particular country's crop has been settled by propinquity – Chile's near-total reliance on Argentine exports (see page 100) may be quoted. But nowhere is the bond so close as between the growers of Papua New Guinea and the consumers of Australia.

Up until the mid-1960s, such tea traffic as there was flowed in the opposite direction. In the course of her general commerce with the territory just across the Torres Strait (for which she was also political trustee), Australia would dispatch an annual 250 tonnes or so in the form of re-exports. But colonisation by *Camellia sinensis* had already begun in the Central and Southern Highlands; by 1968 an area of over 1,000 ha was in bearing and the first significant exports (289 tonnes) had been shipped. Although in that year more than half the crop was consigned to London and only 88 tonnes to Australia, thereafter the balance swung steadily in the opposite direction. Within ten years (1977) the United Kingdom was receiving 2,283 tonnes against Australia's 2,817, out of a total export of 6,196 tonnes, and by 1983 the comparative figures were the United Kingdom 532 tonnes, and Australia 5,273.

Australia does more than offer a bulk market. There are close links with individual packers, such as Bushells (Brooke Bond), and some estates sell their tea under their own labels around the Commonwealth.

Quite recently, Papua New Guinea tea (consigned by the Australian plantation company Messrs W. R. Carpenter) has made its appearance in the London off-shore auctions, fetching prices well up to the average for medium teas. A modest new trend perhaps?

The other significant customers for Papua New Guinea tea in recent years have been Malaysia and Singapore. They first began to figure in the statistics during 1977, but in 1981 took 1,408 tonnes; this was the peak, only 778 tonnes being sent in 1982 and 311 in 1983.

It may well be remarked that distance – even the distance by sailing ship between Canton and the Pool of London – has never inhibited the growth of a commerce in tea, but Papua New Guinea has special problems of cost which make the exploitation of the more remote markets difficult. Transport facilities are still in the development stage and freight charges, both internal and external, are high, while the cost of production has risen so steeply in the wake of spiralling wages, that only a resort to mechanical plucking (using shears, or the Valiant Harvester, on the Japanese model) has kept it within bounds.

Physically, Papua New Guinea is propitious tea territory, combining warmth, abundant rainfall – about 2,540 mm (100 in.) annually in the Western Highlands[5] – and a rich volcanic soil. The estates are nearly all at heights approaching those of Kenya. Yields are good (up to 1,500 kg per hectare in some instances), though the leaf, derived from seed nurseries established about 20 years ago) tends to be on the leathery side and is given severe Rotorvane/CTC treatment in the factories. The ownership of the estates is almost entirely in Australian and British hands.

High costs have not only caused many planting companies to go in for mechanical plucking, but may menace future expansion. Papua New Guinea coffee has a high reputation and, as it can be grown more cheaply, it represents a tempting alternative.

6 Africa – the Twentieth-century Prodigy

Every chapter in a book of this kind is bound to be overshadowed to some degree by the phenomenon of African tea – its dramatic rise, its present ebullience, the riddle of its future.[1] The bold outlines are clear enough; within the lifetime of anyone of middle-age we have seen the supremacy of the great Asian producers challenged by a newcomer which, although its combined output still falls far short of theirs, has penetrated almost all their world markets and has already come near to dominating the largest of them, the United Kingdom.

Nor is there any mystery as to how this has come about. The ambition of the African countries to expand their tea hectarage has meshed precisely with the ever-increasing demand of a teabag-conscious world for the type of leaf which the best of them are perfectly fitted to supply and which they can produce more economically than any of their older rivals. It may be that there are African territories which, in strict commercial or even socio-economic terms, ought not to be growing tea at all, but they are insignificant compared with the big group of thrusting pace-setters and especially with the one which opens our African survey.

Kenya
Development of tea-growing

While 'Kenya coffee' has for years past been a familiar concept, the phrase 'Kenya tea' has never slipped quite so readily off the tongue. Partly a matter of alliteration, no doubt! But it is a fact that if a certain minority of the public was actually aware, say 20 years ago, that Kenya was becoming a significant supplier of tea to the United Kingdom and other markets, this was not necessarily regarded as something to cheer about. The idea that 'good tea' could come only from two or three Asiatic sources died hard.

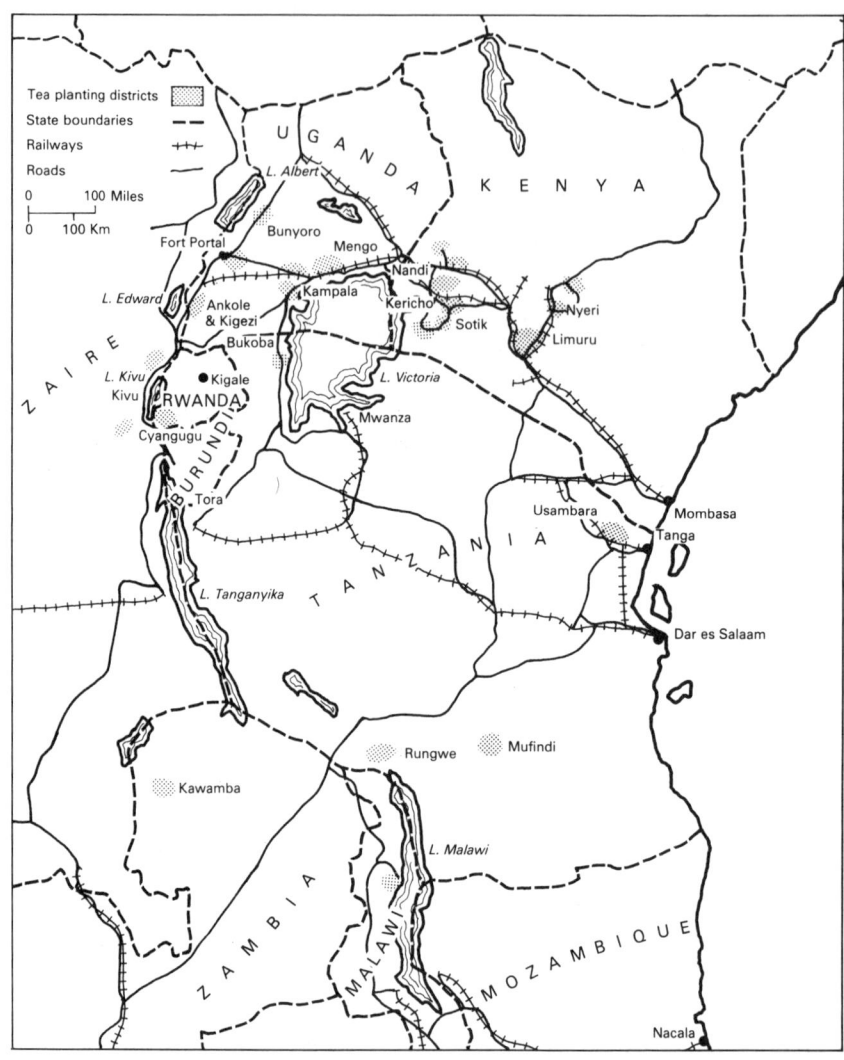

Tea-planting districts of East and Central Africa
Source: *Tea Production in Africa* (Wilson, Smithett & Co., 1969)

Today, such prejudices have been largely overcome. Apart from the fact that a few speciality Kenya blends have recently begun to appear on supermarket shelves, along with familiar Darjeelings, high-grown Ceylons and more exotic Chinas, a glance at the London auction records will show that through the 1970s and into the 1980s Kenyas have topped the price charts with remarkable consistency, even though during the 1983/84 boom India regained the lead.[2] It can, of course, be argued that the Kenyas have flourished because they happen to suit the not very exalted tastes of the

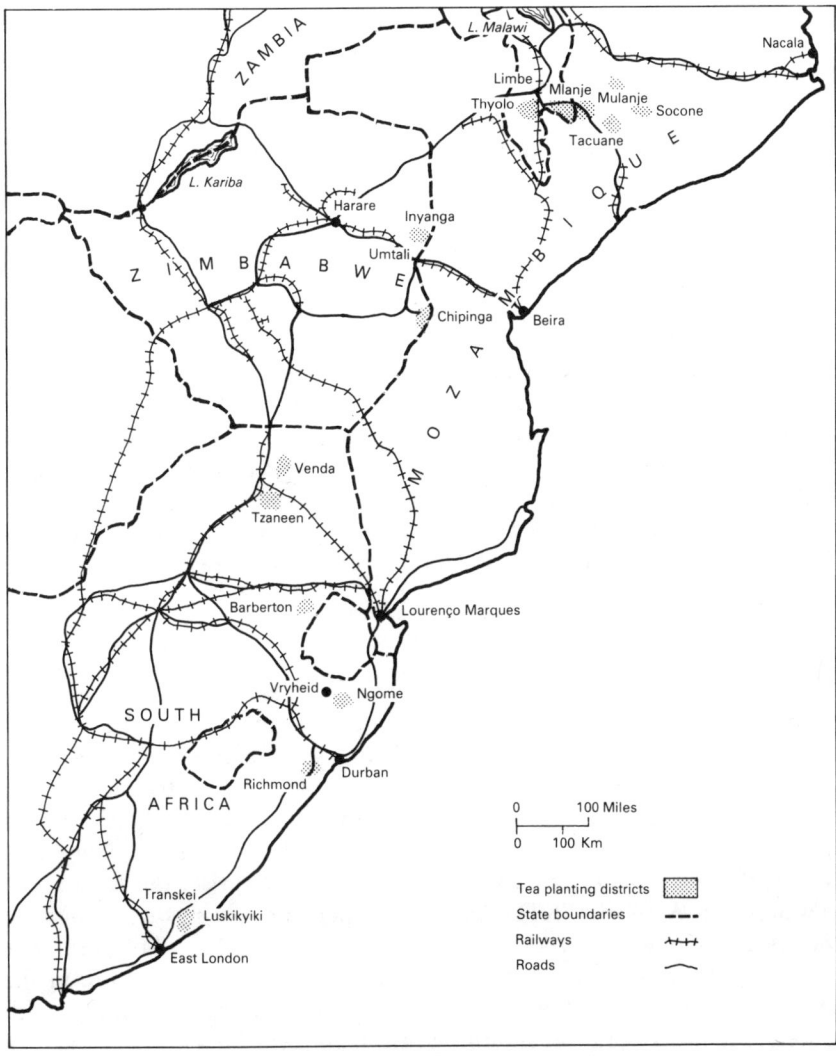

Tea-planting districts of Southern Africa
Source: *Tea Production in Africa* (Wilson, Smithett & Co., 1969)

modern British tea-drinker, but current methods of CTC manufacture in
Kenya do, in fact, produce well-made small leaf which gives excellent flavour
and bright colour, whether floating free or imprisoned in a teabag! Moreover,
appreciation of Kenya quality extends much further than the United Kingdom, since it commands equally good prices in Ireland, the Netherlands, the
United States and Canada and, as we have seen, is sold on an enormous scale
in Pakistan.

Hence, this dynamic tea country deserves rather more of our space than most. The story is supposed to have begun as far back as 1903, when a Limuru settler, C. S. L. Caine, imported seed from India and began to produce quality leaf on a 2-acre 'tea farm'. Other experimental plantings followed, especially after World War I, and by 1928 tea-growing in Kenya was sufficiently advanced for a modest offering to be made (by Messrs S. S. Smith on behalf of the Kenya Tea Company) at a Mincing Lane auction on 18 January of that year.

Thereafter things moved swiftly, with large investments in potential tea land by important overseas concerns and the now famous Kericho, Nandi and Sotik plantings soon began to be recognised.

Messrs Brooke Bond had, in fact, made a start, in a primitive manner, at Limuru as early as 1924 and quickly acquired their first 1,000 acres. Almost simultaneously, Messrs Finlay became involved through the African Highlands Produce Co., which had taken over a large tract of land near Kericho, where BEADOC (British East African Disabled Officers' Colony) was finding it difficult to show a profit on growing flax. Tea was now the favoured crop and in 1928 the first factory was built at Kerenga. Today, Brooke Bond and Finlay own about 6,000 and 5,500 ha respectively and are the country's two largest commercial growers.

Current production
Rise of the KTDA

From Mount Kenya to Lake Victoria, on both sides of the Rift Valley, tea has established its kingdom. This is overwhelmingly a high-grown area, with virtually all the estates lying well above the 2000 m (6,600 ft) line. Further east, between Mount Kenya and Nairobi, are found the equally prestigious districts of Limuru and Nyeri and, to the north, Meru. Here, if anywhere, is the heartland of that remarkable smallholding enterprise, the Kenya Tea Development Authority (KTDA); though it pervades the entire tea country, the first big pilot scheme was, in fact, at Ragati in Nyeri. The whole thing was launched experimentally by the Kenya Department of Agriculture in the 1950s. By 1960, with the help of such agencies as the Commonwealth Development Corporation and the World Bank, which have given financial support ever since, a 'Special Crops Development Agency' had come into being and within four years this had evolved into the KTDA. The part played by the commercial estates in helping to get the KTDA off the ground and in processing and marketing the members' leaf has too often been overlooked.

Today, over 150,000 smallholders tend their plots of less than 0.5 ha each and between them they supply more than a third of all the leaf processed in Kenya. The KTDA, whose shareholders are in effect the growers themselves, exercises a benevolent dictatorship over the whole scheme. It runs large nurseries for the provision of clonal material, an advisory service, buying centres for the receipt of green leaf and some 40 factories (either in operation or under construction). High levels of cultivation and disciplined plucking routines are insisted on and the result is that in Kenya – and probably nowhere else in the world[3] – the standard of smallholders' tea is fully up to that of the commercial estates and sometimes, indeed, surpasses it. A measure of what lies behind such achievements is the fact that during the 1981/82 season the KTDA's field officers carried out no fewer than 16,391 on-the-spot demonstrations.

In Kenya, tea has an edge over coffee as a smallholder's crop because it works through a more open-market system and a much higher proportion of the money it fetches filters back to the grower. Nevertheless, the tea bush is an exacting master, calling for a constant round of cultivation and plucking and there is always the temptation to switch to maize or to another cash crop such as pyrethrum.

Geographical factors

Both smallholdings and estates enjoy a number of blessings: a variety of good soils, for example, with deep friable loams predominating. The 'short rains' from mid-October to December and the 'long rains' from March to June are on the whole reliable (though in recent years they have proved less so[4]) and two visitors from Sri Lanka noted with envy the comparative absence of pests and diseases which are such a problem in the older tea lands.[5] They also observed, incidentally, that weeds were hardly to be seen on the estates which they toured, though this, of course, was due not to nature, but mainly to the 'super' cover of tea being maintained.

Kenya indeed is natural tea country, and, in the climate of optimism which has always enveloped it, indefinite progress and expansion have seemed possible. It may be that we are unlikely to see another decade such as 1969–79, when the area planted with tea doubled from 36,525 hectares to 74,300, and exports rose from 33,000 to 94,000 tonnes. Yet 1979 was in fact a bumper year, with total output falling only just short of 100,000 tonnes. And while it seemed remarkable, in current circumstances, that the 1982 yield, at 95,500 tonnes, was second only to 1979, it soon became apparent that 1983 might break the 100,000 tonnes barrier for the first time. It did so, to the resounding tune of 119,734 tonnes, and 1984 was almost as good.

These recent records have been achieved without any increase in the area under estate tea, though there has been much replanting and in-filling with high-yielding clones. However, under the stimulus no doubt of the general price rise, one leading company announced in 1984 that it intended to put a further 1,500 ha down to tea. It is also going to build another factory. The KTDA, having implemented one development plan after another, seems unlikely to expand smallholder tea much further: certainly until very recently tight finance was having a dampening effect and the programme of KTDA factory building was severely scaled down.

Government intervention

Commercially, Kenya presents the face, rare enough in Africa, of a more or less free enterprise economy. As with those pests and diseases, the planting companies find themselves unplagued by the duties, cesses, corporation taxes and the rest under which they groan elsewhere, and it is in Kenya that they chalk up their highest profits per hectare. Nevertheless, government has its say. At least 20% of all leaf has to be sold through the Mombasa auctions and 15% goes to the state-owned Kenya Tea Packing Factory in Kericho, from which the internal market is supplied.

By African standards, Kenyans are quite heavy tea drinkers – 0.81 kg per head per annum, according to the latest count. Many drink it with milk and sugar, but both *nduvia* (tea without sugar) and *stirungi* (tea without milk) contribute to the social scene.

Auctions

In general, Kenya tea moves in accord with market forces. At a fairly recent count, it was estimated that about 42% of export tea was being auctioned at Mombasa and 16% was shipped to the London auctions, the remaining 42% changing hands by private treaty. It is this last figure which is so significant. Deals between producers and overseas packers, either direct or with the help of brokers, have an enormous attraction today and are carried out with a speed and *élan* which is a world away from the leisurely procedures of the old teamen. A signpost for the future, indeed!

In such deals, nevertheless, prices still tend to be geared to the Mombasa auctions. The latter derive from those first set up in Nairobi in 1957 and only transferred to the coast 13 years later. They form an invigorating element in the African scene, being an outlet not only for Kenya, but for the landlocked states of Uganda, Burundi, Rwanda and Southern Zaïre. Until 1977 only one firm of brokers operated at Mombasa, but the bigger turnover of that year brought two more into the field. By 1981, as many as 93 buyers had registered with the East African Tea Trade Association (EATTA), which runs the auctions, though fewer than 20 are really active. Of the five who buy 60% of the tea, three are subsidiaries of leading UK packing firms. Also to be seen in the auction room are agents bidding on behalf of groups of clients who may prefer to pay a small commission rather than maintain a Mombasa office of their own. Buyers from Somalia seem almost to monopolise the lower grade teas, especially Broken Mixed Fannings, which give a powerful liquor. There is much dividing of lots.

Any comparison between Mombasa prices and those in other auction centres is rendered difficult by repeated devaluations of the Kenya shilling – three within the two years 1981/82, resulting in fluctuations of anything between seven and 13 to the US dollar.

Export

In 1983 some 100,000 tonnes of tea passed through the port of Mombasa, 90% of which was containerised, the prodigious flow being eased by the opening of 'satellite' container depots at Nairobi and Kericho. Kenya has also been the scene of some of the first experiments in 'stuffing' containers at the estate factory itself (see page 111). In the port, new equipment has been installed and operators trained. Altogether, some 9,000 people work for the Kenya Port Authority subsidiary which handles cargo – a measure of what tea and the other plantation crops mean to the country in terms of employment. It is estimated that as many as 1 million Kenyans, out of a total population of 19 million, gain a living from tea or tea-related industries.

After much experiment with cartons, the tide in Kenya seems to be setting firmly towards the paper sack as an alternative to the timber-devouring tea chest. The sacks are locally produced.

On the shipping side, Mombasa is well served, with something like 1,500 ship movements a year, shifting over 7 million tonnes of mixed cargo. Competition between Conference and non-Conference lines is keen and recently, as elsewhere in the world, the trend of rates has been, if anything, downward; for example, in late 1982 the tea trade was able to conclude a new agreement with the EA/UK Conference for a reduced rate of US$1,200 per 20-ft container.

As an earner of foreign exchange, tea has normally been well behind coffee, but this relationship may change. In December 1983 it was forecast that export earnings for the year might almost double to US$245 million.

Tanzania

Tea-growing in what used to be known as Tanganyika is a curiously dispersed affair. Hundreds of kilometres separate the three main areas where *Camellia sinensis* has taken root – Mufundi/Rungwi in the Southern Highlands, the Usambara Mountains in the north-east and Bukoba far away on the western shores of Lake Victoria. The Usambaras represent perhaps tea's only legacy from the Germany of Kaiser Wilhelm II, since the earliest plantings there were made while Tanzania still formed part of German East Africa. The real growth, however, was between the wars, when a pattern of well-found estates under British ownership was established. This still persists, one of the leading plantation companies being Messrs George Williamson.

While most of the Mufundi/Rungwi tea is in the high-grown category, with elevations up to 2,000 m (6,600 ft), in the Usambaras there are several quite low-grown estates. The Bukoba tea is mainly near the 1,500 m (4,900 ft) line.

The Usambaras have a climate not unlike Kenya's, with 'short rains' from mid-October to December and 'long rains' from March to May. In the Southern Highlands there is only one wet season, lasting from December to May. Frosts are not unknown in the drier spells, when production is low. The total area devoted to tea, which for some years has been around the 18,500 ha mark, places Tanzania a level second with Malawi in the African league table.

As in Kenya, a new element has emerged in the shape of smallholders' tea, which has made considerable progress since the early 1960s under the auspices of the Tanzania Tea Authority. Organisation is not yet up to the level of the KTDA and, in spite of World Bank assistance in the formative period, finance has usually been extremely tight. Nevertheless, smallholders, from their little plots of about a third of a hectare, contribute up to 35% of the country's total output of about 17,000 tonnes. Most of their leaf goes to the eight factories owned by the TTA.

Historically, the United Kingdom has always been Tanzania's best customer, the peak being reached in 1979, when no less than 12,459 tonnes were consigned to UK destinations, out of a total export of 15,024 tonnes. Since then, there has been some proportionate decline, but more than half the Tanzania tea sent abroad still goes to the United Kingdom – about 4,000 tonnes of it for the London auctions, where it normally fetches prices about half-way between the Kenyas and the Malawis. Some also used to be sold at Mombasa, but after the closing of the border with Kenya in 1976, that channel dried up.[6]

The great feature today is the growth of private sales to buyers from the United States, Canada, Pakistan and – quite recently – the Sudan. European countries, such as West Germany and the Netherlands, are also customers on a more modest scale. There has been some growth in export sales of tea packeted in Tanzania.

Though the transport position has not been quite so difficult as in landlocked Malawi or Rwanda, 'getting the tea out' has its problems. Usambara is within comparatively easy reach of the port of Tanga, but conditions there are not good, with much congestion and no deep-water wharfs or container facilities. From Bukoba, tea has to be ferried across Lake Victoria to the Mwanza railhead and thence to Dar es Salaam. Leaf from the Southern Highlands is also routed to Dar, via the new Tanzam (Tanzania/Zambia) railway which has certainly eased transport problems for the whole region, but Dar, too, though quite well equipped, tends to become choked up. One must face the fact that the Tanzania tea industry partakes of the common economic malaise of that country, reflected in the fact that for years now estate owners have been able to repatriate only a small percentage of their funds to buy equipment and nothing at all to pay dividends.

Tanzania itself is not a characteristically tea-drinking community, but a promotional campaign is in progress to try to boost internal consumption above its present level of 3,000 tonnes (17% of production). In terms of purchases per head, the Tanzanians' mere 0.19 kg is something on which it should not be too difficult to improve. Locally grown packet tea is marketed through the Tanzania Tea Producers' Association.

Malawi

The former British Protectorate of Nyasaland – independent Malawi since 1966 – was the only territory in East or Central Africa with its tea-growing origins rooted in the Victorian age. As with most things in early Nyasaland, the first plantings seem to have been on a mission farm (1878), but from the late 1880s onwards the commercial cultivation of tea was firmly established in the Mulanje district close to the Mozambique border. Estates such as Lujeri, Lauderdale and Thornwood were in full flow by the turn of the century. An unfortunate beginning made with China hybrid seed was soon corrected.

Current production
Geographical factors

Mulanje is still one of the two districts in the southern part of the country in which tea-growing is concentrated, the other being Thyolo (formerly Cholo) a little further to the West.[7] Of the two, Thyolo's estates, going up to 1,100 m (3,600 ft) on the Shire Highlands, are slightly more high-grown than those of Mulanje, but the latter do somewhat better in respect of rainfall. Production tends to be intensive in the earlier months of the year, which are rainy as well as hot; it falls off in June/July and picks up again somewhat towards October. It is rare for Malawi to go a whole month without rain, but this happened in September 1983 – in fact, there was a no-rain period from 25 August to 15 October, followed by further dry spells, giving some temporary anxiety over crop.

The Malawi tea story during the past 20 years has been of a modest expansion in area planted (18,515 ha in 1982, against 12,507 in 1962). However, production has more than doubled, from between 12,000 and 13,000 tonnes in the early 1960s. For 1981 and 1983, the figure was about 32,000 tonnes; 1982 boasted an exceptional 38,482 tonnes though 1984 came within 1,000 tonnes of it.

Tea Research Foundation

Malawi is, in fact, a classic instance of a country whose tea output has responded to the development of, and extensive replanting with, high-yielding clones. For this the planters have largely to thank the Tea Research Foundation of Central Africa. The Foundation has research stations in both Mulanje and Thyolo, but it also works extremely closely with the commercial estates. Its reputation has, in fact, spread into neighbouring territories, including Zimbabwe and South Africa, which help to support it; we have noted elsewhere the activity of Dr R. T. Ellis, its Director over many years and doyen among tea research scientists, as Tea Adviser to UNCTAD.

The estates and groups, some 40 in number, are almost entirely owned by British-based plantation companies, such as Eastern Produce and Brooke

Bond (who took over the old J. Lyons interests), while a few are still in private hands.

Smallholdings are not so highly developed as in Kenya, but the Smallholder Tea Authority brings together nearly 5,000 farmers, who have some 2,300 ha of tea in bearing. It also owns a factory at Mulanje jointly with the government of Malawi. The Authority is one of the tea enterprises in Africa which has received substantial loans from the UK's Commonwealth Development Corporation.

Export

The Malawi factories today are mainly geared to CTC and LTP production, and there has been much re-equipment with fluid-bed driers. The medium quality leaf such as Malawi sends abroad meets a ready sale, especially in the United Kingdom, which in 1983 took 19,000 tonnes out of 31,000 exported. Other receptive markets are South Africa, Pakistan, the United States and the Netherlands, and these countries are well represented at Malawi's own auctions, founded at Limbe in 1970 and now handling about 35% of the country's tea.

Malawi's burgeoning success as an exporter is the more remarkable since she faces formidable problems in merely getting the tea out of the country. In the first place, the factories are frequently short of chests; Malawi's own timber resources are limited and imported chests get stuck in the bottleneck of the Mozambique ports, so that increasing use is being made of cartons from South Africa and more recently of paper sacks from Kenya.

The country is, of course, completely landlocked and its traditional rail routes to the sea at Beira and Nakala, particularly the former, have long been through guerrilla country, and are in poor condition.

Communications via Tanzania have improved somewhat, but other exits have had to be found. Tea was probably being put into containers (received in the country with imports) sooner than in any other tea territory and in the 1980s a large proportion of these began to be routed by truck and rail right down to Durban on South Africa's east coast. It is a long haul and puts perhaps 5p per kilogram on costs; on the other hand, the port of Durban works at an admirable tempo and anything up to a fortnight can be saved in getting the tea to market.[8]

Moreover, Malawi has consistently been the biggest user of the recently established 'off-shore' auction system in London, and the speed-up in procedure is remarkable. Documents and samples are air-lifted without delay and a container load may be auctioned and paid for within a fortnight of its being put on shipboard at Durban.

Malawi is one of the landlocked countries (Burundi and Rwanda are others) which when prices were right and communications particularly difficult, resorted to the air-freighting of crop in 1984/85.

Though yield per hectare may continue to increase for some time, the area under tea in Malawi is unlikely to show much more expansion. Some estate companies, in fact, have a policy of diversification into various branches of agriculture and a small amount of tea in the more arid zone has been uprooted in favour of coffee.

If statistics are to be believed, there is only the narrowest of gaps between production and export figures for Malawi and consumption in the country is not high, but a number of estates do quite well by selling their own tea to the 'locals'.

Mozambique

Here is a tea territory with great potential which has not fully recovered from the trauma of 'decolonisation' – in this case the withdrawal of the ruling Portuguese from 1974 onwards. At the time of writing guerrilla activity was still rife, its main effect being to disrupt communications between the up-country areas and the ports.

In the circumstances, it is rather remarkable that Mozambique was able to get on with the rehabilitation of many of its factories (all except two of which are nationalised) and to make striking advances year by year in terms of exports.

Development of tea-growing

The story of tea in Mozambique goes back to at least the early 1920s. When Ukers was writing there was already a substantial area under the crop in the district of Milange, just across the border from Malawi's Mulanje, whence indeed the pioneering impetus came. The most rapid development, however, was in Gurue, north-east of Milange, followed by Socone and Tacuane, to the south-east. World War II seems to have given a stimulus to the Mozambique industry and by 1944 exports had passed the 1 million kg milestone.

Current production

Progress after that was steady. By 1961 Mozambique was well ahead of Malawi in terms of area planted (15,128 ha, against 10,600 ha), though production lagged behind and had still not quite caught up when the disruptions of 1974/75 caused a temporary hiccup. Malawi, of course, continued to advance, until in 1981 the comparative figures shown in Table 6.1 were reached:

Table 6.1 Tea production and exports in 1981 (tonnes)

	Production	Exports
Mozambique	22,190	18,000
Malawi	31,965	31,527

However, for Mozambique, as for Malawi, 1981 did not quite represent a peak. In the autumn of 1982 it was reported that during the season ending in

June there had been a bumper harvest 'beating the colonial record by 6,000 tonnes'[9] and that, altogether, Emocha, the state-owned company, had produced 23,000 tonnes of tea. Later figures hardly bear this out, and during 1983/84 drought and disruption took a heavy toll.

In the world's markets, Mozambique tea occupies a peculiar status. Of the rising demand it enjoys there can be no doubt: in 1982 the UK offtake, which had declined rather sharply the previous year, rose to 8,747 tonnes, though 1983 (5,876 tonnes) again reflected a general setback to Mozambique exports. Two other leading customers, the United States and the Netherlands, took 4,351 and 2,289 tonnes respectively in 1983.[10] Yet by that perennial yardstick, the London auctions, the prices given for Mozambiques remain where they have always been – way down at the bottom of the table. During 1982, when Kenyas were averaging 107.1p per kilogram at Sir John Lyon House, they did no better than 66p, and in 1983 the 'concertina' stayed open – Kenya, 148.0p; Malawi, 132.4p; Mozambique, 100.5p.

The fact is that although in terms of elevation, climate and soil, the tea lands of Mozambique are at no particular disadvantage, they fall below most others in Africa in respect of cultivation and manufacture. The 'plain' sorts which are still their staple production tend to disappear, with the humble status of 'reducers', into the lower-priced blends.

Delays of various sorts contributed to the recent rather difficult situation. Apart from the guerrilla activity on the railways already referred to, the ports have had their own problems. Beira, from which Mozambique and many Central African teas used to be shipped, has now been superseded by Nakala, but difficulties with equipment have caused bottlenecks there too. Factories have also found their tea accumulating because of long hold-ups in the delivery of packing material.

In spite of all setbacks, Mozambique seems confident of its future. One reads of considerable expansion plans, which may or may not come to fruition.

Uganda

'Tragic' is not too strong a word to describe the fate of the Uganda tea industry between 1971 and 1979 – the Amin years. Here was a country which in climate and soil was a 'natural' for tea-growing and which had been making progress at a rate which no other African producer could outstrip. The story goes back to the early twentieth century when, with strong government backing, Assam *jats* were tried out on a number of plots at Entebbe, Kampala and Fort Portal. After World War I British ex-service settlers began to substitute tea for coffee and rubber, which were then fetching low prices, and by the 1930s output was sufficient for Uganda leaf to make regular appearances on the London auctions.

Expansion continued after World War II, and the situation on the eve of the 1971 upheaval was that Uganda could show some 50 well-found estates and about 11,000 'outgrowers' – peasant smallholders – who sent their leaf either to special factories owned by the Uganda Tea Growers' Corporation or to the nearest estate factory. Altogether a good 20,000 ha were under tea, with an average out-turn of over 1,000 kg per hectare. Uganda also had the distinction of being the only African country where instant tea ('Fine Brew') was being manufactured and marketed.

But there was one weak spot and it proved nearly fatal to the industry. The Ugandans themselves preferred to work on their own *shambas* and the plucking and cultivating on the estates was done almost entirely by immigrants from Rwanda and neighbouring territories. When chaos broke out they fled to their homelands and have so far not returned. Production became impossible, the estates (all of which had been nationalised) were looted and the tea had to be left to run wild.

Even when order was more or less restored from 1980 onwards, the labour problem seemed insuperable. However, one or two proprietary companies were prepared to 'have a go', notably Messrs Mitchell-Cotts, who entered into a joint venture with the government of Uganda. Under this, the Toro and Mityana Tea Company (TAMTECO) was formed, to be owned by the government (51%) and by Mitchell-Cotts (49%) and the estates belonging to the latter before the Amin era were transferred to it. Mitchell-Cotts would provide the management.

It soon became apparent that sufficient labour could not be recruited, so that early in 1981 the decision was taken to develop mechanical harvesting. At the time of writing Mitchell-Cotts had 550 ha in production. Much of it had been abandoned four or five years previously, but after pruning the tea responded well to the mechanical harvester. All factory production is CTC. Outgrowers are also rehabilitating tea areas and producing leaf for which, until the recent general rise in prices, they were paid 25 Uganda shillings a kilogram.

The eventual target is to bring back into production some 2,000 ha of Ugandan tea and for this loans to the amount of US$5.3 million have been provided by a World Bank affiliate, the International Finance Corporation, with support from the United Kingdom, West Germany and Switzerland and from Uganda's own Development Bank.

World Bank and EEC funds have given much-needed help with the infrastructure and Uganda is one of two tea-growing territories (Malawi is the other) which have qualified for assistance under the Lomé Convention, whereby Third World countries are compensated if their earnings from exports to the EEC fall below an agreed level (the 'STABEX' mechanism). Uganda received the equivalent of US$4,330,000 through this channel in 1979.

As in Tanzania, Uganda's tea lands are somewhat dispersed, but activity is mainly centred round Fort Portal in the west, where the estates of the Toro district mount to 2,000 m on the slopes of Ruwenzori, and in the neighbourhood of the capital, Kampala.[11] Cropping continues all the year round and the principal rains, which as a rule are adequate for all needs, fall between September–November and March–May.

As time went on, exports of Uganda tea showed some signs of picking up: 1,198 tonnes went out through Mombasa in 1982 – twice the 1980 and 1981 level – and 1983 and 1984 were better again. But it all has a long way to go.

Smaller producers

The attractions of tea-growing have been felt far beyond the well-recognised pioneer group – Kenya, Malawi, Tanzania, Mozambique, Uganda – and in this section a number of its outposts are explored.

Rwanda

Close to the Equator, and tucked in between the lake systems of Victoria to the east and Kivu/Tanganyika to the west, are the twin republics of Rwanda and Burundi, formerly a single Belgian Trusteeship Territory known as Ruanda-Urundi. In terms of tea, Rwanda is decidedly the senior partner. By about 1970, when Burundi tea was just heard of abroad, Rwanda had for some years had five sizeable estates in bearing and was already a regular contributor to the world's supplies.

The hills south-east of Lake Kivu proved a good tea-growing terrain. Rainfall is similar to Uganda's and cropping is continuous throughout the year. The result is tea of excellent quality which emulates Kenya's values on the London market. It was something of a landmark when a Rwanda Dust achieved top price at a 1982 Sir John Lyon House sale, and this has happened more than a dozen times since.

The independent government of Rwanda considered it had a sound *rationale* in giving priority to tea production. The country's economy was perilously dependent on coffee and jobs were needed for its fast-growing population, which at 183 per square kilometre is now the densest in continental Africa. Overseas aid was sought and an important contributor was found in the EEC's European Development Fund. Between 1960 and 1979, the EDF invested over 24 million ECUs (European Currency Units equivalent to about US$25 million at the then rates, see Table 6.2) in Rwanda tea. Support was also forthcoming from Middle East sources and from the African Development Fund, which put up a US$1.1 million loan to finance the Ramba-Gaseke project and its factory.

The result is that today Rwanda has over 8,000 ha under tea and there are ten factories in production – nine owned by the Government (OCIR) and the other (Cyohoha) jointly with private enterprise. They operate almost entirely on a bought-leaf basis. Output increased six-fold between 1970 and 1983 (from 1,245 tonnes to over 7,000 tonnes). About a third of Rwanda's tea is

Table 6.2 European Development Fund – aid to tea-growing (values in ECUs)

Country	1st EDF 1960–64	2nd EDF 1965–69	3rd EDF 1970–74	4th EDF 1975–79	Total
Burundi	2,666	4,457	16,840	13,859	37,822
Cameroon	–	50	158	2,840	3,048
Madagascar	–	586	4,501	–	5,087
Rwanda	2,534	5,216	12,982	3,500	24,232
Sudan	–	–	–	8,638	8,638
Zambia	–	–	–	3,100	3,100
Zaïre	–	4,799	5,458	3,030	13,287
Uganda	–	–	–	5,000	5,000
Total	5,200	15,108	39,939	39,967	100,214

Note: The European Currency Unit was worth US$1 up to 1971; from 1972 to 1978 it varied between US$1.1 and US$1.2; in 1979 it rose to US$1.37.

consigned to London, the rest being more or less equally divided between the Mombasa market and private sales.

All went well until the beginning of the fifth EDF period (1981–85). By then the population explosion which had originally set off Rwanda's expansionist tea policy had begun to work in the opposite direction; the government felt it must concentrate on food crops rather than cash crops and the EEC was asked not to put any more into tea. A modest balance left over from the fourth EDF is being spent on technical assistance.

There is quite a brisk internal trade in the country – packeted tea from the Cyohoha factory, for example, is to be found on the shelves of the local supermarket.

Burundi

In Burundi, the motivation towards tea-growing was much the same – a mounting population, much of it unemployed, and an 80% dependence on coffee.

In 1973 hopes were high (in spite of the fact that initially estate work had not been popular with the local people) and the target was to raise the area under tea from 2,800 ha in that year to 4,688 by the end of 1981. This does not appear to have been achieved until some two years later; nevertheless, output rose from a mere 657 tonnes in 1973 to 2,500 tonnes. Some 64% of the tea land represents smallholdings on which about 25,000 families live and work, the rest consists of estates employing about 4,000 labourers. Four factories are active.

Finance has come largely from the International Monetary Fund (IMF) and the EDF, and the latter's commitment to Burundi appears formidable – some 36 million ECUs in the first four EDF periods. About 8 million of this went into creating the agro-industrial complex at Tora, with its 580 ha of tea. Improvements to its heat and energy resources included getting a peat bog operative – peat is quite important in the Burundi economy. It was also planned to plant 600 ha of trees for fuel.

In general, the progress of Burundi tea is regarded as somewhat disappointing, due mainly to local management problems and a lack of experienced tea-makers. So the emphasis now is on consolidation rather than expansion. Out of the 9 million ECUs allotted under the fifth EDF, 2.4 million is earmarked for technical staff – tea-makers, management advisers attached to the Office du Thé de Burundi and a marketing specialist. Fertilisers, lorries and spare parts will absorb most of the rest.

Burundi tea used to be shipped out through Dar es Salaam, 700 miles away, but now makes its way to equally distant Mombasa. It is regarded as less 'useful' than Rwanda's and has not so far achieved the same status on the London market. Some of it has arrived in sacks of woven polypropylene – a good stout material, but tea-tasters view it with suspicion.

Zaïre

While Rwanda and Burundi each cover a modest and compact 26,000 to 28,000 square kilometres, their neighbour to the west, Zaïre (the former Congolese Republic), is enormous, three-quarters the size of India in fact. However, its tea-growing is concentrated close to the Rwanda border, in the mountainous country north-west and south-west of Lake Kivu. Up to the time of Zaïre political upheavals in the 1960s, the industry was making quite good progress and some 22 estates were listed in *Tea Production in Africa*.[12] Since then, many fields have been abandoned and the area in bearing appears to have declined from 12,652 ha in 1970 to 10,300 seven years later. Output is now about 5,000 tonnes per annum.

The EDF moved in to help in revitalising the industry. Two ailing estates at N'gweshe and Kavumu in South Kivu were brought back into efficient production and a new one with a planned annual output of 800 tonnes was planted at Butuke in North Kivu, where a few years ago the splendid red topsoil was giving fabulous yields; it was expected to reach 600 tonnes in 1983.

Having invested some 13 million ECUs in Zaïre up to 1979, the EDF was finding a bit more in 1984 to complete the hydro-electric works which power the factory and possibly to extend the area of tea somewhat.

Like much else in Zaïre, tea has suffered from infrastructure problems, in particular the near-collapse of the road system and the difficulty in obtaining spares and skilled attention when modern equipment like the CTC requires it. Transport of export teas is also hampered, and perhaps it is just as well that there is a home market of 22 million people to absorb a high proportion of the crop.

Zimbabwe

Though the planting of tea in Zimbabwe (Rhodesia, as it was) got off to as lively a start as any in Africa, it was not sufficiently advanced to be brought within the net of the first International Tea Agreement – that distinction was reserved for Kenya, Uganda, Tanganyika and Nyasaland (1934). Somehow the name of the pioneer estate in the Chipinga District on the Mozambique border – 'New Year's Gift' – made its mark soon after the factory was completed in 1933, even though the area under tea was less than 100 ha. New Year's Gift also gained some celebrity as the first 'fully irrigated tea estate', water being drawn from the Tanganda river for the purpose. It was certainly a necessary measure since the local rainfall turned out to average no more than 661 mm (26 in.) per annum, compared with 1,143 mm (45 in.) in other parts of Chipinga, which in itself is well below what is regarded as an acceptable average rainfall elsewhere in Africa.[13]

Other early estates in Chipinga were Ratelshoek, Jersey and Zona, all of which, along with New Year's Gift, are still operated by a local plantation company, Tanganda Tea Estates. A little later the Iyanga district, in the Honda valley 150 miles away to the northward, was opened up for tea, with two big estates; one of them, Luleche, had 800 ha coming into bearing by the end of the 1960s and was turning out nearly 1 million kg of tea. Luleche is now one of the Honda valley properties controlled by Messrs MacLeod Russel.

Currently, Zimbabwe's tea lands extend to nearly 5,000 ha and the 1982/83 season's yield was expected to come out at nearly 11,000 tonnes.

Exports accounted for 60% of total production in 1982, 4,467 tonnes going to the United Kingdom and 1,845 tonnes to South Africa. On the London auctions, prices for Zimbabwe teas approximate fairly closely to the Malawis.

What of the future? The plantation industry in 'Southern Rhodesia' was an example of British colonial enterprise, *pur sang*. As the independence war developed in the mid-1970s, it became increasingly difficult to finance expansion, though output, which had recently risen sharply (thanks to good cultivation and better clones), remained remarkably robust. Changes under Mr Mugabe's socialist-orientated regime were not drastic and British management remained general. Tea has, however, been made a 'controlled commodity' and placed within the orbit of the Grain Marketing Board.

Nigeria

Hitherto, this large and populous country has been curiously inconspicuous in the tea landscape – it has no production and imports about 2,000 tonnes per annum, or a mere 25 g per head for Nigeria's 80 million people.

However, change is on the way. The Lipton periodical *Blend* (Winter 1982) contained a spirited account of the tea-growing project which is in progress on the Mambilla Plateau, adjacent to Cameroon. In this remote spot, 640 km from the railhead and 530 km from the nearest airport, 450 ha have been set out with Kenya clones flown in from East Africa. An eventual yield of 2,000 kg per hectare, compared with Kenya's 2,000–2,700, is looked for when the whole estate is in full bearing. Although there is no actual shortage of local labour, plucking is mechanical (with hand-held machines) as well as manual, the former harvesting 300 kg of green leaf per day, against the manual 36 kg. More land is being set aside for a smallholders' scheme along East African lines.

The factory which serves all this is one of the most modern in Africa and is geared to an LTP/Rotorvane style of manufacture.

Mambilla is already feeding a certain amount of tea into the distribution network of Messrs Lipton, who blend in the country and dominate its market, and the time may come when indigenous leaf could be meeting up to half Nigeria's needs – at the present low level, that is. This leads on to the question of consumption. Up until now Nigeria has drawn on India, Sri Lanka and Bangladesh for her modest supplies,[14] and a survey sponsored by the Commonwealth Secretariat as part of its assistance to the International Tea Promotion Association suggested that it might well be worth while to resume the promotional work inaugurated long ago by the International Tea Market Expansion Board. As a first step, 1983 saw the production of a booklet, *Things Worth Knowing about Tea*, for distribution both to educational bodies and to the general public.

Cameroon

Cameroon has the dignity of being the only territory on the West African coast with an established stake in tea-growing, though there seems no reason, climatically, why other regions to the north and south, besides Nigeria, should not join in. Beginnings were made a quarter of a century ago in West Cameroon, partly at Ndu, over 2,000 m up in the Cameroon Mountains, and partly at Tole, lower down.

The Cameroon Development Corporation, the operative body today, is mainly interested in rubber and oil palm, but has more than 1,200 ha under tea. It was originally financed by the Commonwealth Development Corporation, which has recently combined with the European Development Fund[15] and the French Caisse Centrale de Coopération Économique to provide capital for a new 425 ha estate and factory at Djuttitsa, near the town of Dschang in the Western Province. As in other African countries, such developments are motivated partly by the need to find jobs in the rural areas for young people who are tending to drift away to the towns.

When fully operational, Djuttitsa should add 1,000 tonnes of tea to Cameroon's 2,000 tonnes annual output; most of it will help to supply the local market, but between 10% and 25% may find its way abroad.

Zambia

Zambia has been, and is likely to remain, more famous for copper than for tea and, in fact, quite knowledgeable folk have denied the latter's existence there! But the single plantation project at Kawamba in the north of the country goes back to 1969 and has been run by the Rural Development Corporation since

1974. Help from the EDF has been invoked to consolidate the 300-ha estate and to step up the capacity of the factory. It is planned to allocate a further hectarage to small growers and ultimately production should rise above 1,000 tonnes.

Sudan

The Sudan has a significant status as an importing country (see Chapter 13), but is also taking tentative steps towards becoming a producer in her own right. The area of production is the Imaton Mountains in the deep south. Here a substantial investment of 4.5 million ECUs was made under the fourth EDF to help in the planting out of 435 ha and the provision of seeds and good advice for the outgrowers. There is to be further assistance to the extent of 12 million ECUs under the fifth EDF, partly for the construction and equipping of a factory. The target is an output of 900 tonnes by 1985.

South Africa
Development of tea-growing

Attempts to grow tea in South Africa go back a remarkably long way – in fact, the tea bush was existing (one would not say flourishing) there before most of its other African habitats were even names on the map.

Natal was at first the favoured scene. The earliest experiments belong to 1850, but it was the arrival of the fatal fungus *Hemileia vastatrix*, some ten years after its assault on Sri Lanka, which caused a similar switch from coffee to tea in South Africa. The fact that many of the coffee-growers were 'refugee' families from Sri Lanka no doubt had something to do with the choice of crop, though the necessary seeds were imported from Assam (not a very good *jat*, it is alleged). Planting began about 1877 and soon some 800 ha were under tea in the Stanger district, near Natal's border with Zululand. For a time all went well. More land was planted and in the early twentieth century output reached a maximum of about 1.5 million kg per annum. Not long before World War I, however, the industry showed symptoms of decline – Ukers attributes this to the low prices obtained and the heavy cost of labour, stemming partly from the 1911 ban on imported Indian workers, though growing conditions were never ideal. Decay continued between the wars and finally, in 1948, the last of the Stanger tea was pulled out and the estates went over to sugar.

Current production

Yet only 15 years were to pass before the campaign was renewed. In the matter of tea supplies, as in much else, South Africa is vulnerable to boycott and seeks some degree of self-sufficiency. The fresh start was made near Tzaneen, in Northern Transvaal, in 1963; Barberton in Eastern Transvaal followed and today there is as much as 5,000 ha of tea in Natal, in the Transkei and Venda territories and in Zululand, as well as in Transvaal. Most of the estates are owned or managed by the organisation SAPEKOE. This is a subsidiary of the Industrial Development Corporation, founded by the South African government to sponsor enterprises in which, if successful, the public might eventually participate.

As past history indicates, tea-growing in the Republic faces natural hazards. *Tea Production in Africa* stated the case somewhat bleakly:

All tea areas in South Africa experience extremes of climate between summer and winter, with periods of high day temperatures, moderate night frosts and strong winds. In addition, rainfall is only marginal . . .[16]

The inevitable result is that South African leaf, though well made and of fair quality, is distinctly expensive. For 1982/83 the cost to the packers was R4.40 per kilogram, against Ceylons at R1.78 (f.o.b.) and other growths R1.33.[17]

The South African growers have a captive market, since packers are compelled to take a percentage of local crop pro rata to their own share of sales. In 1982/83, a favourable season, the crop amounted to about 7,500 tonnes, about one-third of consumption.

In defence of this somewhat unreal situation, it can be said that government-sponsored tea-growing in South Africa gives employment to upwards of 10,000 people, brings cash to otherwise backward rural areas and, of course, makes substantial savings on the import bill.

Internal consumption

As the consumption figures indicate, the tea import bill is quite heavy. In 1983 Sri Lanka, with its long history as a favoured supplier, sent 3,056 tonnes – a good deal less than in recent years. Nearly all the balance came from various African territories, headed by Malawi.

A handful of distributors dominate the retail side.[18] Their packs (60% teabags) are heavily advertised and there is uni-national promotion by Sri Lanka, with campaigns directed to all races in the population. Attempts to launch a pure South African blend have met with little success.

Before leaving this interesting market, a word must be said (however reluctantly!) about the product called Rooibos, which because of its alternative name of 'Bush tea', has long been a source of vexation to South African purveyors of the authentic *Camellia sinensis*. Rooibos is, in fact, a tisane, originating in the Clanwilliam district of the Cape, and as much as 2 million kg are marketed annually. Of late years it has even made its way into the health food stores of the United Kingdom (as 'Red Bush – free from caffeine and other harmful alkalis'), though *not* into the London auctions, from which it was expelled with fury as long ago as 1867.[19]

Europe is moving with arthritic slowness towards banishing the word 'tea' from the labels of such concoctions, but in South Africa, it would seem, the ancient name will take some shifting.

Mauritius and Réunion

As might be expected, tea has proved an attractive crop to the farmers and administrators of several sub-tropical islands eastwards of the African continent. Among them, Mauritius (along with its neighbour, Réunion) can certainly claim to be the doyen – there were experimental plantings there as far back as 1817, soon after the British captured what was then known as the 'Île de France'. The pioneer planter was, in fact, a Frenchman, M. Victor Jannet. The industry took root in a modest way and all through the nineteenth and early twentieth centuries one comes across references to Mauritius tea turning up in the West.

One reason why the crop has persisted is that the island's economy is notoriously and dangerously dependent on sugar and there has long been an anxious search for diversification. Besides its usual characteristic of being labour-intensive (Mauritius is over-populated), tea has the local attraction that, unlike sugar cane, it will flourish at elevations well above 400 m (1,300 ft).

After World War II, the British colonial administration took the matter vigorously in hand and both promoted large-scale private planting and encouraged smallholders. To help the latter, 'tea villages' were created, some with co-operative factories attached, though most of the outgrowers' leaf went to the factories of commercial firms. Nevertheless, the build-up from about 2,500 ha of long-established tea, to some 5,800 ha in 1978 was slow and since then economic difficulties and some appalling cyclones have caused a recession and visitors report seeing considerable areas of tea 'let go'.

Currently, about 4,000 ha are in bearing, 2,800 ha under the auspices of the island's Tea Development Authority. The 1,100 smallholders cultivate about 1,000 ha of tea between them.

On the estates, labour costs are high and the official aim of providing employment looks like being frustrated to some extent by a resort to various forms of mechanical plucking. Practically all the Black tea produced in the eight factories at present operating is conventional CTC, and fetches respectable prices abroad. The musical French names of the various estates – Chartreuse, Belle Rive, Bois Chéri – are familiar in the London auction room and one of them, Dubreuil, has figured in off-shore catalogues.

In spite of setbacks, Mauritius is still hoping to make a real 'go' of its tea industry and in 1982 there was news of a joint blending and packing venture with the government of India, Messrs Andrew Yule acting as consultants.

Out of a total production of 6,142 tonnes in 1982, 4,935 tonnes were exported, over 60% of it to the United Kingdom. South Africa was once a prime market, but since it cut down the Mauritius quota in 1978, it takes less than 300 tonnes. In shipping its teas, Mauritius is almost the only country of origin to have apparently settled for cartons rather than paper sacks as an alternative to the conventional chest.

Madagascar

Madagascar, though vastly bigger than Mauritius, is far less active in tea. There is understood to be only one factory, with 200 planted hectares attached. The EDF supplied some finance in 1966–74. The product was mainly intended for local consumption, but two or three years ago a few lots turned up in the London auctions. There are also occasional private deals.

Seychelles

It was a surprise when a well-travelled friend remarked that one of the attractions of a visit to the Seychelles was some quite palatable local tea – 'Island Blend'. Output from the sole estate, which is British-owned, is in fact modest, official statistics recording only 167 tonnes of green leaf plucked in 1980.

7 A Worldwide Plantation Crop

A photograph turned up some years ago, showing long lines of tea bushes cosily bedded down under a foot or so of snow. The scene was probably the Caucasus, but an equally feasible source would be certain areas of central China. A strange environment indeed for our native of sub-tropical forests, as already described in this book! But the hardy and adaptable nature of *Camellia sinensis* was recognised very early and some of the almost frost-proof China *jats* have a long and successful history.

The great Linnaeus was right as usual when, referring to certain bushes naturalised at Uppsala in 1763, he remembered that 'the plant did not appear to be any more susceptible to the cold than a great number of others that grow in our climate, like the syringa [lilac]'.[1] This did not, of course, mean that Sweden was potential tea-growing territory, any more than England or France, where experiments were going on at about the same time, and it is probable that if *Camellia sinensis* actually flourishes in Uppsala today, it is to be found (as elsewhere in Western Europe) safely under glass.

Drought rather than cold is on the whole the worst enemy of tea. The crop is, in fact, grown successfully in areas of wildly varying rainfall, but a downward limit of about 1,270 mm (50 in.) (natural or irrigated) per annum is generally accepted. There seems to be no upward limit – no less than 11,880 mm (467.74 in.) was registered in 1983 on the Jafflong Estate in Bangladesh, not far from Cherrapunjee, credited with being the wettest place on earth (but what about Hawaii?). This was more than four times what is generally regarded as a reasonable mean.

The minimal requirements of a hot summer and reasonable rainfall being widely distributed over the globe, it is not surprising that the empire of tea is equally far-flung. In this chapter we will explore a few regions outside the mainstream areas of production where there is not only enough tea grown for local consumption, but some contribution is also made to the world's export pool.

Iran

It is not easy to say just why the area between the Black Sea and the Caspian should have found favour among tea-growers, though no doubt a learned thesis on the subject lies dormant on some university library shelf. Three countries have concurred in making the experiment and in each case with a measure of success. Russia was almost certainly the pioneer, but because of the complex pattern of tea-trading in the modern USSR, it has been given a chapter to itself later on (see Chapter 12).

Of the other two, Iran was second to Russia in point of time and had bushes out as early as 1898. Real expansion, however, did not come until the 1930s. The tea belt now extends, in scattered fashion, over 150 miles along the Caspian shores between the towns of Rest and Chalus. The Iranian industry was built up on the basis of thousands of small family plots and when the late Dr C. R. Harler surveyed the scene in 1960, he found some truly amazing cultivation practices:

Annual pruning at about 8 in. from the ground is followed by plucking to about 8 in. at the top, and lower at the sides of the plant. As a result many of the bushes are no bigger than cabbages, and since the spacing is about 3½ ft, the waste of soil can be imagined.[2]

The resultant leaf was processed in no fewer than 110 factories, which between them turned out about 8.5 million kg of made tea.

Dr Harler mentions, incidentally, that whereas China and China-hybrid *jats* turn up elsewhere around the Caucasus, the Iranian pioneers got their seed from Kangra in the Punjab and no China seed ever entered the country.

In spite of the eccentric ill-treatment given to the tea bush, the average output per hectare in those days compared well with that in the USSR and Turkey. But in modern times, though up-to-date information from the Iranian tea fields is scanty, the correlation between the last available figure for area planted – 30,000 ha – and an out-turn of 20,000 tonnes does not suggest a high-efficiency industry.

Iran used to be a modest exporter of tea, sending up to 2,000 tonnes abroad in a good year (mostly to the United Kingdom), but she does not, in fact, grow nearly enough to meet her own needs. Imports have risen spectacularly, from 6,167 tonnes in 1970/71 to an estimated 22,000 tonnes in 1983. At one time India and Sri Lanka took more or less equal shares in this trade, but in 1983 the former went well ahead, with 17,000 tonnes against 5,500. Private merchants can and do play their part, with the Iranian end of the deals regulated as to quantity and price: one government agency, the State Tea Organisation, assesses the demand, while the Government Trading Corporation controls imports.

Hardly less important than this heavily regulated commerce is what is politely known as 'unrecorded imports' (or 'a buoyant unofficial trade') from various Gulf States, notably Dubai. Surveys suggest that as much as 9,000 tonnes of tea may slip across the Gulf of Hormuz, thus raising consumption in Iran to 1.3 kg per head and reducing the corresponding figure for the United Arab Emirates (UAE) to a slightly more believable level.

Turkey

The third Caucasian country to join in was Turkey. The Turkish tea lands adjoin the USSR's and continue some way along the Black Sea coast. Soil and rainfall in Turkey are quite favourable, but as might be expected where the climate tends to be bleak, except in high summer, the Caucasian crop season is short, extending only from May until August.

The story of Turkey as a contributor to the world's tea supplies has followed a slightly bizarre course. The first commercial plantings were not made until after World War II, and even by 1950 the out-turn was a mere 208 tonnes. From then onwards, however, production zoomed – 5,450 tonnes in 1961, 13,000 in 1965, 23,000 a year later. And so it went on. By 1975 the planted area was over 50,000 ha, against less than 26,000 only five years before and it was obvious that when all this new material came into bearing, Turkey was due for a tea explosion.

It happened in 1979. The amount harvested that year was so enormous that the factories could not cope and (it is authoritatively reported) *90,000 tonnes of leaf* had to be thrown into the sea. Even so, a lot of mature tea was left unplucked and some growers burned their bushes in despair. The factories, running out of chests, had to bundle the stuff away in plastic bags.

The sequel was that by 1981 – without the magic wand of any International Tea Agreement – production was trimmed to 41,665 tonnes, against 95,889 in 1980 and a peak of 101,955 a year before that, when Turkey's output was the fifth highest in the world. This figure of 41,665 tonnes was, in fact, well below the needs of the home market, but there were obviously substantial stocks to cushion the shortfall. Since then, output has expanded again – 68,000 tonnes in 1982 and 70,000 in 1983.

How was 1981's drastic cut achieved? We have to look behind the mere statistics. Turkish tea-growing was and is a peasant industry and the smallholdings established along the Black Sea coast were largely intended to raise the income of a hard-pressed community. Thus the tea bush was at the mercy of sturdy individualists determined to harvest every ounce of crop and if necessary to bully the factory manager into accepting it.

Sometimes the farmers would completely strip the bushes in May to get cash for their seasonal expenses and visitors have seen factory compounds choked with piles of the resultant leaf.

To achieve such an output, there has been extensive use of scissors or shears, instead of the selective finger and thumb. No wonder it was claimed that the 1979 yield per hectare – 1,902 kg – was among the highest recorded. But at that point the military regime decreed that it must be 'two leaves and a bud' in future and a strictly enforced quota. It is alleged that whereas 1 kg of leaf could be clipped off in a mere ten minutes, it now takes 45 minutes to achieve the same result, which does not suggest a very strenuous approach to the job.

Turkish exports have followed an equally erratic course. The highest figure ever attained was not in 1978 or 1979, but in 1972, when 17,497 tonnes were sent abroad, no less than 15,743 tonnes of it to the Netherlands, doubtless for transhipment elsewhere. The United Kingdom was at that time the only other substantial market. The year 1974 showed a diminuendo, while in 1975/76 (a period of acute domestic unrest) virtually no tea was exported at all.

Nevertheless, since 1977 there has been a recovery, thanks largely to consistent purchases by Iraq, even though for a couple of years – 1979 and 1980 – she was rather suddenly displaced as chief customer by Poland.

It is pleasant to note a small but never-failing stream of Turkish tea flowing to West Germany, no doubt to soothe the homesickness of some of the Anatolian *gastarbeiter*, settled there in their thousands.

Argentina

In 1957 the first tiny offering of Argentine tea reached London; in 1959 exports had leapt to 750,000 kg and the markets had become fully aware of Argentina as a regular source for Black tea. The leaf was often shipped in gunny sacks and at the London auctions earned prices appropriate to a humble 'reducer' – for example, around 24p per kilogram in 1962–64, when the overall average was nearer 50p than 40p.

At first, the United Kingdom and the Netherlands took more or less equal shares – some 2,000–2,500 tonnes at that period. But the British demand soon went well ahead and meanwhile Argentina had found two other highly receptive customers, one of which was adjacent, and the other at least in the same hemisphere.

Just why Chile should drink more tea than any other Latin American country (Argentina included) is not very apparent, but the fact remains that from very small beginnings her thirst for Argentine sorts grew prodigiously. An ITPA survey[3] in 1982 showed an elaborate network of 55 importers (with 45 agents to handle their shipping and paperwork), 500 wholesalers, 250 supermarkets and between 17,000 and 25,000 retailers distributing tea. Total imports of some 13,000 tonnes ensured 1.17 kg per head for Chile's 11 million people, 80% of whom are to some degree regular tea-drinkers. The survey, however, added that tea is predominantly a poor man's drink in Chile; the wealthier classes regard coffee as more dignified. Thus, price as well as propinquity make Chile a natural market for Argentine leaf and by 1980 the trade had passed the 10,000 tonnes mark.

At that stage, almost the same amount was going to the United States where

Argentina has now become the top supplier. The fact is that the Argentine make suits American teabag and instant requirements very well.

Even in the United Kingdom the better manufactured teas were valued for colour under milk – as well as for price – especially in catering. However, UK imports, after breaking the 10,000 tonnes barrier in 1976, went into a decline, until the Falklands crisis cut off the business altogether.

Argentinian tea-growing is almost entirely concentrated in Misiones Province, in the extreme north-east 'finger' of the country between Brazil and Paraguay. Here numerous private proprietors go their individual ways; the names of many of them suggest origins in Central or Eastern Europe and technicians displaced from Indonesia are also to be found.

There is a cold, wet winter and a hot summer, with a cropping season that runs from October to April. The tea itself grows well and is reported generally in good shape, but plucking problems are blamed for the inferior standard of some (though by no means all) of the product.

Plantings here, from China *jat* seed, began soon after World War I, but it was the lack of imported tea during World War II that caused production really to take off. By 1953 imports had become superfluous.

The export pattern is as fragmented as the planting side, with numerous produce merchants fighting for business.

Internal consumption is more or less stagnant at about 5,000 tonnes. Teabags represent at least 50% of the home trade. Total production in 1983 was about 37,000 tonnes – the highest so far recorded.

Brazil

Brazil is the only other country in Latin America to send substantial quantities of tea overseas. Area under cultivation, out-turn and export totals are all about a third of Argentina's, but in contrast Brazilian leaf has always commanded highly respectable prices. This is partly because almost the whole operation centres upon a few large factories which are also responsible for export contracts; even more significant, perhaps, is a strong Japanese influence on both production and business methods. Note also that while there is a good deal of mechanical plucking in Argentina, Brazilian leaf is harvested by hand.

Output statistics show an upward plod from about 6,000 tonnes in 1970 to 10,000 at the end of the decade. Nine-tenths of this goes for export and the 1983 destinations were interesting – 3,617 tonnes to the United States, 1,426 to the United Kingdom, 574 to Chile and 424 to that universal customer, Pakistan; the rest is widely dispersed. The better Brazilian grades are exported in cartons, the 'rough stuff' in sacks.

Peru

Two other countries which grow tea on a much smaller scale are Peru (experimental plantings began as long ago as 1912) and Ecuador. Peru recently benefited from a US$30 million World Bank loan to improve the production of tea and other crops in the Alta Mayo, that is, the Andean foothills.

One of the few to write about Peruvian tea-growing is C. R. Harler.[4] He states that in 1961 the cropping area was about 4,200 acres and output, 2.5 million lb. He mentions two zones of production, one in Cuzco and the other, more favourable, around Tingo Maria, in 'a broad valley at an altitude of 5,000 ft' between the eastern Andes and the Oriental range. The tea was then of the Assam-China hybrid and Assam *jats*. Harler mentions that Peruvian leaf was well received on the London market in 1960, but it does not seem to have reappeared there.

Ecuador

Here, the British firm of Mitchell-Cotts has been involved since 1960. Ecuador has become a regular, if small-scale, supplier to the United States, for 'instant' purposes, though the intake dwindled from 1,161 tonnes to 378 tonnes between 1980 and 1983. Ecuador's 1,400 ha of tea suffers from at least two disadvantages – an excessive rainfall and perhaps the most expensive labour force in the whole tea world.

Guatemala

In Central America, Guatemala is understood to have only one estate, Los Andes, with a few hundred hectares in bearing. Its tea made a début in the London auctions in June 1983 and fetched about the same price as the Brazilians. Leaf is 'Legg cut'[5] and comes in two sizes.

Mexico

Mexico has been the scene of small-scale plantings over many years, but is more significant as a potential importer. At present the Mexicans – nearly 70 million of them – are overwhelmingly coffee-minded, with soft drinks as a vigorous runner-up. Even their consumption of herbal teas exceeds that of genuine Black and Green, which together account for only 0.25% of the total drinks market.[6] Thus a mere 100 tonnes or so of imported Black tea (80% of it from Argentina) is absorbed at present. But consumption is growing, especially among the higher income groups and generic promotion (divided perhaps between iced and hot tea) might well pay off. Instant tea is now being produced in Mexico; its progress will be watched with interest.

The Azores

The island of St Miguel, in the Azores group, provides our sole instance of a tea-growing area forming part (administratively at any rate) of Western Europe. Though little enough appears about it in the literature of tea, the crop has flourished there for a hundred years at least, even if always on a modest scale, and is now in some decline.

Three small factories process leaf mainly from their own plantations, but some is bought from local farmers. In 1983 about 62 planted hectares yielded a total output of 54,000 kg of Black tea, 1,500 of Green and 1,200 described as 'Pearl'. The older bushes are of China *jat* but those from 1940 onwards are of Indian origin, with some experimental hybrids from Malawi.

Most of the Azores tea is drunk locally or in metropolitan Portugal; there is a movement towards export to the United States and Canada.

Such examples naturally provoke the question, Where is the worldwide advance of *Camellia sinensis* likely to end? If tea can succeed commercially in Java and Sumatra (and even in Queensland – see page 175) why not in Sarawak or the Philippines? If in Argentina, Brazil and Ecuador, why not in a dozen other South or Central American countries – or in the southern United States for that matter, where Lipton has long maintained an experimental plantation? Is there any territory in Africa outside the Saharan zone from which tea-growing is climatically debarred?

The sober answer is that the two dozen or so countries from which tea is now exported (plus half as many again where it is a 'home consumption' crop) may already be too numerous in socio-economic as well as strictly commercial terms. To create employment and to earn foreign exchange are laudable ambitions in any developing state, but at this very moment we are seeing how in Africa the imperatives of food production are beginning to impinge upon tea and other apparently attractive cash crops.

Commercially, the main obstacles to profitable operation in some existing territories and to an advance into new ones are likely to be *cost*, especially in harvesting, and the availability of *labour*, particularly where there is no local tradition of plantation work. Such considerations may seem remote in a phase when (as at the time of writing) the world is apparently short of tea and producers almost everywhere are comfortably 'in the black'. But in the long term, it may be wise to envisage a state of things in which our caddies will be filled from tea grown more intensively in somewhat fewer countries than at present.

Part two
*Tea in the
Market-place*

8 *Years of Revolution*

A week is a long time in politics, we have been told on the highest authority. Ten years is not as a rule a long time in tea, that somewhat tradition-bound commodity. Yet the decade 1973–83 was enough to drive anyone almost dizzy with change. In this chapter we will have a brief look at some of the developments, both evolutionary and revolutionary. Sometimes they have played into each other's hands – evolutionary change, for example, in the channels of trade; a revolutionary impact from the container.

Financing and stockholding

Even before the decade started, it was apparent that the age-old system of financing the movement of tea was beginning to break down. It was based fundamentally on low interest rates and the extended credit which they made possible. This applied particularly, of course, to sales through the still predominant London auctions, where the whole process from the time the tea left the estate to the moment it was paid for by the dealer or the packer and ceased to be the grower's responsibility could be measured in months, culminating in the 90 days following auction allowed for final settlement. This 90 days 'prompt' was the first to be trimmed. In 1966 it was reduced to 63 days and shortly afterwards to 42. Finally, a new set of conditions of sale, approved by the then Tea Trade Committee and put into effect on 10 January 1975, laid down that the day of settlement should be the Thursday of the week following sale. The successive reductions in the 'prompt' period, followed by its virtual abolition in 1975, were a clear indication that the days of extended credit in the tea market were over.

Equally significant has been the more recent decline in the stocks which the producers have been prepared to hold at their own expense in London. Until about 20 years ago the end-of-year figure (after the heaviest landings from

India) might be anything up to 100,000 tonnes; in December 1984 it was 46,758 tonnes and even that was above the recent average.

Auction centres

Nowhere else in the world does quite the same financial problem arise. Broadly speaking, teas for the other main destinations are either bid for at auction in one of the producing countries or are the subject of private deals.

The first sales in the various auction centres, so far as they can be ascertained, were as follows:

London	10 January 1839*	Coonoor	23 March 1963
Calcutta	27 December 1861†	Limbe	9 September 1970
Colombo	30 July 1883	Gauhati	25 September 1970
Cochin	4 July 1947	Jakarta	11 December 1972
Chittagong	16 July 1949	Siliguri	29 October 1976
Nairobi	7 November 1956	Coimbatore	November 1980
Mombasa	14 July 1969	Singapore	2 December 1981

Notes:
* First 'free' auction after the fall of the East India Company.
† For an isolated earlier sale, see page 32.

Auctions were revived at Amsterdam after World War II and continued until 10 July 1958. There were also auctions at Antwerp between September 1959 and December 1971 and at Hamburg between October 1960 and February 1965.

The number of auction centres has itself increased in response to the incessant pressure for quick sales. Colombo has always been sufficient to serve compact Sri Lanka but, as we have seen, both North and South India have new centres to supplement Calcutta, the 'daddy' of them all. For Bangladesh there is Chittagong and for Indonesia, Jakarta. Africa has centres at Mombasa and (on a much smaller scale) at Limbe, while the auctions begun at Singapore in 1981 (see Chapter 5) represented a new experiment in a non-producing country.

The proportion of output passing through local auctions varies widely, from virtually 100% in Sri Lanka and Bangladesh to about 60% in North India, 50% in Indonesia and varying amounts from 50% downwards in Africa.

The general consensus is that the auction centres work with speed and efficiency. But when the producer looks around for the quickest method of disposing of his crop and pouching the proceeds, he may well feel that the speediest of all is to sell it straight off the garden to a local merchant or packer. In a country like India, with its huge and heterogeneous internal market, the scope for this is obvious. By selling in this way, the producer not only gets his money sooner, but avoids the expense and the uncertain outcome of a sale at auction; for Assam teas, the saving in selling costs, compared with going to auction at Gauhati, may be as much as 60%, and at Calcutta, 70%. The danger of all this, of course, is that the smaller estate proprietor, 'strapped' for cash, may be tempted to sell his leaf below value, sometimes even to a money-lender to whom he is in debt.

Higher-powered estate owners – companies as a rule – can go further and strike bargains with their opposite numbers overseas. The latter may be actual packers or perhaps merchant firms, particularly on the continents of Europe and North America, who have their own circle of customers. Such deals may be done through the buyer's agents in Calcutta, Colombo, Mombasa, etc., or with the help of traditional brokers; bargains are also struck nowadays by the big growers' own representatives at the importing end, either on sample or on recognised Standards. This is a world dominated by that modern king of communication, the telex.

Forward contracts

As we shall see (in Chapter 18), the tea trade has so far rejected the idea of a 'futures market', but 'forward contracts' are not uncommon, with sellers and buyers agreeing on prices for the delivery of specific quantities of tea due for manufacture within future periods of anything up to a year. Such deals may be on a basis of 'subject to approval of sample' or 'fair average quality', enabling the buyer to reject the tea if, when manufactured, it is found to fall short of the characteristics and quality anticipated in the contract.

Containerisation

All this streamlined trading in tea has been greatly stimulated by what is rightly called the 'container revolution'. The story is a striking one. It originated when the economic and practical benefits of 'unitising' the transportation of tea – that is, movement in block consignments rather than as individually handled chests – began to be realised in the mid-1960s. At that time there were no container services from any of the producer countries, so that the natural first step was 'palletisation'.

Pallets

On a pallet, or wooden platform, easily manoeuvred by fork-lift truck, a neat cube of chests is secured by straps. In the early days, this cube usually comprised 15 chests of the traditional dimensions, $19 \times 19 \times 24$ in. Soon, however, an ingenious change in the most frequently used chest to $50 \times 40 \times 60$ cm not only made it possible to standardise a 20-chest pallet, but enabled any number of chests, from four to 20 (excluding seven), to be made up if necessary into a perfect cube on a 100×120 cm pallet.

Particularly in the case of teas destined for the London auctions, the full benefits of palletisation could only be realised when (as described in Chapter 10) warehousing moved away from the old multi-storeyed buildings by the Thames to modern single-storeyed premises inland, served by road or rail and well-suited to the handling of unitised consignments. Simultaneously, various ports which had virtually replaced London in this trade developed procedures for the discharge of pallets direct from ship to lorry.

One can understand that the concept of unitised shipments was a 'shock of the new'. Its inevitability was only gradually recognised, not least by the shipping lines, whose vessels were then largely old and ill-suited to such methods and who responded with less than enthusiasm to the tea trade's growing demand for a general acceptance of pallets.

But experience soon showed that the pallet could do much to stem the rising tide of in-transit damage to chests. This had arisen partly from a deterioration in chest materials and construction and partly from declining standards of discipline in handling and stevedoring, particularly stowage. An individual chest may be handled a dozen or more times before it even gets on board ship in the country of origin and the same again from that stage until it is opened in the packer's factory and the contents emptied into the blending drum. Unfortunately, in some producer countries, even to this day, handling and stowage problems make it necessary to unitise the chests at the port of shipment instead of on the estate, so that some of the economic and protective benefits of a 'door-to-door' palletised service are lost.

Of course, a pallet, on which all the chests remain exposed, does not in any event provide 100% protection. Also, especially in the early days, when the tea routes were mainly served by ships not designed for unitisation, there was the problem of fitting cubical pallet loads into spaces with sloping sides. The hold of a ship has been neatly compared to 'a warehouse tossed up and down perhaps 1,000 and more times a day', and there were plenty of complaints about damage to loose chests which had been used to fill up odd spaces between and on top of pallets and between pallets and the ship's sides.

Nevertheless, by 1973 it was reported to the UK Tea Trade Committee that 100% of African tea was already palletised, 25% of Indian and a much lower proportion of Sri Lankan, though progress was being made there as well. By 1976, in spite of a shortage of equipment such as fork-lift trucks, the Indian proportion was nearing 50% and the shipping conferences were being urged towards an 'unqualified acceptance' of palletised tea. A 'Code of Palletisation' was produced, aimed at ensuring that chests should be shipped in perfect cubes of tens or twenties with no loose chests left over.

Growing use of containers

Next came the container. Few incidents in the long history of tea are more curious than the timetable of its emergence. In 1976, the idea of shipping tea in containers was still being talked about as a distant possibility; it could hardly be contemplated in the short term – or so the pundits argued – since the capital cost, both of suitable vessels and of the essential shore installations, was surely more than the traffic could bear. At best there was a possibility of small numbers of containers being carried on the decks of existing ships; this was already available to some privately sold teas, 'provided that the buyer was prepared to wait, if necessary, for a suitable vessel and availability of suitable containers'. There were also occasional opportunities for carrying containers in holds, though this tended to be costly.[1]

Faint foreshadowings indeed! Who could have expected 1978 to be hailed as the year in which the 'welcome and inevitable trend' towards the containerisation of all tea began to emerge? Yet so it was. Within the shipping Conferences various member lines were either building or planning the construction of dual-purpose ships, while competition was expected from outside the Conferences, for example a new container-ship operation between India's west coast ports and Rotterdam. The fact was that tea had been caught up in a world-wide movement towards the shipment of goods in container loads, which was soon to dominate the operations of every major port in the world, as well as some minor, but tea-orientated, ones.

The principle of the thing is simple enough. A 20-ft steel container will, with careful 'stuffing', take ten pallets, that is, 200 chests, or 10 tonnes of tea. Once stuffed, no serious harm can reach the chests; the container can be swung ashore straight on to the lorry and delivered in a single operation either to the warehouse of destination or direct to the packing factory. It is at the point of landing that the logic of the system is most clearly demonstrable. It has been calculated that whereas in former days it might take a week to clear a cargo of 50,000 loose chests, the same number, palletised in 250 containers, can now be handled in a single day. A more recent development is the coming of the 40-ft container taking twice the number of chests, though it may sometimes create road transport difficulties at both the sending and the receiving end.

A technical argument still to be resolved is whether 'container tea' benefits or otherwise from ventilation.

In some major producing areas, the fundamental problems of stuffing containers, if not on the estate itself, at least somewhere close to the point of production, remain to be overcome. While the provision of adequate space, lifting equipment and expertise is something which local interests could reasonably be expected to arrange, in many cases the national infrastructure for transporting containers economically does not exist and even at some shipment ports the depots cannot yet provide a streamlined operation. As we saw when pallets first came in, only door-to-door shipment from point of production to inland destination overseas can achieve the full benefits of the container in terms of minimum handling and maximum protection of the cargo.

The picture, however, is by no means unhopeful. Kenya already has inland container depots at Nairobi and Kericho and both in that country and in Malawi it has recently been shown that, in favourable circumstances, tea can be put into containers on the estate itself.[2] In some of the other producer countries, inland container depots are still at the planning (or just the discussion) stage, but it does not seem too over-optimistic to imagine, not very far ahead, containerisation being regularly carried out at, for example, Gauhati in Assam (where an experimental start has already been made) or Hatton in central Sri Lanka.

We have to bear in mind that nowadays it is in terms of container loads that packers are already thinking and planning not only in North America, where the unit has been accepted for years, but also in the London market. The 20 or 40 chest lot, or 'break', may still be the norm there, but off-shore tea is often catalogued in up to 100-chest breaks (two to the container).

The chest and its alternatives

So far this chapter has been written strictly in terms of chests – the immemorial three-ply. But here again the past decade has produced something of a revolution, though it is still far from complete. Plywood is not only more and more expensive, but the production of anything up to 16 million chests per annum for exports alone, plus perhaps the same number for internal trade, is increasingly seen as placing an unjustifiable strain on the world's timber resources. It is India above all that carries the burden at the moment, since her forests not only have to meet the huge indigenous demand, but are a main source of supply for Sri Lanka, whose local tea-chest industry can so far meet only a fraction of the country's requirements. In mid-1984 the Colombo Press was reporting that an order for half a million chests had been placed with the USSR. One estimate is that 4,500 ha of forest must be felled to provide 10 million tea chests.

So what alternatives are there? One uses the plural advisedly. Perhaps the first Black tea regularly shipped in anything other than plywood came from Argentina which, being perennially short of timber, resorted to jute hessian sacks when she began to export in the early 1950s (the tea itself was of utilitarian character, which perhaps muted the general sense of shock).

Hessian sacks, too, have been resorted to from time to time by a few minor producers. However, in some circumstances hessian can impart a taint to the tea and nobody has thought seriously about packing better-class leaf in it.

A note of urgency developed somewhat slowly, but in 1973 it found a focus in London, in the shape of the Tea Trade Committee.[3] Though the problem was, of course, of worldwide dimensions, the TTC, bringing producers and buyers into concert, was perhaps uniquely fitted to grapple with it. A Sub-committee on Packaging was accordingly formed and its proceedings have ever since provided an index to the multifarious developments of the past decade.

The problem was to find a material in plentiful supply, cheaper if possible and more ecologically acceptable than plywood, capable of standing up to rough treatment and giving the tea at least as good protection from contamination and damp. It had also to suit palletised transportation and not cause too many problems to packers.

First in favour was the corrugated fibreboard carton, though people were also dickering over hardboard. The thing was tackled with energy – already in 1974 experimental shipments were being received from Kenya and Sri Lanka and two years later from India, Bangladesh and various African territories. A report presented to the International Standards Organisation conference in Hungary in 1983 recorded that:

Double-wall corrugated board cartons were successfully produced in Kenya by East Africa Packaging Industries and considerable quantities of tea have been shipped in them. Packaging Industries Malawi, in conjunction with Nampak of South Africa, have produced a satisfactory carton which is sold in Malawi. Nampak have also sold their carton to Mauritius.

Another firm which grappled quite successfully with the problem was Rubsteel, of Sweden, and by 1979/80 cartons were being produced on their machinery in Sri Lanka.

In general, however, the carton has never quite made the grade. It is expensive and shows, in fact, only a marginal reduction in cost over the plywood chest. Cartons also tend to bulge and then become difficult to open with existing apparatus in the packing factory.

Thus attention soon turned to the multi-walled paper sack, first heard of at least as early as 1974 but not brought seriously into the picture until several years later. Contrary to what the layman might expect, tea does in fact travel quite as well in such a sack as in a plywood chest, provided that it is carefully packed and palletised and put into a container as soon as possible.

As to cost, a paper sack can be one-third of the price of a made-up plywood chest,[4] though this may be neutralised by import duties where there is not a self-sufficient indigenous paper sack industry. In Sri Lanka, for example, a sack from Europe, carrying 60% duty, costs not much less than a plywood chest.

A problem still not completely solved is the selection of a suitable lining, or 'barrier', to protect the tea against moisture and taint. The earlier shipments were in polyethylene-coated sacks, but buyers were not altogether happy and, especially where the climate poses problems, preferred aluminium.[5] This sends up the price, but there is still a saving over plywood chests.

Quantities of tea are already being shipped from Kenya and Malawi and a few other origins in five-ply paper sacks with the same capacity as chests and fitting as compactly and firmly on to the pallet. This tea is destined mainly for North America and the United Kingdom (where it stands up quite well against chests at auction), but some resistance remains elsewhere. Although most countries of origin are experimenting with sacks, it seems that the tea chest will have to become more expensive or harder to obtain before the change-over is general.

The main obstacle to a more widespread acceptance of the various new materials is in the packing factories, faced with having to mesh the handling of chests, cartons and paper sacks into their smooth and highly geared routine. A standard form of sack will certainly be a necessity.

As to other materials, woven plastic (polypropylene) has made its appearance. In general, plastics are not favoured by tea-tasters, being suspected of tainting the tea or causing it to 'sweat'; also the first polypropylene sacks, being more or less pillow-shaped, were difficult to stack.

Nobody would be bold enough to say that we have heard the last of *any* alternative to the plywood chest – still less of the chest itself. However, as a final, apocalyptic vision, what about teas loaded in bulk into suitably lined containers, sucked pneumatically into hoppers at the other end, whence the blending drums would be fed with a 'mix' of appropriate leaf? The imperatives of cost-cutting have brought worse things than that.

9 *Trends in Retailing*

It is a curious experience to pause in front of the tea section of a large modern supermarket in Britain and to start adding up the number of different packs (brands, blends and sizes) on display. By the time you have got to, say, 54, you will be convinced that you have counted a shelf or two twice over. But no, a choice of anything between 35 and 55 is quite usual. And this goes for much of the continents of Europe and North America as well.

The 'trends' referred to in the heading of this chapter are, in fact, contradictory and confusing. On the one hand, the leading national packers have generally increased their predominance in terms of mass sales, while in most cases reducing their range of blends; on the other hand, we have the spread of 'own-label' or 'store' packs, the vogue for speciality teas and, above all, the proliferation of the teabag in all its varieties of sizes and weights.

Changes in range of teas

Taking these tendencies in order, it was the usual thing until fairly recently for one of the 'giants' to offer a range of up to ten teas, some distinguished by the colour of the pack – 'Blue Label', 'Green Label', 'Red Label' and so on – but actually representing a close-knit scale of prices, rising a penny or two at a time. In the United Kingdom the first serious challenge to this tradition had come from the Birmingham-based firm of Typhoo, when it invaded the market with a single pack just before World War I.[1]

The almost universal 'soft pack', formed by a machine which then measured the tea into it, made shortish runs in these varieties of colour reasonably inexpensive, while the family grocer, with no particular pressure on his shelves, liked to feel he had something on offer to suit every purse.

Moves to rationalise and reduce the ranges began perhaps with the coming of 'small leaf' blends, the selling message of which concentrated on quick brewing rather than minute gradations of flavour and price. But the tendency was powerfully reinforced when the carton, more costly but better adapted to display on self-service shelves, began to oust the soft pack, which became almost a rarity in the developed world.[2] For the record, the carton was also a Typhoo 'first', so far as the United Kingdom was concerned.

Finally, the advance of the teabag rendered any elaborate array of packet teas without special characteristics increasingly superfluous. A representative collection today is perhaps three each from the bigger packers, plus one or two localised blends which still hold their ground.

Own-label and speciality blends

The cupboard would certainly look rather bare but for reinforcement by own-label and speciality blends – that is, teas packed for an individual supermarket chain or group of private grocers, and those which claim to link superior quality with regional characteristics ('Darjeeling', 'Uva Ceylon', 'Formosa Oolong' and so on) and thereby command a premium price. In recent years the two categories have sometimes coalesced, when major supermarket operators have themselves launched speciality ranges to compete with those being promoted nationally and even internationally. Later chapters will show how all this is working out in the various markets of the world.

'Flavoured' blends

But we shall also encounter another competitor for shelf space which may eventually have rather serious implications for those who make their living by trading in tea. This is the 'flavoured' blend. It was about 20 years ago that the idea of selling tea which tasted of something else began to make headway. It originated apparently in the United States,[3] but quite quickly won acceptance on the Continent of Europe.

Tea is certainly susceptible to such treatment. Its own flavour and fragrance are elusive – to vanishing point sometimes in the humbler reaches, it must be confessed. Moreover, there were precedents. Tea drunk with lemon is after all one of the oldest recipes, and Chinas redolent of jasmine or bergamot have always had their devotees. So why not add a dash of orange, apricot, pineapple, blackcurrant, or peppermint to give the too-familiar beverage a 'kick'?

Orthodox teamen were sceptical – 'ghastly stuff' would be a typical first comment – but the less prejudiced kept silence. And sure enough, the flavoured teas began to make their way in the world and to prove their special appeal among the young. We shall have more to say about their proliferation in West Germany and North America (see Chapters 11 and 14). So far, no harm done, and a threat to 'real' tea could only arise when consumers became more interested in the fancy flavour than in the basic beverage. This is actually happening in the United States, though not in the category of flavoured teas so much as through the arrival of some very popular 'mixes' in which the tea content – provided by instant – may be as low as 3%. The next stage after that could surely be a dissociation from the authentic leaf altogether, with mere colourings and flavours taking its already vestigial place.

Inevitably, the coming of flavoured teas has attracted the attention of various regulatory bodies, notably in Europe. In advance of any possible Directive of the EEC, the European Tea Committee arranged early in 1979 for questionnaires to be issued to the trade in its member countries, so that a list could be compiled of the additives used.

This brought into relief the whole question of how the flavouring of teas is achieved. Additives are of three kinds, usually defined as 'natural', 'natural identical' and 'artificial'. Examples of the first category are the jasmine and other leaves used in China from time immemorial; of the second, the oil of bergamot[4] and oil of lemon extensively employed by blenders; of the third, a wide range of synthetics.

The UK trade was one which considered that when it came to labelling, both 'natural' and 'nature identical' additives should be regarded as *natural* and only the totally synthetic as *artificial*.

The next stage was the publication of a Code of Practice for Flavoured Teas by the ETC (November 1979) and of a draft for a Council Directive on flavouring in foodstuffs generally by the EEC (May 1980). Through all the discussions which followed, the question of what should eventually go on to the labels of flavoured teas remained at the heart of the problem and still has not been resolved.

Flavoured sorts apart, there is nothing that can logically bring tea within the purview of even the most rigorous national labelling code, though legislators have often taken some convincing of the fact.[5] Perhaps they are unused to being confronted with a completely natural foodstuff, free from additives or 'doctoring' of any kind. This was not always so and the great eighteenth- and nineteenth-century battles against adulteration[6] were won only because the majority of the trade, even in those *laissez-faire* days, was determined to safeguard the reputation of its product.

Influence of the teabag

Both speciality and flavoured teas, while increasing in popularity, are still marginal in the mass markets of today. The really decisive event has been the coming of the teabag, whether filled with a speciality or flavoured tea or more usually with some nationally advertised blend. It was decisive, as we saw, at the production end, and still more so in the battle for the retailer's shelf space.

As with flavoured tea, the phenomenon began in the United States. According to some authorities, it came about more or less accidentally. In about the year 1908 a New York dealer called Thomas Sullivan started sending out samples to his retail and private customers in small silk bags, hand-sewn. Some recipients thought they were meant for convenience in brewing and criticised the silk. Sullivan then had the idea of substituting gauze – and the teabag was born. By the early 1920s it was fully established and Ukers tells us that, at the time he was writing, packers were using 8 million yards of 'bleached absorbent gauze' annually.[7]

Americans liked teabags, initially, because they made it easy to withdraw the leaf when brewing was complete – an age-long preoccupation which had already given birth to countless infusers and other devices in all the great tea-drinking countries. The teabag became even more functional in this respect when – as happened very soon – it was given a string, with an advertising tag on the end of it, which could be hung over the side of the pot or cup.

Convenience, however, became the dominating theme, once the promotion of teabags had begun in other mass markets, conspicuously the United Kingdom. Identified in the first place with the name of Messrs Joseph Tetley who, though a British firm, had an important associate in the United States, they made their first appearance a little before World War II and were pushed hard after it. The British, alas, no longer took controlled brewing times seriously and seemed quite content to leave the teabag stewing in the bottom of the pot, while adding more hot water from time to time – a practice viewed with shocked surprise by newcomers from the Orient.

Thus the string was now superfluous and the heat-sealed teabag, often made up from perforated paper, took over in a very big way.

In some countries, such as the United States, and indeed throughout most of Europe, string-and-tag still holds its own, while in others, including Australia, the two sorts share the market, with string-and-tag mainly used for cup brewing and stringless going into pots.

This is a reminder that the American teabag originally came in two sizes, 'cup' at a rate of about 200 bags to the pound, and 'pot' at about 150. The amount of leaf in a teabag is still far from standardised internationally; the Netherlands, for example, prefers the 4 g bag, the United Kingdom 3.25, and France offers a choice (2, 2.5, 3).

Even less uniform is the complete pack. The tea shelves in the supermarket are almost dominated by boldly labelled cartons containing 40, 80, 160 or even 240 bags, the latter almost rivalling the soapflakes and breakfast cereal packs in size and flamboyance. We are told that the big sizes are gaining popularity with the housewife, though one cannot help thinking that it is the marketing men who really love them; only with the 'jumbo' teabag carton has tea at last entered the major league of supermarket 'eye-catchers'.

Convenience being such a potent word today, the triumph of the teabag has been almost worldwide, and the graphs move ever upwards. There is, in fact, no known instance – other than a temporary 'hiccup' – of the teabag losing ground in any territory where it has won a foothold. Naturally, its market share is highest in its country of origin (in the United States it has at least 95%, if one excludes instant tea and mixes; in Canada, 90%); in Europe it varies between 45% in Ireland and France, through 68% in the United Kingdom to

85% in the Netherlands and Italy. As to the *speed* of the advance, UNCTAD[8] noted a few examples (see Table 9.1).

Table 9.1 Market share of teabags (%)

Australia	1975	9
	1982	30
Ireland	1977	14
	1982	45
Japan	1966	15
	1980	80

The USSR is one of the few big, tea-addicted countries where teabags are almost unknown and they have still to make their way in the vast internal markets of India and China. The 'Gulf' countries, too, prefer their tea in packet form – so far. But even there there are few centres of population where the teabag is not to be found, catering for expatriate if not for local tastes.

As already hinted, the modern teabag has pretensions far beyond the utilitarian. It has shouldered its way into the speciality field and the idea of 'teabag Earl Grey' is evidently something we have got to live with.

Effects on consumption

One great multinational estimates that, overall, teabag usage is increasing by about 4% per annum. The question of what effect all this is having on tea-making habits in the home and thence on the take-up world-wide was thoughtfully considered in an article by Mr H. H. Godecaux.[9] The teabag contains a carefully measured, and very small, quantity of leaf and the tea-maker has to work in multiples of that quantity. Whether to increase the usage by putting two bags in place of one, or three in place of two, says Mr Godecaux, requires a decision more likely to encourage conservation than happens with the teaspoon – 'just a bit more because of Aunt Flo or for good measure or even good luck'. He concludes that 'when tea-drinkers abandon loose tea and turn to teabags, they will consume less weight of tea'.

It is on this basis that the teabag has been more or less universally blamed for the fall, or at best the stagnation, in imports into every country where it is dominant. Mr Godecaux sets out the equation:

It has long been accepted that an average of 485 cups are made from a kilo of loose tea (220 to the lb). On a basis of 320 tea bags from a kilo, each bag yielding 2 cups (a most conservative figure), 640 cups can be obtained. Expressed as a percentage, teabags will provide 32% more cups than will the equivalent weight of loose tea.[10]

Mr Godecaux's final statistic is that, in his own country (South Africa), teabags are packed at 400 to the kilogram and the trade accepts as a fact that two good cups can be prepared from each bag, giving an extraction rate of 800 cups per kilogram!

What none of us know, of course, is what would happen if teabag users in a specific territory were to be deprived of the device: would they revert to 'loose' tea and the casually generous teaspoon or would they stretch out a lazy hand for the instant coffee jar or the soda-pop bottle? In other words, is the modern consumer more firmly wedded to tea or to convenience? And, if the latter, may not the teabag make up for its severely rationed contents by some increase in the number of *occasions* when it tempts us to put the kettle on?

Packing techniques

In any case, the servicing of the huge teabag market, current and potential, has had dramatic consequences in the packing factories of the world. Not too many years ago, machines turning out 400 bags a minute were regarded as pretty impressive and they still needed a covey of girls to put the bags into cartons by hand. Today, there are machines which have increased the output per minute by just ten times and even the packer who cannot afford such a giant expects at least 2,000 bags a minute as an economical norm.[11] Cartoning as well as bagging has, of course, been mechanised.

It is the tremendous speed and narrow tolerances at which the modern teabag machine works that has made the supply of clean, free-flowing small leaf such a vital preoccupation for the producers.

Rivals of 'real' tea

In connection with 'mixes' in the United States, we made a brief reference to instant tea. Would this product not provide the decisive answer to the convenience problem and beat off the challenge of instant coffee? The fact is that though researched so widely, argued over and test-marketed, 'straight' instant tea has not so far made a significant impact at retail level except in North America. It is important, however, as a basis for flavoured drinks in a number of countries and also in the vending field and its future seems sufficiently firm to call for further discussion (see below).

Soft drinks, whether carbonated or otherwise, with a tea content have an interesting, though still speculative, role; an outstanding example was discussed in connection with Indonesia (see page 69).

We revert, finally, to 'real' tea as an item in the family shopping bags of the world. Its universality is shown in a number of ways, from its still extensive use as a 'special offer', and even as loss-leader, to the ration of subsidised leaf which is regarded as politically indispensible in several West Asian and North African countries. Almost any modern 'trend in retailing', it would seem, must take tea into account.

Instant tea

The origins of instant tea lie in the success of instant coffee, which was held to have eroded tea sales in several Western countries (especially the United Kingdom) during the post-World War II years. If tea was to fight back – so it was argued – must it not also be made available in a similar 'convenience' form?

So began the *spray-drying* of strong Black tea, by processes already familiar in the dried milk as well as the instant coffee industry. It involves: (*a*) passing the leaf through a series of massive cylinders which act as 'percolators' and ensure the maximum extraction; (*b*) pressure-spraying the resultant liquor downward through nozzles in a stream of hot air from the top of a huge stainless-steel tower, 24 m or more high and at least 6 m in diameter. The nozzles atomise the liquor into droplets, from which the moisture is evaporated by the heat, so that what arrives at the bottom is a fine powder.

Freeze-drying, a trickier process, has been extensively tested, but any improvement in quality has not so far justified the cost.

Spray-dried instant tea, produced as above, made a rapid impact in the United States, where it fitted neatly into the local pattern of iced tea and (later) mixes. It also appealed to the vending trade and perhaps 90% of the estimated world output of some 12,000 tonnes of instant tea is consumed in North America.

Hot- and cold-water solubles

Instant teas are normally categorised as *hot-water solubles* and *cold-water solubles*. The difference is that for the former all soluble material is dried in the normal way; for the latter, any constituents which will not dissolve in cold water are extracted and reinstated in more soluble form by a subsequent process. Hot-water instants are regarded as close to a normal cup of tea, whereas the cold-water kinds are ideal for the preparation of iced tea and therefore predominate in the United States.

Not all of North America's supplies come from home production, though powders imported from abroad probably represent less than 5% of the whole. It is when one looks at the origins of these imports that the complexities (and frustrations) of instant tea manufacture become apparent.

Green leaf processes

After some years, it occurred to various inventive people that there was no point in transporting manufactured leaf across the oceans, rehydrating it (so to speak) and then reducing it to a spray-dried powder. Why not short-circuit the whole process by using green leaf in its native lands?

Though sound in theory, this is difficult in practice.[12] Many years and a great deal of money were consumed in experiment. However, viable green leaf processes did eventually emerge in the 1960s. In South India, for example, they were worked on successfully by a subsidiary of Nestlé in the Nilgiris and by Finlay (later Tata) interests in the High Range. India is now the biggest exporter, sending over 1,000 tonnes abroad in 1983 – 780 tonnes of it to the United States.

Sri Lanka was also the scene of two initiatives. One involved a process invented by P. W. Thornhill on Denawaka Estate, but later transferred to Uganda, where it did sufficiently well for the product to be retailed in Britain as 'Fine Brew'. The formula for the other was worked out by the Tea Research Institute at St Coombs and exploited initially by the West German firm of Hälssen & Lyon (the factory is now in the hands of Unilever). In this case, the brand name chosen was 'Ceytea'. Sri Lanka's output of instant has fluctuated widely over the years. It peaked in 1974 at nearly 291 tonnes, but recently has only once reached 200 tonnes (1980). Of the 151 tonnes exported in 1983, the United Kingdom and West Germany each took nearly a quarter, the rest being dispersed between the United States, Japan, Canada, Australia and other destinations.

In Africa, apart from the Uganda enterprise, Kenya has long been part of the instant tea picture, again with erratic results in terms of tonnage. A more steadily expansive era may have been reached with the installation of self-contained withering and spray-drying facilities at the Finlay factory at Mara Mara. In 1983, in fact, Kenya's exports jumped from 126 to nearly 364 tonnes; 101 tonnes went to the United Kingdom and the rest to the United States.

Obstacles to growth

It will be seen that we are not talking big business, even though the financial returns from instant are obviously higher than from the equivalent amount of leaf. The long-term trouble with instant tea is that is has more going against it than for it. To begin with, there are still technical problems, including the fact that in its 'natural' state it is a small, dense powder, only a tiny quantity of which – 0.5 g – is needed to produce a cup of tea, as against 1.8 g for instant coffee. This would make life impossible for the user, so that the granules have to be blown up (usually with dextrose) into something bigger and lighter.

More seriously, whereas instant coffee appeals in its own right and not just as an ersatz, the only instant tea that can make much sense is one which approaches real tea flavour and that is hard to achieve. Even in the vending context, where instant ought to be a 'natural' and where most of it is absorbed, there is the additional hazard that the 'whiteners' used nowadays as milk substitutes blend quite nicely with instant coffee, but are death to instant tea.

And so it comes about that in most places outside the United States where instant tea makes the supermarket shelves, it tends to be in disguised rather than straight forms, for example as the basis of beverages like 'Lift', produced by George Payne at their Swindon plant. There also appears to be a niche for speciality instants, including the ubiquitous Earl Grey, exported with some success by Nestlé, particularly to France.

10 *The United Kingdom and Ireland*

The United Kingdom
Mincing Lane

During one of the 1983 sessions of the BBC's ever-popular tournament in mental agility, 'Mastermind', the question came up: 'Where is the head-quarters of the London tea trade?' Answer: 'Mincing Lane'. One mark. Chances of catching out the 'Mastermind' team must be rare indeed and it was rather surprising that only a few corrective letters were received by the BBC. An attentive stroll down Mincing Lane today (including a detour into Plantation House, which dominates its west side) reveals that the number of name plates visibly relating to tea can be counted on the fingers of one hand.

It happens that, without being too fanciful, one can assign precise starting and finishing dates to the identification of the famous little street with the buying and selling of tea – 20 November 1834 and 8 February 1971, a period of just over 136 years. It all began with the first auction held at the London Commercial Salerooms after the breakdown of the East India Company's monopoly;[1] the end came with the last sale in the Plantation House 'auditorium' before the auctions moved to Sir John Lyon House, fronting the Pool of London, and took most of the London tea trade's offices with them. The answer to that 'Mastermind' question should have been 'High Timber Street', though little enough remains of that particular alley between Upper Thames Street and the river.[2]

As long as auctions were held at the East India House, teamen tended to cluster round it, with addresses in Gracechurch Street, Leadenhall Street and Coleman Street, as well as Rood Lane and Philpot Lane, where they remained much longer. Mincing Lane, through the centuries, had been a haunt of wine merchants and sugar brokers and it is a painful fact that the only *soi-disant* tea merchant to be found there before 1834 was a sly gentleman who had been arraigned the previous year for selling 'British tea' gathered from the hedgerows.[3]

Mincing Lane filled up rather slowly with teamen, but it is proof of the tremendous hold which their product took on the nation's consciousness from the mid-nineteenth century onwards that this inconspicuous thorough-fare, into which probably nine out of ten Londoners never ventured, should have become as much a synonym as Fleet Street or Harley Street.

Mincing Lane and its immediate environs were mainly garrisoned by people regularly involved with the auctions – brokers and dealers – but the trade as a whole was concentrated to an astonishing degree within a radius of two or three miles. Year by year millions of tea chests were discharged into bonded warehouses on either bank of the Pool, there to be weighed and inspected and to have samples taken from every chest by archaic processes which, though drastically streamlined, did not finally vanish until the last vestiges of the Tea Duties were abolished in 1964.

Samples having been collected by brokers, dealers and other interested parties, voluminous documentation was passed down the line, though this was mitigated when the invaluable Tea Clearing House, where samples and documents are collected centrally, was instituted in 1888. Sale by auction followed and in due course most of the tea found its way to packing factories within a short cab-ride of Mincing Lane. Goulston Street for Brooke Bond, Leman Street for the Co-op, Bethnal Green Road for Allied Suppliers, City Road for Hornimans, Wellclose Square for Twinings, Mitre Square for Ridgways and Kearley & Tonge – such were just a few of the once familiar destinations.

Even at the outbreak of World War II, only two major packers were beyond the tightly drawn circle – Lyons, who had moved to Greenford in Middlesex in 1920, and Typhoo in their original Birmingham fastness.

This is not, of course, to ignore the vigour of the non-metropolitan trade, not only the powerful clusters of packing houses in such cities as Glasgow, Liverpool and Birmingham, but also numerous wholesalers, local chain stores and even individual grocers, who still boasted a 'tea department', often with a London-trained taster in charge. It is doubtful, though, if they ever during the present century represented in aggregate more than 10% to 20% of the market and inevitably they bought almost all their tea directly or indirectly from 'Mincing Lane'.

The general dispersal which has removed importers, warehousemen and packers alike from their traditional haunts was described in some detail in *Tea for the British* and will be referred to from time to time; sufficient to say that, apart from all other considerations, the chance of creating one or more modern installations on a 'green field' site has been strongly attractive to all sections of the trade.[4]

We can now take a general look at Britain's tea supplies – where they come from and how they are being handled in the last quarter of the twentieth century.

Sources of supply

To record simply that in 1983 the United Kingdom imported tea from between 30 and 40 different countries would, of course, be highly misleading. As tea-growing has proliferated around the world, everyone from time to time sends a bit to London. But the main strands in the network are clear enough. There are some comparative figures in Table 10.1.

Table 10.1 United Kingdom imports* from leading suppliers (tonnes)

	1962	1972	1982	1983
Totals	252,808	211,814	207,697	184,261
India	122,507 (48%)	62,104 (29%)	54,425 (26%)	43,190 (24%)
Sri Lanka	79,316 (31%)	34,717 (16%)	18,722 (9%)	8,876 (4.8%)
Malawi	10,356 (4%)	9,227 (4%)	21,007 (10%)	19,053 (10.4%)
Kenya	9,136 (3.6%)	32,736 (15%)	47,958 (23%)	51,046 (27.7%)
Mozambique	6,887 (2.7%)	12,174 (5.7%)	8,747 (4%)	5,876 (3%)
Indonesia	3,615 (1.7%)	6,976 (3.3%)	7,615 (3.6%)	6,924 (3.8%)
Tanzania	3,188 (1.25%)	6,555 (3%)	5,772) 2.8%)	7,375 (4%)
China	1,602 (0.5%)	2,233 (1%)	11,804 (5.7%)	15,045 (8%)
USSR	–	–	2,414 (1.2%)	3,478 (1.9%)

Customs and Excise Statistics. Copyright HM Stationery Office.
*Gross, imports, before allowing for re-exports of 17,538, 19,714, 24,000 and 29,078 tonnes respectively.

It will be seen that, even allowing for some general falling-off, there have been highly significant changes between individual suppliers. India's contribution is down by two-thirds; there has been an eight-fold decline in Sri Lanka's contribution, contrasted with a more than five-fold rise in Kenya's and the doubling of Malawi's and Indonesia's; above all, we have China's ten-fold advance. Some ground regained by Sri Lanka in 1984, and further progress by Indonesia, left the broad picture unchanged.

Such switches at the head of the field have not of course come about by chance; they can be related to: (*a*) altered requirements in types and prices of leaf demanded by the UK market, with an overall swing towards the medium and lower ranges; (*b*) new trading patterns in the producing countries, especially Sri Lanka; and (*c*) interplay between (*a*) and (*b*). Some light has been shed on this already, and more will be diffused as we go on, but the plain and visible fact is that whereas 20 years ago India and Sri Lanka were supplying three-quarters of the UK's tea, that figure is now down to less than a third, while Africa's share (after minor producers have been added on) is very nearly half.

Ports of entry

There are great developments here, as everywhere else, and the figures again are eloquent. In 1962, 76.16% of all the UK's tea came in through London, 12.33% through Liverpool, 5.5% through Bristol (Avonmouth). By 1971, Avonmouth had jumped to 31.79% and Liverpool was still 12.33%, while London's share was only 39.1%. But a significant part was now being played by Hull (2.3%) and Felixstowe (2.2%) and 23 other ports were being listed. Observe the scene in 1982 and 1983, as revealed by Table 10.2!

Table 10.2   Ports of entry – United Kingdom

	1982		1983	
	Kg	%	Kg	%
Felixstowe	68,862,462	33.16	63,668,167	34.55
Avonmouth	59,765,305	28.78	51,804,716	28.12
London	32,173,839	15.49	27,901,525	15.14
Southampton	13,594,543	6.54	21,654,080	11.75
Ipswich	5,780,481	2.78	4,682,495	2.54
Hull	3,236,298	1.56	3,293,709	1.79
Liverpool	3,883,267	1.87	1,989,575	1.08
	187,296,195	90.18	174,994,267	94.97
Other ports	20,400,726	9.28	10,266,246	5.03
Total	207,696,921	100.00	185,260,513	100.00

Customs and Excise Statistics. Copyright H.M. Stationery Office.

In 1973 *Tea for the British* described Avonmouth, that progressive port on the Bristol Channel, with the great motorway interchanges close at hand, as 'the almost perfectly functional location'.[5] Fair enough – in the pre-container era. A major feature of containerisation is that it reduces the number of ports which it is logical to use. If, for example, a shipping line can service the greater part of Northern Europe by quick discharge and turn-round in say, Antwerp, Rotterdam, Hamburg and one British east coast destination, it will obviously do just that. What is almost shocking to the historically minded is that the 'British east coast destination' concerned is likely to be not the once mighty port of London, but inconspicuous Felixstowe, once known mainly for Edwardian holiday hotels and a girls' school!

The tea trade was not directly affected by the gradual closure of the entire system of London docks other than Tilbury, because, from the creation of the latter in 1886, practically all consignments were landed there, then lightered upstream to the warehouses along the Pool. But the forces behind the dock closures – mainly labour problems and high costs – operated equally at Tilbury, and Felixstowe has been able to provide a well-organised and trouble-free alternative. Not that Felixstowe would recognise itself as a 'tea port' as such; since about 1957 it has simply been handling containers in ever-increasing numbers, without any particular concern about what is inside them.

Avonmouth still has its regular callers – an example is East German ships from Mombasa – while Southampton has been landfall for vessels bringing Malawi and other Central African tea, routed via Durban.

By 1982, the number of 'other ports' involved in the trade had risen to no fewer than 36. Newport in South Wales – considered at one time a strong contender – headed the list with 2.7 million kg, followed by the Medway (Rochester) with 2.4 million and Dundee[6] with nearly 2 million, while Manchester, Newhaven, Middlesbrough and Holyhead were all above the 1 million mark. In 1983, Grangemouth (1.5 million kg) and Dundee (with 965,000 kg) took the lead, with the Medway and Newport still prominent, but Manchester had dropped out. Millions of kilograms may sound impressive to the layman. But bearing in mind that a single cargo – containerised or otherwise – may consist of up to 60,000 chests, or 3 million kg of tea, no UK port outside the four leaders can have received more than two or three fully loaded vessels during the year. Much of the rest simply represented transshipments from the Continent.

Warehousing

Even after World War II, when the riverside warehouses felt the full force of the blitz and tea had to be diverted far and wide, many of the old wharves with their evocative names – Orient, Bull, Colonial, New Crane – were back in action and it was only from the late 1950s onwards that the new pattern began to emerge. Broadly speaking, tea warehousing now takes place in four main locations – on the London perimeter at Dagenham (Dagenham Storage Co.), Chadwell Heath (Arbuthnot Storage) and Greenford (Buchanan Butlers); in North Oxfordshire (Banbury Tea Warehouses); at Avonmouth (Smith Warehousing, also Buchanan Butlers and Banbury Tea Warehouses again); and at Liverpool (Henry Diaper and Cory).

The contrast between these modern installations and the old multi-storeyed warehouses is sharp enough – nowadays it is all a matter of fork-lift trucks, wide avenues and tiers of 'palletised' chests, though a new problem has arisen with the coming of paper sacks, which cannot be stacked more than two pallets high without racking. Weighing and sorting procedures are fully mechanised. Much tea, however, remains in its containers until the auction room or the importer's instruction decides its destination.

Many container loads, moreover, go direct from port to factory for immediate use. Blenders have been able to reduce their stocks of original teas very considerably and the public warehouses, being much less used to hold buffer stocks, have lost a good deal of business in recent years. However, this all means that tight schedules are worked by the blenders and, should their shipping arrangements be disrupted for any reason, it is more important than ever to have spot tea available for them through the London auctions.

Auctions and private sales
Decline of the London auctions

With the United Kingdom still the magnet for teas from all over the world, the London auctions, in spite of their shrunken state (to which one has to make repeated reference), are an irreplaceable 'thermometer' of price and quality. During 1983, consignments from 14 of the 35 or so countries exporting to the United Kingdom were catalogued – often, of course, in very small quantities. But whereas up to 20 years ago some 80,000 'packages' (chests) were still being disposed of over three days – Indian and other growths on Mondays and Wednesdays, Ceylons on Tuesdays – nowadays a single Monday sale is sufficient to deal with an average of about 20,000–25,000 packages coming forward, exclusive of off-shore.[7]

The decline in the London auctions is, in fact, out of proportion to the reduction in UK imports, powerful influences being the desire of the countries of origin to build up their own auctions and the producers' need for the quickest possible return on their crops. Naturally, *price* comes into the equation at every stage; if a grower thinks that at a particular juncture he is going to do better in Calcutta or Mombasa than at Sir John Lyon House, he will simply make a switch.

Off-shore auctions

Despite every effort to simplify procedure (shown by successive revisions of the 'conditions of sale'),[8] there is an irreducible minimum of time needed to get teas landed in London and then warehoused, sampled, catalogued and auctioned. To alleviate this problem, a very interesting innovation was launched in 1982 – 'off-shore' auctions, whereby containerised tea is sold against samples airmailed to London along with the necessary bills of lading and other documents. Such teas can be catalogued immediately they have been put on board ship, sold the following Monday and paid for on Thursday.

Fundamentally, off-shore auctions were designed to take the utmost possible advantage of the well-known benefits of containerisation: improving sellers' cash flow, cutting out double handling and facilitating delivery direct to the blender's plant. Moreover, a container, while afloat, can be diverted to one of several 'option ports' on the Continent or even to North America.

The value of this system is especially felt by landlocked countries, like Malawi, Zimbabwe and Rwanda, whose teas may have already suffered delay in getting to the coast, and Malawi has indeed been its strongest supporter so far. India has not yet sold 'off-shore' and Sri Lanka has done so only to a modest extent.

In comparison with the weight of 'landed' tea dealt with in the London auctions during 1984 (49,561 tonnes), 8,498 tonnes of 'off-shore' sounds like 'small beer', but the build-up continues to be good and may yet help to restore some of the entrepôt trade to the United Kingdom, as well as providing a new lease of life for the tradition – now three centuries old – of selling tea by auction in the City of London.

Maintenance of standards

Apart from simplification of procedure, the conditions of sale have also been amended to include a minimum standard for teas on offer, based on British Standard 6048 (International Standard 3720 – see Chapter 16). The idea behind this was to discourage the shipping to Britain of sub-standard teas. As from April 1981, any doubtful samples could be submitted to a screening panel, which in turn would decide whether they ought to be analysed. In the event, the volume of such dubious imports has been extremely low. During the first two years of the scheme, only seven samples went forward for analysis; of these, five were rejected.

It had been intended that the scheme should eventually cover private importations as well as auction teas, but as this would be far more difficult to operate and might involve legislation, the idea remains in abeyance.

Selling brokers

There has inevitably been a concentration in the world of broking, beyond that recorded in *Tea for the British*, published in 1973.[9] Then there were five selling brokers, against 14 in 1951; now there are only four with catalogues – Thompson Lloyd Ewart; George White; Wilson Smithett; and Haines. The first of these is the most important historically, since 'Thompson' is a name that can be placed alongside 'Twining' in tea's British annals.[10] John Thompson was produce broker to the East India Company as long ago as 1760 and the first of a series of six William James Thompsons, in direct succession, occupied the 'box' at the auctions which immediately followed the end of the East India Company monopoly. The present composite name reflects a number of amalgamations over the years. George White (formerly Gow White) is another firm with a lot of history embedded in it. On the other hand, Wilson Smithett (pioneers of 'off-shore') have remained one and indivisible since their foundation in 1865.

Selling brokers have usually been identified to some extent with teas from a particular country, but without rigid demarcation, and the rise of the Africans has provided new scope for them all. In addition to their multifarious services to the producer at the London end, they have for many years had broking interests in countries of origin.

Buying brokers and their customers

Buying brokers tend to be a more diversified group than their selling confrères. About ten of them (including one or two who do both) operate in the Sir John Lyon House auction room, if only, in some cases, through the 'chair'. Often they have been identified with individual big buyers – Stansand with Lyons Tetley, S. S. Smith with Brooke Bond, Meriden with Typhoo, G. Harrison with the Co-op, are modern examples – but broadly speaking, any buying broker will represent any dealer, merchant or packer who requires his services. In recent years the convention of anonymity has been breached and the client's name will be heard, as well as that of his buying broker, but the latter continues to look after samples, contracts, etc., and to pay the bills.[11]

The dealer, in the old sense of an individual or firm buying tea at auction and holding a stock for resale down the line, is almost extinct today, killed by high costs and interest rates. There are still those who act as merchants or intermediaries, negotiating 'back to back' transactions between growers and exporters on the one hand and packers and distributors on the other. All such an operator needs is a thorough understanding of the market at both ends and (almost as important) some expertise in currency movements, to which an international commodity like tea is so sensitive. For such intermediaries, the container – '200 chests in a box' as one of them put it – provides an admirable unit of operation, but unlike the old-time dealers, these men usually tend to operate outside the ambit of the London auctions. The latter essentially serve the packers.

Packers

Mention was made earlier of the influence on all aspects of tea trading in Britain of a comparatively few nationally distributed brands. They have shown remarkable staying power throughout the present century, though some of their earlier rivals have disappeared.

The rise and fall of mighty Mazawattee, which would certainly have figured in any 'Big Four' between 1880 and 1914, is a classic instance. There were special circumstances in that case,[12] as also in the comparatively low-key 'presence' of the great name of Lipton in its country of origin, while another early leader, Horniman, is now the speciality arm of Lyons Tetley.

How were these empires built up? In the first place, of course, by advertising and sales promotion on a scale only equalled by that other universal commodity, soap. The latter, indeed, provides more than one instructive parallel. Take 'blended to suit the local water'. This used to be reckoned a good selling point for tea, but was surely even more logical as applied to soap. And, in fact, soaps for hard water districts and soaps for soft were widely purveyed until the genius of William Lever swept them away with 'Sunlight – Blended to suit all Waters'.

But, like soap, the national tea packs owed their success more to extraordinarily intensive distribution than to any other single factor. They had a massive base on which to build. Selling tea was already almost a cottage industry – no fewer than 194,000 persons 'had their letters up' when the licensing of tea retailers was discontinued in 1869. At that stage, much of the tea would be weighed out in pennyworths. But as time went on a 'Lyons Tea' or similar plaque would appear alongside 'Sunlight Soap' on the walls of the humblest store in the remotest village, while by 1930 Brooke Bond were claiming that their 'little red vans' served 190,000 shops (back to 1869!) in their itineraries.

Simultaneously, Typhoo, while not neglecting the grocer, uncovered a new dimension in tea-selling when they convinced thousands of pharmacists of the medical virtues of their 'leaf-edge' blend and persuaded them to stock it.

The English and Scottish Joint Co-operative Society Ltd, as the tea-packing wing of the Co-operative movement persisted in calling itself until quite recent times, could not, of course, cast its net quite so wide, but with the potent aid of the 'divi', built up sales which embraced almost – though not quite – every branch of every society.

Market share

The results of all this in 'market share' are plain to see and have sometimes, in fact, found their way into official documents. When the old Prices and Incomes Board (already on the way out) reported in August 1970 on competition and efficiency in the tea industry, the 'line-up' was: Brooke Bond, 43% of the market; Typhoo, 18%; Lyons, 12%; Co-op, 12%. A combined share, in other words, of 85% – quite a spectacular rise, since the previous inquest (by the Monopolies Commission in 1956) assigned them only 70%. The 85% figure (if it was ever completely accurate) has hardly held since 1970 and there have been changes in proportion between the 'Big Four' – notably an advance by Lyons (now Lyons Tetley), with Tetley teabags as the spearhead. In its annual report for 1982, Brooke Bond claimed a third of the UK market.

It is a sign of the financial times that for a decade or more there has not been a completely independent tea firm among the leaders. In 1968 Brooke Bond teamed up with Liebig (the 'Oxo' people) and Typhoo with Cadbury (later Cadbury-Schweppes). Ten years later Lyons, having absorbed Tetley in 1972, became part of the Allied Breweries complex. In 1984 came the 'battle for Brooke Bond', eventually won by Unilever. The numerous Lipton companies throughout the world are already subsidiaries of Unilever and that name sometimes appears in tea transactions; in the United Kingdom, however, the Lipton retail shops, together with Maypole, Home & Colonial and others in the old Allied Suppliers group, passed to Cavenham Foods in 1972 and thence to Mr Gulliver's Argyll Foods.

It may be that something of a stalemate has been reached in the long-drawn-out battle, 'Big Four versus the Rest'. The latter have, beyond doubt, benefited from the vigorous resurgence (described in the previous chapter) of own-label and speciality teas. This has been markedly linked with the rise of the great supermarket chains – Sainsbury's, Waitrose, Fine Fare, Safeways, Tesco and Asda among them. They tend to sell more main-line national packs than anything else, but their house blends are highly competitive and they make increasing play with speciality teas, whether their own or other people's. In the smaller self-service stores, a wholesaler's label is often featured.

Speciality teas

'Delicatessen' is a magic word in modern food selling and there are plenty of teas which qualify. In fact, they have been estimated to represent, in sterling terms, a £40 million share of the UK's £400 million market. One of the curiosities of the trade over the past decade has been the proliferation of Earl Grey, once regarded as no more than a slightly esoteric – not to say élitist – survivor from the past. There was a time when only two famous speciality firms, Twining and Jacksons of Piccadilly, packed it; which came first is a matter of argument, though Jacksons claim to have been given the formula by one Earl Grey and the right to use the name by another. But there is more than a suspicion that initially the famous Reform Prime Minister was invoked as a publicity ploy, like the 'Winston Churchill' and 'Queen Mary' blends which sell so well in other lands. Anyway, packer after packer has adopted the formula (in which oil of bergamot is the essential ingredient) and it is now by far the most widely diffused of all speciality teas in the United Kingdom. So far, however, 'instant Earl Grey' (see page 122) is strictly for export!

Otherwise, 'scented' teas have not taken anything like the strong hold which we shall see them achieving elsewhere, but their pioneers persist with them, new ranges continue to appear and it may be that by sheer availability they will achieve a vogue. The general range of speciality blends, which used to cover traditional Chinas, Darjeelings and high-grown Ceylons, has lately been enlarged to include other Indian growths and a few Kenyas.

Such initiatives provide a useful outlet for some of the diminished band of packers who carry on outside the circle (and well below the output) of the 'Big Four'. Names of past, as well as present, significance are R. Twining, part of Associated Foods (Weston) since 1964, and Ridgways, more recently acquired by Tate & Lyle. The old 'London trade' is represented by firms like David Lloyd Pigott, Brash Brothers, George Payne (packers to Sainsbury's but long since controlled by Messrs Finlay), James Ashby and very few others. Even where they continue to pack their traditional brands, the bulk of their business today – and it can be substantial – comes from supplying own-label blends to supermarkets and other retail chains and groups and from servicing caterers.

Regional packers

Outside London, there is a scattering of packers in most regions. The special vitality of North-west and North-east England can perhaps be typified by a couple of concerns, both bustling ahead, though very different in function – Gold Crown Foods of Liverpool and Ringtons of Newcastle upon Tyne. Gold Crown is heir to those two remarkable 'Liverpool Welsh' enterprises, David Jones and Morris & Jones, whose splendidly Victorian origins were traced in

Tea for the British.[13] They eventually came together as packers to the Mace grocery group and Gold Crown now forms part of the Argyll Foods empire. Ringtons, on the other hand, remains independent and, besides conducting its unique door-to-door operation[14] over a wide swathe of the North-east, is a packer by contract, notably for Marks & Spencer.

Scottish packers are down to less than half a dozen. They are headed on the east coast by the venerable Melroses of Leith (it has changed hands, but is still known internationally) and by R. Drysdale; in the Glasgow area by Matthew Algie, continuing on its independent way and with a great-great-grandson of the founder in the chair.

Re-exports

It is the packers who are responsible for more than two-thirds of the UK's re-export trade in tea. The International Tea Committee gives a stupendous list of 52 countries (in addition to others not separately named) to which tea is consigned year by year from UK ports. Twining claim to export Earl Grey to 90 countries. Re-exports include of course bulk leaf for subsequent blending, but in 1983 (something of a peak year) 16,841 tonnes out of 29,078 re-exported took the form of 'tea in packets not exceeding 3 kg', as the official rubric has it. We shall be constantly coming across this British 'tea in packets' during our worldwide explorations.

Re-exports have tended to expand recently and have become even more important in percentage terms. Their share of all tea reaching the United Kingdom increased from less than 7% 20 years ago to 11.6% in 1982 and as much as 15.8% in 1983. Money-wise, one obviously cannot equate imports f.o.b. directly with exports c.i.f.,[15] but it should be recorded that while in 1983 the UK's teamen paid the equivalent of US$352 million for tea brought in, the value of tea sent out was US$142 million. All but US$32 million of this came from the packet and teabag trade.

Retailing

Since the purveying of tea in the high streets and by-streets of Britain is almost entirely governed by those 'trends in retailing' surveyed in the previous chapter, it would be an unprofitable exercise to go into much more detail here. If there is one outstanding feature of the trade which has persisted through all vicissitudes, it is its competitiveness. Tea may not often figure as an actual 'loss leader', but the more popular (and well advertised) a blend, the more likely it is to be the subject of price-cutting exercises. This goes for every section of the trade and a stroll through six or seven assorted supermarkets, chain grocers and private shops in one's home town is likely to reveal six or seven different price tags, not only on run-of-the-mill teabags, but on the best known specialities.

Well over 50% of all tea sold in the United Kingdom today goes out through the supermarket chains, headed by those mentioned on page 131, and after the Co-ops have taken their share (perhaps 14%) the rest is spread somewhat thinly over an enormous range of outlets. The system of buying through voluntary groups of private retailers has helped to keep the 'corner shop' grocery and village store alive, even in dwindling numbers, and though most of the groups have their own-label range, it usually seems to lead a somewhat hole-and-corner existence on the self-service shelves.

While there has not been the flurry of 'tea boutiques' recently observed on the Continent, Britain still maintains a few chains of specialist tea and coffee shops, of which Importers Ltd (a Lyons Tetley subsidiary) is perhaps representative. The proliferating 'health food stores' may have an instinctive leaning towards herbal concoctions, but most of them admit the presence of *Camellia sinensis*, preferably with 'free from . . .' something or other on the label. Finally, a limited range of own-label packs is thought indispensable to stores of the Marks & Spencer, Woolworth and British Home Stores type.

United Kingdom Tea Council

In the light of all this activity, it might be assumed that the United Kingdom is also an unassailable Kingdom of Tea. Unfortunately that is not quite so. The British tea-drinking cult probably reached its apogee in 1956–58 when, with war and post-war restrictions at last shaken off, it attained a prodigious average of 232,500 tonnes per annum, or 4.5 kg per head for every man, woman and child in the British Isles. Then came slow decline, much of it attributed to the competition of newly fashionable instant coffee.[16] This decline led in turn to the formation of the United Kingdom Tea Council in 1965. For the first time it brought producers, importers and distributors into full concert, but as Chapter 17 will show, such harmony in generic ('tea as tea') promotion is always hard to sustain. Twice already – from 1970 to 1975 and from 1982 onwards – differences of opinion over funding have forced the Council to retreat from an aggressive advertising campaign to a comparatively low-key public relations role. This was unfortunate, since advertising had shown itself capable of changing attitudes and influencing sales. Between 1979 and 1981 consumption was held fairly steady at about 3.20 kg per head.

Even with its resources slashed, the United Kingdom Tea Council has displayed considerable verve and ingenuity in keeping the virtues of tea – good, well-prepared tea in particular – in front of the public. Just one example has been the spirited tea-making contest in which 500,000 Cub Scouts from 5,000 Packs across the country took part; this was followed by a similar competition for Brownie Guides, with 10,000 Packs competing. Schools and colleges have also been extremely well serviced.

Catering

The subject of catering tea in the United Kingdom is somewhat nostalgic, since its finest flowering, the chain teashop, born in the last quarter of the nineteenth century, finally expired in the third quarter of the twentieth. ABC, Lyons, Express Dairy . . . let us not weep. In any case, tea is still served by the cup or pot through an enormous range of outlets, where it remains even further ahead of all its rivals than it does in the home. Catering absorbs at least 13% of all tea imported into the United Kingdom; some 10 billion cups are dispensed every year and hospital patients will not perhaps be surprised to learn that the biggest single consumer is the National Health Service.

Quantity does not always mean quality, however, and the Tea Council is painfully aware of the fact. Hence, its interesting scheme whereby catering teas are submitted for test and placed in three categories or grades. There has been good support from the trade and the Tea Council reports that since the system was introduced in 1979 the proportion of catering tea achieving the highest grade has risen from one-third to two-thirds. The same method of grading now obtains in Canada. As a further stimulus to better catering tea, the UK Tea Council in 1984 launched a national Afternoon Tea competition for catering students at 250 colleges and met with an astonishing response.

The consumption figures given above do not include cups dispensed from vending machines, the majority of which are made from instant tea. The problems which 'whiteners' cause in this connection have already been noted and, after much experiment, a fair number of machines are now in service using leaf tea and even, in some cases, liquefied milk powder. Tea Council surveys have shown that where instant is dispensed, tea claims only 10% to 12% of all beverage sales; with leaf, this goes up to as much as a half.

Ireland

The song of the tea kettle has a very special place in the domestic mythology of Ireland. One image handed down through the generations was of the 'peasant' of the Gaelic-speaking West, dependent otherwise on the potato for sustenance, choosing his sole luxury, his tea, by expert exercise of eye and nose. One still encountered this legend in tea trade circles 30 years ago. The fact that the 'peasant's' choice usually fell on some whole-leaf grade from North India, is faintly reflected to this day in the predilection of the Irish for the larger broken grades in their packet tea.

But there was another reason why such a preference lingered on long after the rest of us had been converted to the quick-brew, small-leaf mentality. It goes back to World War II, when the British imposed what were regarded as unfair restrictions on tea supplies to the neutral Republic. With the coming of peace, the Irish government retaliated by permitting the trade to buy only in countries of origin and not in Mincing Lane (as was). The embargo was not lifted until Ireland entered the EEC in 1973.

Consumption

The renewed freedom to do business with London did not attract immediate flotillas of tea chests across the Irish Channel, but it helped to accelerate that trend towards modern tea-drinking ways which is symbolised by the teabag. Commanding less than 5% of the trade 20 years ago, it claims at least 45% today and crystal-ball-gazers see it going up to 68% at no distant date.

Already, teabags have had their usual effect on 'apparent consumption'. While the United Kingdom's amazing 4 kg plus per head began to shrink in the 1960s, Ireland, which had always come a very close second, remained steady and even increased its per capita figure slightly. Then came figures for the 1968–70 period: Ireland 4.04 kg and the United Kingdom 3.99 kg. In both countries there has since been a falling-off, but the gap has widened and the Irish are now incontestably the top tea-drinkers of the Western world.

Sources of supply

Moreover, appreciation of *quality* in tea is still maintained and the really cheap and nasty finds no market. This in spite of the fact that the old aristocratic large-leaf teas have gone beyond recall. India remains the number one supplier, but Africa, headed by Kenya, has come up fast; an Irish packer with probably the biggest current growth rate trades in Africans only.

Here again, the teabag is partially the clue. One thing it cures you of is bothering too much about what your tea leaves look like. Consumers, finding that African CTCs provide, according to our teamen, a 'brightly coloured liquor with freshness and briskness' in the soft Irish water, rather lost interest in the old North Indian Orthodox with its 'attractive leaf appearance and thick creamy liquor'. And, of course, CTCs give a quicker infusion, whether or not that is what is really demanded by the tempo of Irish life . . .

Packers

If tea-drinking habits have moved with the times, so has the machinery of distribution. In both cases, there has been gain and loss. In the early 1950s, when the present writer was staging 'tea weeks' and similar shenanigans in Dublin and points south and west, there were some 50 packers or merchants supplying the retail trade. Now only four survive – two are located in Dublin, two in Cork and it is no secret that something like 60% of the entire trade is in the hands of a single company, J. Lyons (Ireland) Ltd. They and the other merchants proceed by the method of direct van delivery to individual shops, so that the wholesaler plays a very minor role.

Retailing

The retailing system is made easier by the fact that the number of grocery outlets has decreased from 2,300 in 1971, to less than 1,500 today. Nearly half the trading in tea is, in fact, done by seven supermarket chains, whose share has risen from 17% to 47% in the same period. The chains manage to enliven their tea shelves with own-label blends packed for them by the Irish merchants; these tend to be lower in price and their appeal is somewhat limited.

One reason why the Irish trade continues to deal mainly with countries of origin is that the cost of moving tea from the United Kingdom to Ireland is quite considerable and the London price needs to fall correspondingly below the level of the out-markets to make it attractive. Not more than 25% of all Irish tea is bought through the various auctions of the world; nearly all the rest comes direct from the producing companies or their agents, of whom five are still active in Dublin.

Containerisation

Ireland is one of the countries sharply affected by the coming of the container and the consequent reduction in the number of ports served, as described in Chapter 8. Twenty years ago Dublin used to receive 12 direct shipments from Calcutta during the growing season; in 1983 there were three, all containerised. From Mombasa there was a direct break-bulk service for many years, but now nearly all the ships are containerised and in 1984 only one in four was routed direct to Dublin. The time may come when all African teas will have to be transhipped, probably at Felixstowe (as the Sri Lankans are already), and the Indonesians at Rotterdam.

11 *Western Europe*

For a continent whose liquid intake is at least commensurate with its standard of living, Europe (always excluding the United Kingdom and Ireland) makes no spectacular contribution to our subject. When the Belgian National Institute of Statistics carried out a survey in 1981, it discovered that Europeans were absorbing 483 litres per head per annum of everything other than tap water. The tally included: beer 145 litres; coffee 130; soft drinks and minerals 96; and milk 88, whereas the combined shares of wine, spirits, tea and 'other beverages' came to a mere 24 litres.

This puts European tea-drinking into rather surprising perspective. In that particular pond (appropriately liquid metaphor) swim three sizeable carp and about a dozen minnows. The Netherlands and West Germany have always been significant as tea traders and/or consumers, France somewhat less so; none of the other West European countries shown in Table A.7 (in Appendix 4) approaches them in either weightage or cuppage, so to speak, though some of them are of moderate interest to the pedlars of speciality teas. This applies particularly to Scandinavia. Of the 'big fish', seniority beyond all doubt can be claimed by the Netherlands.

The Netherlands

A heavy weight of history, in tea as well as in other terms, rests on this small country. Almost from our opening page, we have been aware of Dutch voyagers and traders as among the first to bring tea to Europe and almost as soon we encountered them as pioneers of planting in competition with China.

Amsterdam

It was from Amsterdam, almost certainly, that the future giant among consumers, the United Kingdom, received its earliest supplies in the 1650s and up to World War II that city could claim to be the tea capital of Continental Europe. There, in the old mercantile quarter, were to be found the head offices of the great plantation companies of the 'Dutch East Indies'; there, too, long-established auctions were held, rivalling London's in age and not far behind them in importance. These were serviced by that unique institution, the Pakhuismeesteren van de Thee, with its gigantic warehouse on the waterfront. At their height, between the wars, the fortnightly sales attracted home and foreign buyers in almost equal proportions.

After the shattering events of World War II an attempt was made to resume the auctioning of tea in Amsterdam, but the Indonesian exporters, at whom, of course, these auctions had always been angled, were on the whole disappointed by the prices obtained. From a maximum of 6,535 tonnes in 1951, offerings had dwindled by 1957 to less than half of that amount. A fresh initiative at Antwerp (in September 1959) also foundered and the same fate overtook a brief experiment at Hamburg (October 1960–February 1965). The fact was that independent Indonesia was far more interested in building up its own auctions than supporting any in Europe. At first the PTPs (see page 67) sold most of their tea privately, but 1972 saw the launch of the now flourishing weekly sales at Jakarta.

Rotterdam

Since World War II the focus of the Netherlands' tea trade has shifted from Amsterdam to Rotterdam, always important, of course, on the entrepôt side. Anything up to 70,000 tonnes of tea passes through the great harbour in a year – roughly 9,000 tonnes of it for internal use, some 12,000 to be re-exported after intermediate storage and sometimes blending, and the remainder simply to be trans-shipped for the United States and numerous other destinations.

Such trans-shipments have become more significant than ever in the age of the container. Rotterdam is one of the handful of Northern European ports to which the big container ships deliver tea and from which 'feeder' services can conveniently redistribute it. Rotterdam has also benefited from time to time when currency fluctuations have made it more profitable to consign tea there than to the United Kingdom direct. Recently, freight rates from Indonesia have slightly favoured Rotterdam.

Even the massive figures quoted above do not represent the whole of Rotterdam's slice of the world's commerce in tea. The city is also at the heart of a very large 'triangular' trade whereby leaf may be bought in the various producing countries and shipped to importing destinations without ever coming to the Netherlands.[1]

It is remarkable, in fact, how with the end of the 'colonial' age a new era of Dutch enterprise in tea has opened up.

European Tea Committee

Rotterdam's leadership in tea has received further recognition by being chosen as the headquarters of the European Tea Committee (Comité Européen de Thé), as well as of the International Tea Promotion Association (see Chapter 17). The ETC, founded in 1966, differs from many of the international bodies now concerning themselves with the product in that, as its statutes say, its object is mainly 'to protect effectively . . . the interests of the tea trade and industry' by establishing a common policy between associations in EEC countries. In addition to the EEC members, Sweden and Switzerland are Associates. The Committee plays a unifying role in a whole range of technical matters, such as food legislation, labelling directives, a possible future International Tea Agreement and so on. In recent years it has owed much to the leadership of its Secretary, Mr Rukus van de Meeberg, veteran of the Dutch trade and extremely knowledgeable about all aspects of tea.

Consumption

The internal situation in the Netherlands is not quite as bright as the external trade. What should be a flourishing market has been affected by a trend towards weaker tea. This is usually traced back to World War II. Families had to 'stretch' their desperately meagre supplies; often they drank their tea without milk and the taste for a brew comparable to the British 'cuppa' has not returned. Consumption per head has remained remarkably static over the years, drifting downward, if anything, from 66 to 64 g during the past decade. Even so, this compares well with anywhere else in Western Europe, outside the United Kingdom.

Teabags make up nearly 85% of all tea drunk in the Netherlands and it is curious, in view of the taste for a weak brew, that a 4 g bag is the general rule, in contrast with lighter weights elsewhere. But it means that Dutch families tend to use one 4 g bag where at least two 3 g or 3.5 g bags would be needed for a good, strong pot. Recently a 'two bag' campaign has been launched by the Netherlands trade, to persuade housewives and caterers to fortify their brews.

This is a reminder that the Netherlands is one of the two countries (Nigeria being the other) where the International Tea Promotion Association started to campaign. In conjunction with the packers, it formed the equivalent of a Tea Council, with the intention of making young people and caterers its special targets. Among much else, a permanent pavilion was built at the Flevohof Agricultural Exhibition in the north of the country, attracting some 800,000 visitors a year, mostly school children.

Holland is a price-conscious market and pays rather less for its leaf, on the average, than most European countries, though the statistics need to be used with care.

Sources of supply

In terms of gross imports, in 1983 the USSR, with 3,990 tonnes, headed the field for the first time (a notable landmark). Argentina came a close second with 3,971 tonnes, while Mozambique, which had established a formidable lead in 1982 with 4,686 tonnes, now sent only 2,289 tonnes. This compared with 2,623, 2,2442 and 1,636 tonnes respectively from the three more 'up-market' origins, Kenya, Indonesia and Sri Lanka. But it is probable that a large part of the cheaper leaf disappeared again as re-exports (about 15,000 tonnes in all) and that the internal market was mainly serviced with Kenyas, Indonesian and Sri Lankan teas of medium quality, supplemented on a smaller scale from Malawi and Brazil. Sri Lanka is trying hard to improve its modest share. In 1984 the USSR and Argentina maintained their lead in gross imports.

Packers

There are some 18 tea-packing firms in the country, great and small – mostly the latter. The market leader, Douwe Egbert, claims more than a 50% share, with the venerable concern van Nelle and the recently amalgamated Drie Moller and Niemeyer some distance behind. In the big stores they have to compete with own-label packs at a lower price, which now claim a growing percentage of all sales. There is a tradition – handed down, no doubt, from colonial days – for tea packers to trade also in coffee and tobacco and recently (as in Britain and America) they have found it expedient to become part of national and even international conglomerates.

Retailing

At first glance, the shelves of the big supermarkets, whose chains have grown at the expense of traditional grocery outlets, give a more 'de luxe' impression, with their array of handsome local packs (many of them with names suggesting a 'ye olde English' connection), supplemented by indubitably British speciality tins. But the fight for shelf space is keen and 'special offers' abound.

West Germany

Politically, there are now two Germanys; 'tea-wise', there are three. East Germany (the 'Democratic Republic') is an unimportant tea territory, as we shall see in Chapter 12; West Germany (the 'Federal Republic') comes in the middle range, but encapsulated in it is that unique entity, Ost (East) Friesland.

Ost Friesland

Tucked in between Bremen and the Dutch border, the Ost Frieslanders were for long a somewhat isolated community of farmers and fishermen with a modest standard of living, for whom tea was one of their few luxuries. A parallel with the west of Ireland immediately springs to mind, but the difference is that whereas the 'peasantry' of the Gaeltacht have now been absorbed into the general pattern of Irish tea-drinking, the Ost Frieslanders still stand alone. A mere 450,000 of them account for about 8.5% of West Germany's consumption, and at 3 kg per head per annum they rank alongside the Irish and the British at the head of the European league. They appreciate quality as well as quantity: it is the best Assams that provide their favourite tipple.

Quality indeed (and the high prices it implies) has been until very recently the hallmark of West German tea-trading as a whole. No country in the world has paid more per kilogram for its bulk supplies, whatever their origins. The average in pre-boom years worked out at a dollar equivalent of US$3.50, against, for example, Ireland's US$2.50, the United Kingdom's US $1.80 and the Netherlands' US$1.60. This went right through to retail level, topped up by a system of taxation guaranteed to keep prices sky-high. Its chief feature was and is a consumption tax of DM4.15 per kilogram. Being a flat-rate duty instead of the more usual *ad valorem*, it has naturally tended to encourage the importation of the high-priced teas. Like the Dutch taste for weak tea, this system of taxation goes back to World War II, or rather its aftermath, since it was created by the occupying powers in 1945–47 and subsequent West German governments have perpetuated it.[2]

What has undermined the veneration of tea as a 'quality' product to some degree of late has been the energetic promotion of certain simply packaged, low-price blends, but the veneration still takes its characteristic forms. As in the Netherlands (and indeed in Japan), but much more so, blends which may not have any particular United Kingdom connection are given prestigious British names like 'Windsor Castle', 'Sir Winston' and 'Milady'. Then there is the cult of First Flush Darjeeling, small parcels of which are flown in each year and parachuted down amid ample publicity. The mystic stuff is retailed at the equivalent of up to US$80 per kilogram.

Much of West Germany's high quality tea, with its strong emphasis on flavour, is not sold via the supermarket shelves in the orthodox way, but is dispensed loose and in quite small quantities at 'boutiques' specialising in this line. These now number some 1,500 and represent perhaps 10% of the total trade. They are also the focus for a development which has gone far towards changing the face of West German packing and retailing in recent years – the growing craze for flavoured tea.

Up to the mid-1960s the only instances of this were the usual Earl Greys and Jasmines, but when orange and lemon flavours were cautiously introduced they quickly found a market. Others followed – no doubt on the analogy of ice-cream, strawberry and vanilla proved particularly popular! – and today a leading firm like Hälsson & Lyon of Hamburg claims to have over 100 varieties available. These exotics have still captured no more than some 15% of the market, but they have done a valuable job in introducing young people to the beverage. It does appear that the 'youth market' – that 'will-o'-the -wisp' of tea promotion worldwide – has for once been corralled.

German Tea Council

Some of the credit at least must be assigned to the German Tea Council (Gesellschaft für Teewerbung). Generic tea promotion in West Germany goes back to the earliest days of the International Tea Market Expansion Board, but the present Council has been operative only since 1952. Its sponsors are the Tea Boards of India, Sri Lanka and (from 1981 onwards) Kenya, together with representatives of the West German Tea Association. In recent years the Council has had a budget of about DM1 million, three-quarters of it provided by the producer countries and the remainder by some 35 trade 'sponsors', whose contributions ranged from DM1,500 up to DM20,000. This is not big money in modern advertising terms, but the Council can fairly claim that its prolonged and systematic approach to generic promotion (largely in the public relations and educational spheres) has contributed to the steady rise in West Germany's tea imports, from 3,725 tonnes when the Council started, to 17,603 tonnes in 1982 and comparable figures thereafter.

Sources of supply

In spite of the flavoured tea vogue, traditional Black blends, more than half of them in teabags, continue to provide the trade with its 'bread-and-butter'. West Germany has always been an important market for India, which in 1983 supplied 5,387 tonnes while Sri Lanka, with 3,746 tonnes, fell behind. The 'dark horse' in this race, as so often, has been China, sending less than 100 tonnes up to 1968, but cantering steadily on since then and currently in third place with nearly 2,500 tonnes. Some of this is in the form of Fannings, used as 'reducers', but there are also leaf grades which go into the flavoured teas, as well as into some highly-esteemed specialities.

Most of this tea is shipped in container loads to Hamburg, second only to Rotterdam as a European tea port and centre for the entrepôt trade (its experiment with auctions has already been mentioned), but Bremen is another important location.

If any orthodox teamen of Hamburg or elsewhere are a bit 'sniffy' about flavoured teas, what can be their reaction to the so-called 'health' teas which are also enjoying something of an explosion? They have nothing whatever to do with *Camellia sinensis*, but are herbal concoctions claiming to work wonders for most of the internal and external organs of the human body. A long fight to get the word 'tea' banned from their labels has been lost.

Belgium

In comparison with their neighbours across the Netherlands border, the Belgians are minuscule consumers of tea. In 1982 they were credited with gross imports of 1,845 tonnes, and, after allowing for a sizeable element of re-exports, their per head absorption has remained static for a number of years at no more than 0.11 kg.

As might be expected, there is a greater tradition of tea-drinking in the northern, or Flemish, segment of the country centred on Antwerp (significant as a tea port and the scene of auctions between 1959 and 1971). Nevertheless, tea is said to be made noticeably weak in those parts and stronger brews are to be found in Brussels and points south.

Lipton is a powerful influence, partly no doubt because of its packing factory in Brussels, and though a good deal of Douwe Egbert seeps in from the Netherlands, the United Kingdom is the biggest single source of Belgium's supplies, with Twining and other specialities prominent. As in France, Green tea has become quite significant, stimulated by the influx of workers from North Africa.

In spite of its modest standing as an importer, Belgium has taken a lead in trying to enforce a total ban on tea in which the smallest trace of pesticides can be detected – a matter on which the local trade sought the help of the European Tea Committee in 1982.

France
Sources of supply

If Dutch and West German families get a mild kick out of the idea that they are drinking 'English' tea, those of France have, if not a 50–50, at least a 40–60 chance of actually doing so. Excluding the Green variety, with its specialised market among North African immigrants and mainly supplied from China, over 2,500 tonnes out of a Black total of 6,909 tonnes imported into France in 1983 reached her from the United Kingdom, mainly blended there and shipped in packet form. Such teas are retailed either under their own long-familiar names – Lipton, Tetley, Twining – or as local brands in British ownership, including the popular 'Thé Eléphant' (Lipton).

As to origins, the prevailing taste in France has long been for Ceylon or Ceylon-character blends and this is, of course, reflected in the import statistics (2,675 tonnes from Sri Lanka – whether via the United Kingdom or direct – and that was just half of the 1983 Black total).

Significant today, however, is the quiet erosion of the market by China. As already mentioned, her main contribution is in Green tea, but her shipments of Black have steadily increased and they now average 1,000 tonnes per annum – leaf of fair quality at prices below those of comparable growths from elsewhere. This pressure is unlikely to relax.

Consumption

It must be admitted that tea in France has no more than a minority appeal. In the perspective of history this is a little strange, since we have the testimony of Mme de Sévigné, among others, that the late seventeenth-century cult of tea-drinking was at least as strong there as anywhere in Europe and it long remained highly fashionable. But today coffee is king and surveys suggest that only 15% of households now drink tea regularly (accounting for 90% of total consumption), while half of them never touch it at all.[3]

The overwhelming majority of housewives who do put tea on their shopping lists resort to chains of supermarkets and self-service stores; about 45% of sales are in teabag form, though with considerable variation in weights, 2, 2.5 and 3 g bags all being available.

Promotion

The prospects for tea in France are far from being all doom and gloom. Looking back over the past 20 years or so, it has, in fact, made a respectable advance; the figure of 0.14 kg per head per annum may seem humble compared with the Netherlands or West Germany (let alone Britain), but up to the 1960s it was no more than 0.05 kg. Throughout this period the Association of French Tea Importers (CEFREPIT) has worked hard to spread the gospel, particularly by sponsoring the sports events which make such a strong appeal to young France today.[4]

On the French Tea Council, CEFREPIT originally sat with representatives of the Indian and Sri Lankan Tea Boards, but Sri Lanka now prefers to 'do her own thing' and negotiates directly with leading importers and packers to push Ceylon blends.

There seems to be a general feeling that with a bit more money put into promotion, tea could resume quite a respectable place in Europe's most food-and-drink-conscious economy.

Switzerland

As visitors will be aware, Switzerland is a fairly expensive place in which to drink tea. 'Store brands' predominate, notably those of the influential retailing organisation, Migros, and also the Co-operatives, which between them command perhaps 40% of a less than 2,000 tonnes market. The United Kingdom tops the list of origins with 822 tonnes, Sri Lanka being close behind.

Recently the whole business of tea-drinking in Switzerland has become mixed up with the vogue for flavoured teas, instant mixes and herbal infusions. An announcement made in 1981 that the Swiss Tea Association was to be reconstituted as an 'Association for Tea and Herbs' was perhaps significant.

Scandinavia

Here is a group of countries whose peoples have had an influence in the world which cannot be measured by their numbers – let alone by their prowess as tea-drinkers! In history, in commerce, in the arts, they stand proud. But the figures which concern us, as shown in Table 11.1, are incontestable.

Table 11.1   Scandinavian imports and consumption (averages, 1979–81)

	Population (millions)	Tea imports (tonnes)	Consumption per head (kg)
Sweden	8.32	2,880	0.35
Denmark	5.12	2,340	0.46
Finland	4.80	820	0.17
Norway	4.10	770	0.19

A 1983–85 average would probably show little significant change. Thus, the space which can be given to Scandinavia in the present book must be trimmed to that measure.

The task is made easier by the fact that the main characteristic of each of the four markets is common to all – like the French, only more so, they prefer to get their tea from the United Kingdom. The tradition may not be so strong in Denmark as in Sweden, Norway and Finland, but it is broadly not unfair to regard Scandinavia as a modest, but significant, extension of the distributive network for UK packet teas.

The four countries can be taken in order of population.

Sweden

Here, the British connection is a good deal closer than the import statistics, as published, would suggest.

Prima facie, Sweden in 1983 got 1,647 tonnes out of its 2,856 tonnes of tea from Sri Lanka. But a survey carried out for the International Tea Promotion Association made the specific point that careful enquiries in 1979, when the corresponding Sri Lankan figure was 2,177 out of 3,051 tonnes, showed that the major distributors imported 'negligible' quantities direct from countries of origin:

The recorded imports from Sri Lanka, India or Kenya are in fact blends which the Certificate of Origin describes as 'mainly Sri Lankan' or 'mainly Indian' tea. In other words, where 51% of the tea content derives from a single source of origin, the blend will be so designated.[5]

This is surely an important caveat!

There are, in fact, only two indigenous tea packers of any substance, of whom the Kooperativa Forbundet claims some 15% of the market for its own blend and distributes up to a quarter of all tea sold in Sweden. Recently the KF has launched an ultra-cheap 'no brand' line.

It was the other substantial local packer, Kobbs AB, which headed a trend which has greatly influenced the strategy of the UK exporters. Until recently, the latter had relied on handsomely designed tins to catch the eye of the consumer. But when Kobbs abandoned tins in favour of lower priced 'pouches', or paper bags, they were so successful that everyone had to follow suit. There is actually an ecological slant to all this – Swedish people (and it applies to Danes too) don't like the waste of the earth's resources which the use of tinplate for packing tea seems to imply.

Also characteristic of the Swedish tea scene today is the number of specialist shops and health food stores selling all manner of obscure packs, including a strange variety of flavoured leaf – the usual lemon, orange, blackcurrant, etc., plus such exotics as mango and banana – not a lot, but some! Flavoured teas under the Lyons 'Horniman' label are packed locally.

Teabags account for 35% of overall sales.

Denmark

Denmark is top of the Scandinavian 'per head' table. Here is another small but competitive market where 'pouches' have sharply reduced price levels and the demand for tins is now only marginal. The proportion of imported packs from the United Kingdom is probably 50%; three Danish packers headed – as in Sweden – by the Co-op (FDP) supply most of the rest. Major outlets are limited, but here again a number of small vendors are getting into the business. For many years both Sri Lanka and India carried on uninational promotion and more recently the International Tea Promotion Association earmarked Denmark for one of its first generic campaigns, but all such plans have had to be suspended (see page 195).

Norway and Finland

Norway and Finland are UK-dominated markets, on a smaller scale still.

In relation to population, Norway has a large number of minor grocery outlets – over 8,000 served by five buying groups. This no doubt reflects the country's strung-out pattern of villages and difficult communications in the past. In 1982, 542 tonnes out of 846 tonnes imported came from the United Kingdom, though Sri Lanka (hitherto inconspicuous) was planning a push with directly imported packets.

The Finns traditionally fortify themselves with coffee, a thumping 13.3 kg per head per annum compared with only 0.17 kg of tea. What is more, 'Finland uses only the very finest of fine Arabica. It is without any doubt the most discriminating coffee-drinking country in the world'.[6] A tough competitor indeed for tea and some 'missionary' work appears to be called for – perhaps by the UK firms which sent the Finns 354 tonnes out of their 917 tonnes of imports in 1983.

Italy

With the second highest population in the EEC (57 million, against West Germany's 62 million), Italy ranks only sixth in tea consumption, well behind the United Kingdom, Ireland, West Germany, the Netherlands and even France. For some years the gross import figure has teetered around the 4,000 tonnes mark. In 1982 it was 3,855 tonnes (or 3,400 after re-exports), representing a ration per head of no more than 0.06 kg, or, in old-world Anglo-Saxon terms, under 2 oz per annum – say, 0.5 lb for the whole family. And that is a generous estimate. Few readers will be surprised that the corresponding figure for coffee would be 32 lb! The mind's eye hardly catches a typical Italian in the act of pouring out a cup of tea. And while tea made a modest advance throughout the 1960s and 1970s, coffee marched ahead much more briskly.

Various reasons have been given from time to time for tea's relative unpopularity – from hard and heavily chlorinated water (more easily disguised in coffee) to its image as a drink not only lacking in the precious Italianate aura of 'virility', but also having a positive identification with hospitals and convalescence. As might be expected, tea-drinking has taken a somewhat stronger hold in the industrial north-west, centred on Milan and Turin, than in the less internationalised south.

Italy draws, substantially, on only two sources for its tea, Sri Lanka and the United Kingdom – 1,708 tonnes from Sri Lanka in 1983, and 670 tonnes from the United Kingdom. Sri Lanka is reaping the benefit of consistent promotion over a spread of years, including carefully cultivated relations with individual importers and packers. British interests are represented mainly by the usual handful of international names, Lipton, Fortnum & Mason, Twining, with the last named specialising in the promotion of its decorative tins. They all work hard in the field and reap some reward, but are somewhat swamped by the two leading indigenous firms, Star and ATI-PILETI, which between them control 55%–60% of the market. Both of them are partly nationalised, which considerably strengthens their position.

Out of Italy's 18,000 more important food distributors, 97% are estimated to stock tea, though it is obviously not a significant line with most of them. Italy is perhaps second only to Spain as the most 'teabag conscious' country in Europe – market share is as much as 85% and probably rising. Bags vary in weight between 1.5 and 3 g.

Portugal

The Iberian peninsula can hardly be regarded as tea territory, though Portugal long had the advantage of association with Mozambique and even obtains a small amount of tea from the Azores. Imports vary but appear to be approximately 300 tonnes a year, which represents no more than 0.01 kg per head for the inhabitants. Imports are under strict government control and as licences tend to be issued annually on the same terms as the year before, it is difficult for any individual trader to expand his business. Nevertheless, the well-known labels of the multinationals, with Tetley and Twining among the more prominent, do appear on the self-service shelves. Leading local blends bear the euphonious names of Sambique and Chali-Cungo.

Spain

In Spain, the nature of the market is well illustrated by the fact that it has what is almost certainly the highest proportion of UK imports of any country outside Scandinavia – 459 tonnes out of 718 in 1981. For historical reasons,

Horniman remains the most potent brand name – not the Lyons Tetley speciality range under that title, but leaf brought in to be packed locally. Sri Lanka has the biggest share of direct imports and is doing all it can to promote its packets and teabags. The latter, incidentally, rule supreme in Spain – something like 90% of the market.

Yugoslavia

Finally, Yugoslavia, poised between East and West, is a rare example of a Communist country which is trying to operate something like a mixed economy – and undergoing severe economic strain in the process.

Tea ranks low on the Yugoslav diet sheet and though scores of importers are theoretically free to bring it in, only about a dozen do so. Some 2,600 tonnes spread among 23 million people works out at a mere three or four teabags per head per annum; a few drink it regularly, but most seem to treat tea as just one more of the herbal concoctions which are traditional in the country and take it for their colds and flu.

Big distributors like Franck of Zagreb may have a range of mint, camomile, lime and rosehip 'teas', with *Camellia sinensis* bringing up the rear.

As to origins, India (1,759 tonnes) and the USSR (745 tonnes) shared the lead in 1981 and it was reported in that year that India was planning to set up a large warehouse in conjunction with the state trading company OMNICO, from which tea would be distributed to Southern and Eastern Europe.

12 *The USSR and Eastern Europe*

The USSR

It has been quite a puzzle to decide just where in this book the Russian chapter should be located. The USSR is unique for the triple role it plays – in descending order of significance – as importer, producer and exporter of tea. All three are intertwined, but especially the first and last, and to them the story of tea-growing in the USSR will serve as a convenient prologue.

It began as part of the general development of the tea lands between the Black Sea and the Caspian, from which Turkey and Iran have also benefited. W. H. Ukers went into considerable detail about the first experimental plantings from 1847 onwards and the emergence by the end of the century of a Russian tea industry which was to become 'one of the most important sources of wealth in Transcaucasia'.[1]

Current production

In the modern geography of tea, 'Transcaucasia' signifies the Soviet Republic of Georgia, though the crop is also cultivated in Azerbaijan to the east and in the cumbrously named Russian Soviet Federated Socialist Republic (RSFSR) to the north.

Much of Georgia, famous for wheat and wine as well as tea, enjoys Russia's nearest thing to a Mediterranean climate. The weather tends to be dry in the principal harvesting months from May to September, though there are usually good midsummer rains and the main flush starts then; the best quality period is in July/August (corresponding to the North Indian second flush). There are sharp winter frosts which have always influenced the choice of *jats*. Much work has, in fact, been done by the Tea Research Institute of the USSR on the breeding of productive and frost-resisting clones; these included Assam, Kangra Valley, China and Japan crosses in remarkable diversity.

Up until World War I, the Georgia industry was a mixture of biggish estates and peasant holdings and when it emerged from the chaos of the Revolution the traditional families continued to harvest their own leaf, as they do today, though under a co-operative umbrella.[2]

The actual plucking, however, is almost wholly mechanised, with the help of an apparatus peculiar to the USSR (see page 19), most of the tea being conveniently planted in dome-topped hedges. Partly at least because of this, the quality of most of the Georgian tea is not high. It is frequently criticised in the Russian press and, as we shall see, is hardly regarded as a choice product abroad. An exception, apparently, is the district of Khrasnodar, which, because it is well up on the Caucasian slopes, has defied mechanisation and yields a small quantity of high-grown, hand-plucked and carefully manufactured leaf. Output there is expected to rise to some 1,400 tonnes.

In the main areas of Georgian tea production, the factories, usually operating on a 'bought-leaf' basis, produced in 1983 143,000 tonnes of tea from perhaps 80,000 planted hectares. About 30% of this was Green tea. In the Black grades, the factories turn out an average of 44% Broken Orange Pekoe, 35% Orange Pekoe and Pekoe, 10% Pekoe Souchong, 8% Fannings and 3% Dust – a highly orthodox, not to say old-fashioned, range! The Fannings and Dust, not being acceptable to the Russian housewife, are sent summarily into exile, mainly to the decadent West.

The factories themselves exhibit a variety of machinery, mostly of conventional origin, but modified to secure something like continuous withering and rolling. Quoting Messrs Thomas:

Machine withering (three machines) is standard practice, functioning like the action of a drier. After withering (six hours) tea enters the rolling room. Rolling consists of three rolls each of 45 minutes (18 rollers). In the case of coarse leaf, a fourth roll is sometimes used. Fermentation lasts from $3\frac{1}{2}$ to 5 hours.

Imports

Home-grown leaf is not sufficient, and never has been, to keep the samovar bubbling. A decidedly readable book could be written about Russia's tea-trading through the ages. Apart from misty beginnings in barter along the Mongolian border, a real start was made when the Empress Elizabeth established a regular caravan route in 1735. At a stately 25 miles per day, the trains of camels, each loaded with four chests, took 16 months to cover the 11,000 miles between China and Old Russia, including an appalling 800 miles across the Gobi Desert. Slow camel to St Petersburg, indeed! The final completion of the Trans-Siberian railway brought this picturesque procession to an end.

Simultaneously, the trade in brick tea was reaching vast proportions. At first it was bought from Chinese manufacturers in the ordinary way, but after 1861, when the port of Hankow was opened to foreign commerce, numerous Russian firms set up their own factories there. Brick tea was also produced by Russian and British companies at Foochow (Fuzhou) and so enormous was the demand that Dust was imported in quite substantial quantities from India, Ceylon and Java, to supplement local supplies.

By the turn of the century, Czarist Russia was the world's third largest importer (after the United Kingdom and Australia) and was supplementing her 120 million lb from China – leaf and brick – with some 18 million lb bought in Colombo and less than half of that amount in various Indian markets. No wonder that one of the earliest propaganda ploys of the Ceylon planters was to establish an agent in Moscow – and to send him on a regular promotional mission to the great Nijni-Novgorod Fair.[3] By this time, in fact, the 'Moscow tea merchant' ranked in dignity with the 'old Mincing Lane hand'.

Up to World War I, there seemed to be no limit to the potentialities of the Russian trade, but, of course, the 1917 Revolution was as devastating to external commerce as to home production and a quarter of a century went by before imports crept back as far as the 50 million lb mark, most of it from China.

We must pass with speed to modern times. For some years after World War II, the flow of foreign tea into the USSR remained largely a matter of comradely deals with her newly 'communised' neighbour. But, as was seen in Chapter 2, the great ideological split of 1961 and the outlawing of China tea in the USSR has benefited India rather than that former favourite supplier, Sri Lanka (see Table 12.1).

Table 12.1 USSR imports and re-exports – 1983 (tonnes)

Imports from:		Re-exports to:	
India	61,932	Czechoslovakia	320
Bangladesh	1,853	Germany	520
Sri Lanka	3,784	Poland	3,160
China	1,652	Mongolia	4,720
Vietnam	5,341		
Other countries	2,179	Other countries	16,596
Total	76,741	Total	25,617
		Net imports	51,124

The USSR's current absorption of so much of the best of Indian tea, from fine Darjeeling to the better CTCs of Assam and the South, not only represents a dramatic shift in world trade, but also expresses the conservatism of Russian tastes. Shops in the USSR remain a thriving market for packet teas of the type that are losing out to the teabag in so many parts of the world. Messrs Thomas report the existence, early in the 1970s, of nine factories churning out nine types of Black and eight of Green packets, in sizes ranging from 25 to 100 g. The urban housewife seeks her pet brands and blends in the local supermarket, favouring particularly those based on whole-leaf grades such as Orange Pekoe.

Teabags are not unknown (one reads of a single IMA machine operating in Moscow and three Constantas at Tbisi, centre of the Georgia industry), but they mainly cater for the tourist and the expatriate.

Adding home production (at 143,000 tonnes) to imports (less re-exports) at 51,124 tonnes (1983), it seems likely that the USSR's annual consumption is in the order of 200,000 tonnes, and rising. This adds up to some 0.75 kg per head for her 268 million people, but that certainly does not represent the scale of the tea-drinking habit in the average Russian household. Since time immemorial, the beverage, taken extremely weak, has been on tap throughout the day, the family teapot being kept going with boiling water from the samovar. The tea is made at normal strength, but the glasses from which it is drunk are only half filled and are topped up, again from the samovar. Tea is drunk with lemon, seldom, if ever, with milk.

Exports

There remains the third role of the USSR, as a trader in tea. For exports overall we have no statistics, though some rather scanty re-export figures indicate that, as might be expected, neighbouring Communist countries are among the recipients. Only Poland (see page 154) and Mongolia take any substantial tonnage.

More interesting is the fairly recent incursion of the USSR into the market places of the West. It was in 1968 that UK imports of Russian tea suddenly jumped from near-nil to 2,060 tonnes, and since then they have averaged round about the 3,000–4,000 tonne mark. And the quality? Messrs Thomas refer rather scathingly to a 1976 shipment of a 'very mixed consignment of Dusts and Fannings' (but with some 'delightful leaf', whatever that was) to a big UK dealer who resold it at 26p per kilogram as a 'price reducer'. Russian leaf has certainly helped to fill that role since the successive disappearances of Turkish and Argentine leaf from the London market. The best of it perhaps has characteristics comparable to Malawis.

Though direct shipments to the United Kingdom have sometimes figured as re-exports in the USSR statistics, it seems fairly certain that most of what is sent to London is the unwanted Fannings and Dust from Georgia and parts adjacent.

Russian tea, as delivered by Russian ships, is usually packed in 40-kg chests, 480 to a 40-ft container, or smaller quantities in 20-ft containers.

Much could be written about the 'terms of trade', since most of such shipments come to the West as part of those mysterious barter deals in which razor blades or synthetic fur coats are exchanged for honey, jam, edible starch or tea. Since the latter more often than not passes thereby into the hands of European speculators with no experience of or interest in the commodity, the disposal of it tends to become the perquisite of one or two British firms which have made this particular business their own.

Czechoslovakia

Only two of Russia's East European satellites, Poland and Czechoslovakia, rate a regular listing in the International Tea Committee's 'Apparent Consumption of Tea' table. The Czechs, as a matter of fact, only just scrape in at 0.14 kg per head. But it is interesting to see some of the places from which their modest 2,544 tonnes of leaf came in 1982 – 732 tonnes from the USSR, 463 tonnes from China, 382 tonnes from India and 204 tonnes from that rather ideological source, Vietnam.[4]

Poland

Poland, on the other hand, as Europe's biggest consumer next to the United Kingdom, takes its tea-importing arrangements seriously. There are the usual Russian 're-exports', of course (2,700 tonnes annually in recent years), but the 'Polish buyer' is also a familiar figure at the Calcutta and South India auctions, favouring for the most part the medium ranges. When the annual trade protocol between India and Poland was signed late in 1982, a big increase in commerce between the two countries was envisaged. Later, the Polish representative said that tea consumption in his country was increasing and the quota for Indian tea would be raised from 17,000 to 23,000 tonnes – a slightly academic gesture since, at any rate up to the end of 1981, shipments had never topped 14,000 tonnes. They did increase to 16,544 tonnes in 1982, but then came a surprising about-turn.

China has usually come second to India as Poland's biggest supplier, but, after some fluctuations, their share rose suddenly in 1983 from 3,337 to 7,828 tonnes, while India's dropped to 11,816 tonnes. Of other sources, Turkey came rather abruptly into the picture in 1979 and 1980, with 3,856 tonnes and 3,031 tonnes respectively, and then disappeared again. Bangladesh is the only other substantial supplier, averaging about 1,600 tonnes in 1980–83. As with India, Poland uses the auctions at Chittagong to acquire Bangladesh tea, which is then blended locally to a fixed standard before being shipped.

But there is another interesting spin-off from the tea-consciousness of Poland, that fundamentally most civilised country. In recent years British packers of speciality teas have made fruitful contacts with the official Polish importers and some highly respectable brand names from what might be called the 'Fortnum & Mason' end of the spectrum are to be seen on the shelves of the supermarket chain set up to handle imported consumer goods. 'Turkish Earl Grey' also makes a surprise appearance – not very like the real thing, we are assured. The remainder of Poland's 45,000 retail food outlets deal almost entirely in domestically blended and packed brands.[5]

The net result of this varied activity was 24,547 tonnes of tea from all sources entering Poland in 1981 (rising to an estimated 28,000 tonnes in 1983) and a consumption per head very different from Czechoslovakia's – over half a kilogram, in fact. It is notable that, reversing the trend in Western Europe, 'real' tea has made inroads into the sales of the herbal concoctions which have hitherto been popular. Both, incidentally, are called *herbata* and the sign 'Herbata Anglieska' may be seen outside the few cafés where tea is served by the pot, strong and with milk.

13 *The Great Gulf Market – and Beyond*

Some call it 'the Middle East' (ignoring the fact that most of it is in the Near East); others, more fashionably, talk of 'West Asia' (thereby excluding the North African component); others again use 'the Gulf' as a sort of shorthand for anything west of Karachi and east of Khartoum.

The fact is that there is no comprehensive term to cover the great block of some 14 contiguous and mainly Arab countries which, whatever their political differences, have at least one thing in common: they are part of a 'growth area' for tea consumption without parallel outside the two mighty home markets of India and China. Overall, they offer approximately 140 million people who consume over 180,000 tonnes of tea every year at an average per head of 1.29 kg.

To maintain some law and order in this chapter, it may be best to start with the two formidable powers, Iran and Iraq, before plunging into the Gulf proper, and thence passing onwards to the west.[1]

Iran

Iran (population 42 million) need only be glanced at here, as it has already made its appearance among the producers (see Chapter 7). For obvious reasons, no up-to-date import figures are available, but producers' export statistics suggested that Iran would be looking for at least 20,000 tons of Orthodox leaf during 1983, most of it likely to come from India. To the region as a whole, Iran mainly figures as the presumed recipient of large quantities of 'unrecorded imports' from countries as diverse as Bahrain, Kuwait, Dubai and Pakistan.

Iraq

In tea terms, Iraq (population 13.5 million) is the great phenomenon of our day. When in 1980 imports from her chief supplier, Sri Lanka, alone reached 22,793 tonnes, this was reckoned to be a matter of strategic stock-piling, but the tempo has if anything increased. 1982 saw over 28,000 tonnes of Sri Lankan and 5,000 tonnes of Indian leaf shipped to Iraq. In 1983 there was a change of emphasis, 15,000 tonnes out of a record total of 37,500 tonnes coming from India, but 1984 saw a prodigious 33,876 tonnes shipped from Sri Lanka alone. With modest contributions from China, Indonesia and elsewhere, it is probable that total imports will continue to rise at least in parallel with the increase in the population – that is, 3.5% per annum.

No wonder it is variously reported that tea is the principal hot beverage in Iraq, that consumption is virtually universal, that it is regarded as highly refreshing and that it is a traditional part of Iraqi life! Tea and sugar, boiled up together, form a rich and pleasing syrup, considered wholesome for children, no less than for adults.

Tea is a state monopoly and buying is mainly done through offices in Colombo and Calcutta. Most of the tea is shipped in bulk, to be put into 1 kg cellophane packs in a fully automated local plant. Teabags are being produced in small quantities. But it is interesting that in 1982 Iraq swung a little way back towards her earlier practice of importing packeted tea from Sri Lanka.

Jordan

Jordan and Syria are neighbours with contrasting philosophies, the former offering a free, the latter a controlled, market. Perhaps as a natural consequence, a good deal of tea flows unrecorded from the one to the other and it may be assumed that not all of Jordan's official import of a little over 3,000 tonnes represents tea actually drunk in the country. There are five recognised brands, but 'a variety of traders in other products enter the market speculatively, when an opportunity for profit is detected'.[2] However, Jordan also brings in about half of its Sri Lankan tea in prepacketed form.

Syria

Syria presents a typical growth picture, with 'imports for consumption' more than doubling (4,161 tonnes to 9,000 tonnes) between 1972 and 1982. As hinted above, statistics are unreliable. Imports are normally at least 90% from Sri Lanka, but very recently the State organisation, which controls tea completely, started buying some of the medium sorts in South India. Syria takes a certain amount of tea in packets – about 500,000 kg from Sri Lanka and much smaller quantities from the United Kingdom.

The Gulf

We can now move on to 'the Gulf', which for present purposes can be taken to comprise:

Qatar
Kuwait   The United Arab Emirates (Dubai and Abu Dhabi)
Bahrain   Oman

There is a special touch of *The Arabian Nights* about the statistics for all these very important tea territories, especially concerning their 'per head' consumption. Nobody actually believes that the good people of Qatar – men, women and children – get through 6.50 kg each in the course of a year, almost twice as much as the European record-holders, the Irish. Or that Kuwait comes second with a whopping 5.22 kg. The fact is that both of them, with all their Gulf neighbours, are essentially entrepôt centres, with small resident populations, but an extremely active forwarding trade.

Qatar

Qatar is an oil state, of which only about half the population of 180,000 is indigenous. Wages are high and tea comes from a variety of sources in elaborate packages, including teabags from the United Kingdom which are considered superior to those from the producer countries. Imports, which in 1979/80 totalled over 1,500 tonnes, with India as the main supplier, were less than half that figure in 1981/82.

Kuwait

Kuwait presents much the same picture on a grander scale. Here we have 1.3 million people, half of them immigrants or temporary residents, and all benefiting from the highest per capital income in the world, but probably consuming no more than half of the country's import of tea (6,500 tonnes in 1983). In 1981, when the figure was 6,000 tonnes, all but 1,254 tonnes of it came from Sir Lanka.

UK speciality teas accounted for 469 tonnes. It seems an anomaly that both in Qatar and Kuwait some tea is made available in subsidised form.

Bahrain

Bahrain (population 358,000) is a typical entrepôt community, whose tea statistics have sometimes been distorted by her re-exports to Saudi Arabia being delayed.

It is a very free-wheeling market, with a rich miscellany of packs (mostly orthodox Indian leaf) and as much as 25% in teabags. Bahrain is typical of the whole group of Gulf states into which Lipton, for example, import string-and-tag teabags from the United Kingdom and packet tea from India. Speciality teas by several of the leading British packers are to be seen in the shops and booths. Television commercials provide a modern promotional touch.

The United Arab Emirates

In the United Arab Emirates (UAE), both Dubai and Abu Dhabi are India-orientated. There is substantial local consumption of about 2.2 kg, but the Emirates are heavily enmeshed in the re-export trade, especially to Iran.

Dubai, with its 40 supermarkets and displays of teabags (many of them locally packed), as well as the other concomitants of modern living, is an ultra-sophisticated market. Brooke Bond of India has an important stake.

Oman

Finally, Oman figures as another small but rich oil state, where multinational proprietary packs are highly popular.

The number of inhabitants is not exactly known (the official figure of 1.5 million may be on the high side), but they all drink tea, absorbing about 1,500 tonnes at a personal rate of 2 kg per annum. India, at the most recent count, had 71% of the market and the UK speciality blends about 12.5%. A lot of cross-border trade goes on.

Saudi Arabia

With Saudi Arabia one travels once more into the consumer rather than the distributive zone. As the world well knows, this is the kingly Arab state *par excellence*, where modernity is on the march and the gains of tea at the expense of traditional coffee are most strongly marked. As an importer, Saudi Arabia is not yet in the Iraq class, but its absorption of 15,494 tonnes of tea makes it a significant customer, especially for Sri Lanka, which currently holds at least 70% of the market.

The retail trade in tea is in a rapid state of evolution. Up to 80,000 small grocery stores and equally numerous teashops are supplied by localised wholesalers, working on low margins and heavy volume discounts. New brands and labels proliferate, all on much the same level, though Lipton teabags dominate that particular segment. Peculiar to this market are 'family' packs consisting of two polythene pouches of 750 kg in a single kraft box. Teabags come from the Dubai packing factory or from the plant set up in Riyadh itself (jointly with a Hong Kong company) and equipped with six machines of West German type.

'Loose tea', which used to figure largely, is now more or less extinct; in contrast, the United Kingdom has taken a rising share, with the result that Saudi Arabia is now second to Canada as Britain's best re-export market. Television advertising is potent and it is a curious sidelight that Radio Monte Carlo is reported to be popular with teenage audiences.

Egypt

Egypt, with her 45 million people, is often listed as the biggest consumer in Africa, though her orientation, in this as in other matters, is rather towards West Asia and the Gulf. Whereas the people of Kenya or Southern Africa tend to make and enjoy their tea after the 'English' fashion, Egyptians, like Iraqis, prefer to boil up leaf and sugar together, and to drink the resultant brew from a glass. This encourages them to look for a good, deep colour in the liquor, so that imports are dominated by CTC Fannings and Dust.

Just what those imports amount to is a debatable question. The ITC Bulletin (1983) showed an average consumption for the triennium 1979–81 of 30,560 tonnes, or 0.73 kg per head. This was based on official import figures, but *exports* to Egypt recorded by the main producers were in fact very much higher every year. ITC recognises the discrepancy, and in its 1984 Bulletin presented the situation in export terms, reaching the impressive figures shown in Table 13.1.

Table 13.1   Exports to Egypt (tonnes)

	1981	1982	1983
India	18,700	13,600	14,300
Sri Lanka	17,400	24,200	31,000
Indonesia	10,800	8,400	2,100
Kenya	2,600	4,600	7,000
Total (all growths)	53,000	57,300	65,000

Whatever the true facts about consumption, it is undeniable that tea is truly the national beverage, whether in town or village, and, though soft drinks are making some headway among the younger folk, they cost anything up to three times the price of a glass of tea.

Naturally, so lively a market has attracted the attention of the publicists. Both India and Sri Lanka maintain offices in Cairo and carry on uninational propaganda, and Egypt was one of the first countries pinpointed by the International Tea Promotion Association as crying out for a generic campaign.[3]

Egypt is among the few countries where tea is treated as an essential commodity. A regular subsidised entitlement of 0.5 kg per head is distributed through ration shops; this is in addition to unsubsidised tea, available in the stores and bazaars in the usual way and as a rule of superior quality.

The 'public sector' predominates in what is essentially a socialist country, though with some relaxation towards private enterprise in recent years. A government agency buys tea abroad; government factories pack it. Even where bulk tea imports by the private sector are allowed, the packing has to be done by the state organisation or by licensed packers in the Free Zones of Egypt. Prepacked tea is also being imported in increasing quantities; profit margins on it are controlled by law – currently, 6% to the importer, 4% to the wholesaler and 10% to the retailer.

Egyptian officialdom, conscious of the importance of tea in the national diet, has been alert to any shortfall in manufacturing standards. Early in 1983 there was something of a furore over the rejection by the health authorities of a large consignment of Indian tea on the ground that it contained excessive quantities of metal particles. As explained more fully in Chapter 16, CTC and LTP manufacture does, in fact, tend to produce slightly more of such particles than Orthodox rolling, and special care has to be taken to eliminate them from the Fannings and Dusts of the type so popular in Egypt.

Sudan

Sudan, the largest African territory in area, and with a population of some 20 million dedicated tea-drinkers, has a strong claim on our attention. But though its people may sip away all day at their glasses of sweet tea, it is not easy to be precise about how much they actually consume. Published per head figures – 0.71 kg in 1978–80, only 0.42 kg in 1979–81 – are unreliable, partly because of the 'unofficial imports' which notoriously slip across the borders from East and Central Africa. Just as in the case of Egypt, her chief supplier, India, records sending 11,508 tonnes in 1980 and 8,057 in 1981, or 19,585 tonnes for the two years, whereas Sudan purports to have received only 7,085 tonnes in the same period.

Figures for the other two important suppliers are hardly more consistent, but it seems that China tea, procured under barter deals, has lost some of its popularity, imports having fallen from 4,706 tonnes in 1980 to only 661 tonnes in 1981, with a further decline since. Sudan has often been seen as a logical outlet for African exports – official as well as otherwise! – and, in fact, 2,906 tonnes was listed as coming from Kenya, Uganda and Tanzania combined, though the records of the individual countries suggest higher figures. Recently there has been a very steep fall in all tea purchases, due to the shortage of foreign exchange and general economic weakness.

Up to the end of 1980, imports were a state concern, those from India being the monopoly of a single concessionaire, the Sudan Tea Company. The arrangement was fraught with many difficulties and Indian suppliers had to wait two years and more for their money. The private importations which are now allowed must be paid for in what is called 'parallel market currency', that is, there is an official exchange rate linked to the US dollar, but also a premium rate for which currency can be bought and sold on the open market.

The pattern of distribution is very much as one might expect – loose tea still popular in the country, packets in the towns. Distribution to the former is distinctly erratic and both government and private stores are often out of stock. Nevertheless, the Indian Tea Board has found it worth while to do some advertising in order to counteract any swing towards Kenya and

Tanzania and in 1981 Bangladesh, whose tea had scarcely been heard of in the territory, sent an introductory mission.

Libya

Egypt's western neighbour, Libya, has all the characteristics of a strictly controlled economy. Only the National Supply Corporation can bring tea into the country and it likes to deal with state export organisations under government-to-government agreements.

In the case of the Sri Lanka, for example, all purchases are channelled through the nationalised agency Consolexpo, and Libya is, in fact, the most important outlet for prepacked Sri Lankan tea. However, India now appears to have taken a two to one lead in this 10,000–12,000 tonnes market, though up-to-date statistics are lacking. China also sends variable amounts – her peak was in 1974 (3,883 tonnes), but recently this has dwindled to under 1,500 tonnes.

Algeria

In Algeria the pattern is much the same, with a state trading body, ONACO, responsible for all imports. As almost everywhere in this region, consumption per head seems to be going up steadily, though from a fairly low base – only 0.29 kg in 1974–76, 0.47 kg in 1979–81. The total is still not more than 9,000 tonnes.

Tunisia

This is a much livelier scene, since Tunisia offers perhaps the most convincing example so far of China's ability to take over a market previously dominated (though in erratic proportions) by the two traditional suppliers, India and Sri Lanka. China began to appear on the scene in the early 1970s and by 1977 was sending 2,050 tonnes of tea, against India's 1,223 and Sri Lanka's 2,684. By 1982, Sri Lanka's exports to Tunisia had dwindled away to nothing. India's were still fairly strong at 1,926 tonnes, but China's had leapt to 8,100 tonnes. Early in 1983 it was reported that the Tunisian state monopoly (OCT) had signed a contract for the import of 12,000 tonnes of Broken Orange Pekoe from China and since the average yearly consumption in the country during 1978–81 was recorded at only about 9,500 tonnes, these figures, if taken at their face value, would suggest that other suppliers are about to be squeezed out altogether.

As individual consumers, the Tunisians are certainly way out in front among North African peoples and indeed their 1.5 kg per head places them high in the world league.

Morocco

And so to Morocco, where Chinese penetration is of longer standing and has recently taken an unexpected twist. Not only have imports of China tea increased enormously of late (a jump from 11,779 tonnes in 1980 to 19,431 in 1981), but Morocco is planning to *grow* tea under Chinese auspices. A report in the American trade press in 1983 stated that the country's first tea factory was due to begin production soon.[4] It is sited at Larache, on the Atlantic coast south of Tangier. The plantation from which it will draw its leaf has only 90 ha in bearing so far, but its 1984/85 target is 860 ha. Output will be entirely of the Green tea, which has always been the Moroccans' favourite refreshment (with or without the addition of mint and ample quantities of sugar). Machinery for the factory, together with some 20 technicians to train the local staff, is also being supplied from China. The progress of this remarkable enterprise, so remote not only from its country of origin but from any other tea-growing area, will be watched with considerable interest.

It should be mentioned that mainland China does not yet have a total monopoly of imports; Taiwan, which used to be strong in Morocco, still sent 1,200 tonnes at the last count (1982).

Unlike other North African countries, Morocco is a free market, the importers suffering no state interference, except that a 25% deposit (reimbursed after six months) is required on all consignments.

14 *North America*

Only two countries are involved here, and we must necessarily begin with 'Big Brother'.

The United States
Historical developments

If tea is part of the mythology of Ireland, the United States holds a unique place in the mythology of tea itself. How could it be otherwise, when folklore traces back the very origin of those States to the arrival at Boston in 1773 of 284 chests of Hyson and Bohea?

Given that the Boston Tea Party was not an isolated event and that Charleston, Philadelphia and Annapolis, for example, equally witnessed the violent rejection of British-shipped tea and the 'accursed duty' which it bore, the proceedings in Boston Harbour on that December night had a profound symbolic value. The British government had completely misjudged the 'colonists'. It could not see that the retention of a 3*d.* impost on this one article, when all other import duties into America had been waived, left their main grievance intact, since the yield was earmarked towards paying the salaries of British officials and maintaining their independence of local legislatures.

Thus, when the East India Company, happening to find itself vastly overstocked with tea in London,[1] obtained permission to dump some of it with American merchants, an explosion of some kind was certain. Up until that time, and even beyond it, there was no majority feeling in favour of 'rebellion' as such, but this affair of the tea duty touched hearts, minds and pockets together and nothing could ever be the same again.

Not only British colonialism suffered a setback; the status of tea on that side of the Atlantic was never quite the same again, either. It had been an extremely popular beverage, especially with the Dutch-descended burghers of New Amsterdam, among whom tea-drinking was a cult long before the British captured the place and rechristened it New York. Five years before the Boston Tea Party, imports had risen to the then prodigious figure of nearly 900,000 lb, but political agitation and boycott ensured that they sank to 226,156 lb in 1769 and only 108,629 lb a year later. The United States, as W. H. Ukers remarks, came into the world with a 'prenatal disinclination to tea' and the heirs of the East India Company – the tea producers – are still paying the penalty.

A flurry of American interest in the China trade marked the later years of the eighteenth century, but the weight of tea shipped was not large. However, over the next half-century there was a slow recovery. The import of a little under 7 million lb in the year 1830, representing a per capita consumption of 0.54 lb (or 0.24 kg), compares not too unfavourably with the current American consumption of 0.36 kg. Pending serious competition from coffee, tea then made quite steady progress until the end of the nineteenth century. The peak figure, in per head terms, was between 1881 and 1896, with an average figure of 1.34 lb.

The story after that was one of more or less consistent decline, followed by virtual stagnation, at between 0.36 and 0.38 kg during the past decade. One stresses the 'per head' factor, since this has after all been the target of the laborious and largely frustrated efforts, made over a very long period, to conjure a bonanza for producers and distributors alike out of the huge growth in the population and prosperity of the United States.

Consumption today

In tonnage terms, the United States certainly occupies a respectable place. The 1983 'net for consumption' figure of 77,140 tonnes kept her third to the United Kingdom and Pakistan in the world league; otherwise only the USSR imported anything approaching a comparable weight of tea. An analysis of current absorption, however, holds out no very grand hopes for the future. As is well known, the United States is the original home of two phenomena, teabags and iced tea, neither of which is calculated to send imports soaring, especially in the quality range. Up until the mid-1960s, Indian and Sri Lankan teas, mostly in that range, took more than 60% of the market; now they are down to a sad 17% (see Table 14.1).

Table 14.1 Imports into the United States: teas 'passed by the examiners for admission'[2] (tonnes)

	1962	1972	1982	1983
India	12,950	7,431	2,189	2,128
Sri Lanka	22,908	20,546	13,667	8,672
Total (all growths)	58,092	69,445	82,664	75,147

In 1984, which saw a modest recovery to 82,484 tonnes, there was little change in the Indian and Sri Lankan shares.

Sources of supply

Where have all the orders gone? The answer is significant in a number of ways. The United States normally imports from 25 countries in a given year. After overtaking Sri Lanka in 1980, Indonesia remained the number one supplier until 1982 (13,961 tonnes – slightly less in 1983), while China advanced from a mere 557 tonnes in 1972 to 6,845 tonnes a decade later. Kenya staked a steady claim, averaging some 7,000 tonnes over the same period, though 1983 showed a decline to only 4,665 tonnes. But the greatest single beneficiary in the swing away from Indian/Sri Lankan teas has beyond doubt been Argentina. In the six years 1976–82 her share increased nearly seven-fold (1,815 tonnes to 11,823) and she was pressing the leaders hard, but in 1983 she came out decisively on top at 15,122 tonnes; since total imports of Black tea had fallen to 71,709 tonnes, this represented no less than a 21% share. In fact, with Brazil weighing in to the tune of 3,807 tonnes, plus minor contributions from Ecuador and elsewhere, tea now provides an unexpectedly significant strand in the pattern of 'hemisphere' trade. The trend was fully confirmed in 1984.

Nor is it just a matter of tonnage; there has been an obvious shift in price. One has only to contrast Argentinas valued at US$1.13 per kilogram in 1982 (before the boom period, of course) with Sri Lankas at close to US$2 or the Indonesian average of US$1.60 with Indian growths touching US$3. Apart from the countries already mentioned, much low- or medium-priced tea from various sources comes in through Rotterdam.

The pattern of trade in the United States is complex at all levels and gives ample scope for wheeling and dealing in these comparatively cheap teas. Some 36 importers and packers, representing the cream of the trade, are listed as supporting the Tea Council of the USA, where they sit alongside representatives of India, Sri Lanka, Indonesia, Kenya and Tanzania. Sharing the same offices is the US Tea Association, the trade's very active co-ordinating body, with a total membership of 146.[3]

Apart from a few major firms which organise their own channels of supply, packers buy mainly through dealers and brokers. The ranks of the latter have been swelled of late by newcomers (often with coffee and/or cocoa interests as well). They may be offering first-hand tea acquired through a few contacts in the producer countries, but they are also to be found peddling second- and third-hand parcels in the 'sticks'.

Retail distribution

On a more serious level, the United States has for many years been something of a Lipton fief – the firm of Thomas J. Lipton was founded by old 'Sir Tommy', as a personal property, in 1893, long before he had begun competing for the America's Cup. Later it passed into Unilever ownership and is still thought to command as much as 45% of the market.

It can hardly be said that there are any other 'national brands', promoted coast-to-coast, though some widely known names are those of Salada Foods (owned by Kellogg), McCormick, Brooke Bond and Tetley. It was the last named, though of British origin, which 'colonised' the United Kingdom with teabags from its American base. The 'Tenderleaf' brand was recently acquired from Nabisco by Procter & Gamble. At retail level, two or three supermarket chains are making the greatest headway and may have obtained up to 85% of all sales. Some 600 wholesalers service innumerable corner stores and catering outlets.

The leaf tea handled in this way (we are not at the moment talking of instant or 'mixes') comes overwhelmingly in the form of teabags – more than 95% at the latest count and still rising, though at a slower rate than over the past decade. 'Loose' (that is, packet) tea can be said to be on the way to extinction, except perhaps in a few southern States – Georgia, Mississippi, the Carolinas. Teabags (usually of the string-and-tag variety) come in a wide range of sizes and prices. Competing with established packs are teabags filled with medium- or low-quality leaf and sold in plain, white boxes at a price which may be no more than US$1 for 100 bags.

Iced tea

It is the use to which they put all these teabags (packets of tea too, for that matter) that distinguishes the consumers of the United States from those of any other major country. Despite the challenge of cola and similar soft drinks, iced tea, drunk from a glass, can still be described as the classic American summer beverage, enjoyed by perhaps 80% of all households.

Lemon and sugar are important elements in the iced-tea-brew and this has led to the production and vigorous promotion of compounds in which all the ingredients are brought together in a powdered and pre-measured combination.

Less desirable (certainly from the grower's point of view) is the vogue of so-called 'mixes', in which the authentic tea element may be no more than 3%. Obviously, these do not compete directly with the genuine article, either iced or hot, but they may well mislead the younger generation as to what tea is all about.

Into this environment, instant tea fits a good deal better than anywhere else. If one has no very intimate acquaintance with – even reverence for – the flavour of 'real' tea, the idea of spooning a powder into a pitcher or glass, sweetening to taste, adding water and either pouring the liquor over ice or popping it into the refrigerator, has a powerful appeal to the American way of life and the resultant beverage is perfectly acceptable and refreshing.

In addition to instant manufactured internally (Lipton and Nestlé predominating), the United States is by far the biggest importer of powders produced elsewhere. Out of 1,028,264 kg exported by India in 1983, 780,201 kg went to American destinations; for Kenya, the corresponding figure was 262,646 kg out of 363,825 kg. Much smaller, though variable, quantities come from Sri Lanka. Sales of instant seem to have reached their peak across the United States in 1975, when it was claiming a 'leaf equivalent' of about 41 million lb, as against 70 million lb for bags and 10 million lb for packets, in retail food outlets. Recently there has been a decline and in percentage terms instant held only 21% of the 1982 market, compared with over 30% seven years earlier. Much of the powder is brought in in the form of micro-crystals and then 'blown up'.

Specialities

As in every country with an old tea-drinking tradition, mass-produced teabags, mixes and instant do not represent the entire presence of *Camellia sinensis* – it would be sad if they did. There have always been a lot of curiously evocative entries in the import lists published by the Food and Drug Administration of the US Department of Health – Scented Black, Scented Green, Scented Canton, Spiced Tea, China Jasmine, Oolong, Japan Gunpowder, Russian Green . . . Compared with the usual bulk shipments, some of these hardly amount to a row of caddies, but Green tea in general still has a good market, especially on the West Coast, with its substantial Japanese-American population. Of the 5,385 tonnes of Green passed by the examiners in 1984 – a much enhanced figure – 2,180 tonnes came in fact from Japan, but the lead was taken for the first time by China, with 2,654 tonnes.

Speciality teas, in the widest sense, are arousing increased interest today and are appearing in 'class' shops and boutiques hitherto only concerned with pushing fancy coffees. One operator in the field recently claimed to have 133 varieties available, including flavoured teas, natural and traditional teas and about thirty kinds of decaffeinated tea. British speciality firms have shared in this 'boomlet' to a modest degree and Mr James Norwood Pratt has sprightly references to the impact of Twining, which now has a packing factory of its own in the country.[4]

The question remains whether the sellers of 'real' tea – speciality or otherwise – carry enough clout to resist the tendencies which might seem to be turning the beverage into just one more 'soft drink'. Iced tea, though so important socially and to the industry, can be seen as the first fateful step in that direction. When you add a miscellany of flavours and confuse the issue with mixes and their ultimate offspring, 'Iced tea n'lemon on a stick', what becomes of the delicate individuality of tea 'like Mother made'? Someone has described *fruit juice* as having the most perfect American characteristics, 'naturally healthful, tasty, cold, low in calories',[5] but one cannot help feeling that the more tea aspires to the condition of fruit juice, the more tenuous will be its hold on what should be a magnificent market.

Canada
Consumption

An article by Mr Gordon F. Reynolds, Executive Director of the Canadian Tea Council, in the *International Tea Journal* (October 1982) was embellished with a slightly melancholic graph.[6] It showed consumption per head moving almost uniformly downwards between the mid-1960s and the late-1970s and had it been extended to cover the past five years, the slippery slope would have continued unchecked. The latest estimate we have is a triennial average of 0.78 kg for 1980–82, compared with 1 kg in 1964–66. Another table in Mr Reynolds' article revealed that the 'percentage of the population over ten years of age drinking tea on an average day' had fallen year by year from 64% in 1959 to 48% in 1978.

Thus, any review of the Canadian tea scene, as it was and is, must take the form, if not of an inquest, at any rate of a serious medical report.

Superficially, tea might be thought to have something of a head start in a country which in spite of a recent infusion of Germans, Italians and Asians, is still so largely populated with families of UK descent. But it has always been up against a rival tradition of coffee-drinking, with roots both in France and across the US border, whence also has come the competition from cola and other soft drinks. In one way, too, the image of tea as a 'British' institution has been a positive disadvantage; the lady of leisure, entrenched behind her well-appointed tea table, must always have been a minority figure and in the modern social and economic climate she has virtually disappeared. Wives work and when the middle-class family does reassemble in the evening, the increasing tendency is to go out for their meal – and not necessarily to drink tea with it. Tea probably remains, however, the most popular beverage from lunch-time onwards.

The curious result of all this is that Canadian tea-drinking today is broadly identified with the lower-middle and lower socio-economic levels and makes a poor showing at the upper end of the spectrum. Geographically, although British Columbia is always regarded as living up to it name, consumption there is markedly less than in the Atlantic region, while Quebec, of course, is coffee country. Some comparisons are shown in Table 14.2.

Table 14.2   Tea consumption by regions

Region	Population (%)	Tea consumption (%)
Atlantic	9	15
Quebec	29	22
Ontario	35	35
Prairies	17	15
British Columbia	10	13

Tea-drinking outside the home has been mentioned. That is where 25% of all food expenditure is located, but where only 11% of all tea is drunk. Some think it is because of poor standards both of leaf and service. To improve the former, the Canadian Tea Council has borrowed the UK system of voluntary grading of catering teas and this has been hailed as one of the most dramatic and effective initiatives by the industry for decades.

Packing and retailing

The trading picture is predictable. It includes over 90% teabags (predominantly 120 to the pound '2 cup' bags), plus an array of cheaper 'economy' bags in cellophane packs, some of them at 150 and even 180 to the pound. These include own-label blends and also nameless generic packs as in the United States. They are said to be on the decline now, but they must have contributed to tea's status as a 'down-market' commodity.

'Mainstream' tea is purveyed by a handful of major firms with international connections – Brooke Bond ('Red Rose'), Salada and Tetley. Tetley have recently made a considerable impact with their teabags imported complete from the United Kingdom. An array of smaller, localised packers share most of what is left (perhaps 35%), but some British speciality teas command quite a strong minority taste.

It is not an easy market to break into. In spite of the size of the country, the distribution chain is short, most retailers buying direct from importers or packers; Canadian or US brokers supply the rest. Eight chain stores make up to 85% of all retail sales and to get 'listed' on their shelves means guaranteeing payments based on any shortfall below a pre-agreed volume and giving discounts for promotions. Market leaders have gained their place at various times by aggressive, competitive schemes.

Sources of supply

It is not surprising, given the tenor of these paragraphs, that Canadians show no great preoccupation with the sources of their tea. Time was when India and Sri Lanka enjoyed a peaceful share-out of the market, though up to the time of World War II, Japan and other Greens made quite a powerful showing.[7]

Nowadays the Canadian trade buys wherever prices may be attractive. Sri Lanka still has a 20% stake and so has the United Kingdom, while India, Indonesia, Kenya and the South American countries supply most of the rest of fluctuating proportions. Some traders believe that China may reach a 10% share within a year or two.

Total retained imports in 1983, at 15,787 tonnes, were the lowest yet, and it is only a partial consolation that the per head consumption of 0.78 kg already referred to still keeps Canadians vastly ahead of the United States (between 0.36 kg and 0.38 kg).

The final conclusion of an independent survey of the market carried out on behalf of the Commonwealth Secretariat was that, while the Tea Council was already working from a well-thought-out base, it needed and deserved more funds for consumer research and for an educational drive both to schools and to the food service sector.[8] This might prepare the way for intensive promotion later on.

15 *The Australasian Scene*

We go 'down under' for the last of our regionalised surveys of the world's tea-drinking communities. There are plenty more, from Iceland to Tahiti, but to cover them all would require at least a couple of volumes on W. H. Ukers' scale. Enough – one feels the reader will agree – is enough.

Australia

Here is yet another country where tea-drinking is part of the national legend. It is rooted in the 'outback', where, as that indestructible 'Waltzing Matilda' will never cease to remind us, the lone prospector sang as he sat and waited till his billy boiled. Rudyard Kipling, in one of his World War I stories, attributed the 'ornery' Australian character to drinking 'stewed black tea with their meat' three times a day.

That image has never quite been effaced, even though the typical Australian took to town life very early, and today 60% of the population finds a congenial habitat in the spreading suburbias of just five great cities – Sydney, Melbourne, Adelaide, Brisbane and Perth. This development has laid Australian society open to a number of influences which have not been for the good of tea.

Imports and consumption

First, however, let us look at the actual situation. The statistics are certainly a cause for concern. Taking the past 20 years alone, imports have shrunk from 29,000 tonnes in 1961/62 (the Australian 'tea year' ends at 30 June) to a little over 23,000 tonnes in 1981/82[1] and 21,500 in 1982/83. Meanwhile the population has continued to rise (10.5 million in 1961, 15 million in 1982), with the sad mathematical result that consumption per head has dwindled from 2.5 kg per annum to little more than 1.5 kg.

Australia's suppliers have shared unevenly in this decline, as Table 15.1 makes clear. Two reasons are generally given for the overall drop in the weight of tea brought into the Commonwealth – the changing beverage habits of the people and the rise of the teabag. In a way, the two things interlock.

Table 15.1   Australian imports (tonnes)

	1961/62	1971/72	1981/82	1982/83
Sri Lanka	18,994	13,243	5,908	3,432
Indonesia	5,839	10,282	8,355	8,137
India	2,866	3,375	1,782	2,612
China	574	447	1,953	1,918
Papua New Guinea	–	94	4,843	4,669

It has often been pointed out – and rightly – that the arrival after World War II of numerous 'New Australians' of European rather than of British origin must inevitably have led to a trend towards coffee. Coffee has, in fact, advanced until it is now neck-and-neck with tea in 'kilogram per person' terms, though that, of course, leaves tea still well ahead in cuppage. Of European origin, too, is the impressive increase in wine-drinking (from 9.8 litres per head in 1972/73 to 16.5 litres in 1978/79 and no doubt rising still), while beer – almost as traditionally Australian as tea – and soft drinks remain more or less static.

Though Australia has from time immemorial been a packet tea market, the teabag, first introduced in the late 1960s, has been making inroads, not to the same extent as in Europe or North America, but with perhaps a 35% share at the time of writing and a growth rate of about 2% a year. Even within the teabag field there is a civil war – 'no-string' versus 'string-and-tag'! So far, string-and-tag seems to have a slight edge, particularly with the younger generation. Most of the stringed bags go into cups, no-strings into pots.

Both packets and bags share an unfortunate characteristic – the contents have been bought on price rather than on quality. Values of teas imported into Australia in recent years have shown a sharp decline and one fears that the advance of the teabag has merely facilitated this. Cuppage may have held up better, but less leaf goes into each cup.

Sources of supply

As Table 15.1 shows, the main sufferers from the changing patterns of Australian imports have been Sri Lanka and India, particularly the former. The 19,000 tonnes figure for Sri Lankan tea in 1961/62, out of a total import of 29,000 tonnes, was to some extent misleading. Before World War II, Sri Lanka was certainly an important supplier, but two-thirds of Australia's needs were, in fact, met from the Netherlands East Indies and it could be said that it was the disappearance of the latter and its tumultuous rebirth as Indonesia that gave Sri Lanka its chance. Now Indonesian tea is flowing once more in a natural southerly direction, meeting on its way a highly significant tributary from the highlands of Papua New Guinea. Comment has already been made on the forces of propinquity which brought Papua New Guinea so powerfully into the picture and on the links with Australian packers which have been forged (see Chapter 5).

In an attempt to halt the slide, both Sri Lanka and India have made Australia the target for 'value-added' campaigns – the importation of prepacked teas. India has been especially active in this field and in 1982 reported one of the largest orders ever secured for packets and teabags of South Indian origin.

Retailing

Yet it must be admitted that the vast majority of the packs which appear on the supermarket or grocery store shelves – the main outlets – are standard blends of no distinctive character, so far as origins are concerned. Brooke Bond influences (through the local firm of Bushells) are strong in the packet field; Lipton is strong in teabags. Tea has featured only too often as a 'loss leader' in the popular segment of the trade.

Promotion

The question naturally arises – what, if anything, can be done to improve Australia's standing as a tea market? It was explored in a 1980 survey carried out by the United Nations Development Project (UNDP) for the International Tea Promotion Association (ITPA). According to this survey any generic campaign on behalf of 'tea as tea' would have to be mainly defensive – to prevent further erosion of the market, rather than in the hope of increasing it. Even so, there would have to be a strong combined shove by producers (whether members of ITPA or not) and the entire Australian trade. Thus a *sine qua non* would be the revitalisation of the Australian Tea Council, which in 1963 took over from the energetic campaigning begun by the 'Empire Tea Growers' of 30 years before (see page 193) and continued by the International Tea Market Expansion Board,[2] but the Tea Council's efforts were hamstrung when the largest contributor withdrew in 1970.

The UNDP considered that television advertising, though expensive, would have to be the spearhead. It should be aimed mainly at the under-35s, for many of whom tea-drinking is still an old-fashioned habit, beloved of their parents, but sadly lacking in glamour for themselves. Some believed that a summer iced tea campaign might play a useful part.

A realistic budget for all this was put at A\$1.6 million a year for five years. By far the greater contribution would have to be made by the producer countries, so, all in all, the forward path looks stony. Yet the final thought must be that in spite of all the unfortunate trends described, every Australian ('New' or otherwise) still drinks over 500 cups of tea each year and that is surely something to build upon.

Production

A by-way of tea production about which many people even in Australia know little is that for some years the Commonwealth has been growing its own tea – on however modest a scale. In point of fact the first plantings go back as far as 1960, when Dr A. P. Maruff set out a nursery at Innisfail, about 150 m (500 ft) up, close to the coast of North-east Queensland, the only region in Australia where sun and rain combine to simulate tea's sub-tropical home-lands. Even so it was found that 70% of Innisfail's 3,556–3,810 mm (140–150 in.) of rain fell in the first six months of the year and irrigation would be needed in the second six. A factory was built in due course and the tea was purveyed locally.

The present 'state of play' is apparently that there are eight plantations destined for tea – four on the Atherton Tableland and four on the wetter tropical coast, but only one estate, of 140 ha, is actually in bearing.[3] Two more factories were under construction in 1983. Yields are high – with exceptionally good weather they may touch 4,000 kg per hectare – and the leaf is regarded by Australian blenders as of good medium quality.

Work on the estate is highly mechanised, and we referred in Chapter 1 to the claim that 23 men do all the field and factory work, while a further 12 are engaged in blending and packing. Queensland would like to see more investment in this promising development, for which some 30,000 ha of suitable land are available.

New Zealand

The same 'Anglo-Saxon attitudes' which made Australia a tea-drinking country in the first place are observable also in New Zealand, where a British-style way of life has, if anything, been less subjected to change.

W. H. Ukers recorded imports of nearly 11 million lb of tea annually in the 1930s, with per capita consumption at about 7.4 lb – a steep rise since the beginning of the century.[4] The latest figures show imports up a little (in metric terms, 6,244 tonnes against rather less than 5,000 tonnes in Ukers' day). Consumption per head, on the other hand, has gone down from about 3.50 to 2.07 kg; the decline has been gradual and must be attributed mainly to the competition of other beverages.

In contrast to the Australian pattern, New Zealand always was and remained until very recently an overwhelmingly Sri Lankan market. Before World War II, 75% of her tea was shipped from Colombo – there was no strong 'Dutch East Indies' presence as in Australia – and that was still the pattern up to about 1971. Since then, Sri Lanka's market share has contracted, while Indonesia and, more recently, China have made themselves felt in a decisive way (see Table 15.2). India, which at one time topped the 1,000 tonnes mark, is now down to an inconspicuous 105 tonnes.

Once again, all this spells just one thing – price. Packers who used to buy

Table 15.2   New Zealand imports (tonnes)

	1971	1976	1981	1983
Sri Lanka	6,368	4,009	2,408	1,796
Indonesia	716	477	1,063	1,040
China	123	1,033	1,695	2,290
Papua New Guinea	–	107	285	690

off-grade Fannings in Colombo, turned to China for the kind of leaf they wanted at the prices they were prepared to pay. Educational campaigns and in-store promotions on behalf of Sri Lanka may have done something to stem the tide.

The possibility of packet tea imports from producer countries has been opened up by a reduction in New Zealand's import duty on such teas – one of the few still imposed.

Teabags have made just about the same advance as in Australia and, generally, New Zealand conforms to the almost worldwide pattern of a brand-orientated, price-conscious consumer market. Something, it seems, that tea has got to live with.

16 *The International Framework*

Background to restriction

The moment Indonesia entered this narrative (see Chapter 5) some reference was inevitable to the days before 1933 when the producers in three territories, the Netherlands East Indies, India and Ceylon, virtually controlled the supply of Black tea to the world at large and when two governments, those of Holland and the United Kingdom, were in a position to control *them*. That they did not actually do so was due, of course, to the *laissez-faire* philosophy which reigned during the period of tea-drinking's greatest expansion in the West. In practice, producers and distributors alike went on their own sweet way, subject only to the restraints of Customs and Excise, labour and anti-adulteration legislation and the like. Even the emergency controls necessitated by World War I seemed to leave little permanent mark.

There is no knowing how long this happy state of affairs might have continued – though the rise of Asian nationalism would certainly have put paid to some aspects of it – had it not been for the slump in tea prices which gathered pace during the late 1920s. Once the effect of post-war decontrol had worked its way through, supply and demand remained in reasonable equilibrium between 1922 and about 1928. But while acreage and output registered only modest advances in India and Ceylon, in the Netherlands East Indies they both showed explosive increases. Exports zoomed from 102 million lb in 1920 to 160 million in 1929.[1]

Much of these exports came on to the London market in the form of 'clean common' tea and, since in those days the United Kingdom absorbed 50% of all Black leaf exported from the East a slump in the price of 'clean common' was inevitable. From a reasonable 17*d*. per pound in 1926 it sank to just over 1*s*. 3*d*. in 1927, 1*s*. 2*d*. in 1928 and only 10½*d*. the following year. Meanwhile stocks representing over six months' supply had accumulated in London.

At that point the producers' associations (but not as yet their governments) put their heads together and agreed that for 1930 they would reduce exports by some 57 million lb on the current total of 903 million lb. India was to contribute 36 million lb of this cut, Ceylon, 11.5 million and the Netherlands East Indies, 10 million. In the event, India sent 24 million lb less tea abroad and Ceylon 8 million, but the Netherlands East Indies sent only 1 million less.

Worse, any scaling-down by the big estates in Java and Sumatra was offset by more lower-grade material from smallholdings reaching the 'bought-leaf' factories – the exact reverse of what had been aimed at! Not surprisingly, the price of 'clean common' tea in London continued to wilt, reaching 9*d*. in 1930 and a derisory 6½*d*. a year later.

The first Agreement

Voluntary restriction had clearly failed; the next move was towards compulsion. It was, in fact, the traditionally libertarian Dutch who in October 1932 put proposals before the India and Ceylon Associations in London. The latter obtained the assent of their members and, with a speed which today would seem miraculous, by 9 February 1933 the first International Tea Agreement was ready for signature. Its central provision was that *standard exports* should be established for each of the three participants, based on the highest figures attained during the years 1929–31 as follows:

India	338,594,779 lb
Ceylon	251,522,617 lb
Netherlands East Indies	173,597,000 lb

For the first regulation year (April 1933 – March 1934), the quotas were set at 85% of standard. There was to be no control of *output*, but in practice the three countries assigned 'standard production' figures to their estates, so as to spread the export quota equitably. Acreages were 'frozen' until further notice. The Agreement also made provision for *promoting* tea internationally (see Chapter 17). Governments only came into the picture because, in order to make the scheme effective, the respective legislatures were required to pass a series of Acts and regulations, which had subsequently to be policed.

Administration was in the hands of a newly-created International Tea Committee, which held its first meeting in London in July 1933. The members soon had the satisfaction of seeing a net decrease in exports of 162 million lb in the year ending March 1934 and the price of 'clean common' climbing back towards its 1929 level. It is relevant to the 'politics' of possible restriction today that the ITC always denied that it had a 'price objective', though that could only have been true in strictly formal terms.

The word 'net' in relation to the reduction in exports should be noted. Under the original Agreement, no mention was made of producing countries other than the three signatories, but during 1934 it was realised that cognisance must be taken of what was going on in Africa and, to a much lesser degree, in Malaya. Tea estates were already springing up in Kenya, Uganda, Tanganyika (now Tanzania) and Nyasaland (Malawi), and, although exports from these British colonial territories had been negligible when restriction was first mooted, by 1933/34 substantial quantities were on the way. Accordingly they were now brought into the scheme, but with generous export quotas and permission for a 25% increase in total acreage.

The result of all this – plus smart work by various Far Eastern producers, such as Japan, Formosa (Taiwan) and French Indo-China (Vietnam), in taking advantage of the situation – was that, though the three regulating countries reduced their exports by 171 million lb in 1933/34, the 'outsiders' made a gain of 9 million lb. Africa, of course, went marching on: by 1935 exports (mainly from Kenya and Nyasaland) had passed the 11 million lb mark and had nearly doubled again by 1938 – trifling figures in relation to world output, but a thunderous portent of what was to come.

Malaya was no problem – its handful of producers undertook not to extend their 3,000 acres of plantations for the time being, and were left to get on with it.

Developments since World War II

The original Tea Agreement was for five years and since, with various minor adjustments to the quotas, it worked with reasonable efficiency, it was renewed for a further five years from 1938. World War II naturally put the whole thing into cold storage, though there was a nominal extension until March 1948 just to keep the administrative machinery ticking over; after that an interim Producers' Agreement between India, Pakistan, Sri Lanka and Indonesia went into effect for a further five years. The same four countries signed a new Five Year Agreement in 1950, but in terms calculated to 'ensure maintenance of production' rather than to restrict it. An interesting provision was that new extensions on land not hitherto planted with tea were limited to 5% of the 'permitted acreage'; replacements were allowed up to 10%, but had to be accompanied by simultaneous uprooting of a corresponding area of old tea.

By 1955, when the five year period ended, prices were in a boom phase, nobody saw any reason for further regulation, and the Agreement was allowed to lapse. However, all the governments and producers' associations agreed that the International Tea Committee should be kept in being as a centre for the collection and dissemination of statistical and other data – a function which it has continued to perform with admirable efficiency up to the present time. A hard-worn copy of the current ITC *Annual Bulletin of Statistics*, together with as many of its predecessors as he can get hold of, is part of the furniture of every tea historian's desk. More importantly, the *Bulletin* and its *Monthly Statistical Summaries* provide an indispensible service to all concerned with the buying and selling of the product worldwide.

In 1983 the ITC celebrated its 50th anniversary (and the 25th year of service of its statistician, Peter Abel); more information than there is room for here about the 'old days' is to be found in its jubilee publication, *International Tea Committee – the First Fifty Years*.

To resume the saga of the International Tea Agreement, actual or potential, by the mid-1960s, when prices had again become unremunerative[2] and a possible restriction of exports was being bandied about, new forces had come into play. The Food and Agriculture Organisation (FAO) of the United Nations, seated in Rome, had begun to take an interest in tea and convened a series of *ad hoc* consultations, beginning in Sri Lanka in 1965. The third of such meetings, held at Kampala in Uganda in January 1969, led to the establishment of a new Consultative Committee on Tea and this became involved in the preparation of temporary export quotas, pending a long-term pact.

However, the initiative gradually passed to another UNO body, the United Nations Conference on Trade and Development (UNCTAD). With head-quarters in Geneva, it is more specifically charged with producing an 'integrated programme for commodities' which would help to stabilise world markets and improve the earnings of developing countries. This programme was eventually formalised at UNCTAD's fourth session, convened at Nairobi in May 1976, tea being one of the score or so commodities in which the developing countries were rightly held to have an interest.

Recent negotiations

Meanwhile, the United Kingdom government had taken the lead in promot-ing a new International Tea Agreement. This had as its background a somewhat controversial report (published May 1975) about conditions on Sri Lanka tea estates and the alleged low earnings of the workers.[3] The report seems to have had some influence upon the then Prime Minister (Mr Harold Wilson) when he urged the Commonwealth heads of government, meeting in Jamaica, that there ought to be an Agreement aimed at stabilising world trade in tea and making the crop more remunerative to the growers and their employees.

The response to soundings made among Commonwealth producers was not very enthusiastic, mainly because the forecast for the next few years was for a marginal shortage of tea, and that brought into action the industry's instinctive reliance on the 'supply and demand' mechanism.

Nevertheless, the United Kingdom was able to put to the FAO's Inter-governmental Group on Tea an outline of an Agreement based on export quotas, to be triggered if prices fell below an agreed level. Nothing happened immediately, and it is a sobering fact that, in spite of a welter of conferences and reports since then, the situation in 1984 was little different from that of years before.[4]

Proceedings at Geneva in May 1982 give as good a glimpse as any of the 'state of play'. Here, UNCTAD's 'Third Preparatory Meeting on Tea' was attended by delegates from no fewer than 40 member states, to whom were added representatives of the FAO (Food and Agriculture Organisation), IMF (International Monetary Fund), GATT (General Agreement on Tariffs and Trade), OECD (Organisation for Economic Co-operation and Development) and the European Tea Committee. A report from UNCTAD's Inter-governmental Group of Experts on Tea, which had preceded the session, showed that 17 countries, representing 95% of world exports, had been involved in negotiations on possible quotas. If one recalls that the three signatories to the International Tea Agreement of 1933 controlled 90% of such exports, against only 63% at the time of the Geneva meeting, one understands how it is that any step forward today is a step taken through treacle.

But, of course, it is not just a question of percentage shares. The countries which, in their own view, have least to gain by an International Agreement include those whose tea production is still in a dynamic phase. Chief among them, needless to say, is Kenya, now supplying nearly 12% of the world's markets. There are conflicting views about the degree to which Kenyan production can continue to expand, but some growth there will be, accompanied by a robust suspicion of any attempts at limitation or control. Given political stability, it is probable that other African territories, such as Malawi and Mozambique, will also wish to expand their exports to meet the world demand for tea at their particular price levels.

Agreement objectives

However, the May 1982 meetings in the Geneva Palais des Nations did attempt to construct a solid framework for action. It would accepted that any future International Tea Agreement would have the following objectives:

1. To promote an orderly expansion of world trade in tea, while maintaining prices at levels which are remunerative and just to producers and equitable to consumers.
2. To balance import demand and export supply and avoid excessive price fluctuations.
3. To improve market access for tea.
4. To ensure adequate supplies to consumers.
5. To maintain, and improve where necessary, the quality of teas traded internationally.
6. To encourage the efficient development of the world tea economy by seeking to facilitate and promote improvements in the growing, processing, marketing and distribution of tea.
7. To promote and increase the consumption of tea.

Under 1 and 2 above, price objectives and intervention levels would be established, using an 'indicator price' computed on all teas sold on the Eastern and Mombasa auctions. Each year, a global export quota would be agreed between exporter and importer members of the Agreement, taking due account of the price objective of that year. Quotas would only apply to countries whose average annual exports during the previous three years were equal to or greater than 10,000 tonnes. Currently, this formula embraces India, Sri Lanka, Kenya, Indonesia, China, Malawi, Argentina, Bangladesh, Mozambique and Tanzania. Left outside are a whole array of minor, but aspiring, producers, including Brazil, Burundi, Cameroon, Ecuador, Mauritius, Papua New Guinea, Rwanda, Turkey, Vietnam, Zaïre and Zimbabwe, which collectively add over 50,000 tonnes to the world's supplies.

Green tea exports would not come under the quota system, and a major loophole seems to be the proviso (to which the EEC spokesman expressed a reservation) that 'export quotas will not apply to trade in tea traditionally undertaken on an inter-governmental basis between CMEA [East European bloc] countries'.

No general view has yet emerged either on another aspect of regulation – the possible creation of an international *buffer stock*, such as is featured in certain other commodity agreements, but there is little enthusiasm for this among importers.

If the achievement of a quota system under objectives 1 and 2 appears difficult, though not impossible, some of the remaining objectives would seem to have an almost visionary quality. Everyone will agree that if market access to tea is being impeded it should be improved; that consumers should be assured of adequate supplies; that the quality of teas traded internationally ought to be maintained; that there should be improvements where possible in the growing, processing, marketing and distribution of tea; and that increased consumption should be encouraged. Such aims are easily stated; to implement them would surely tax a global organisation with dictatorial powers. There is no such central authority, of course, least at all in the world of tea, where policies are more than ever today shaped by the forces of nationalism on the one hand, and the imperatives of the market-place on the other.

Standards for tea

However, some useful machinery, of a modest kind, does exist, bearing especially on the improvement of the quality of tea and promoting its consumption. The latter is dealt with in the next chapter; the former claims a few paragraphs here.

Tea has for some time attracted the attention of the International Organisation for Standardisation (ISO) and of various national bodies affiliated to it, notably the British Standards Institute (BSI). As a result, an International Standard for Black Tea (ISO 3720) has been hammered out, and was circulated to the members in August 1975. Most of them approved it, though with technical reservations in certain cases.

The aim of the Standard was the limited one of specifying the plant source of the leaf from which Black tea is to be produced and setting requirements for various chemical characteristics which, if met, would indicate satisfactory manufacturing practices.

As to plant source, the unique and authentic status of *Camellia sinensis* (Linnaeus) O. Kuntze was expounded in the Prologue. On chemical characteristics, the main elements (or parameters) which ISO 3720 covers are as follows:

1. *Water extractable solids.* The quality and colour of brewed tea depends on the quantity of chemical components extracted. Teas containing a lot of stalk, etc., will tend to have an undesirably low content of soluble material. ISO 3720 specifies 32% as the minimum quantity of extractable solids which should be present.

2. *Crude fibre content.* This is defined as that part of the plant material that does not dissolve in acid or alkali and provides an index to the quantity of the more mature portions of the plant which have been used in the production of a particular tea. For example, coarse plucking up to the fourth leaf will obviously produce more crude fibre content than fine plucking.

3. *Ash content.* This represents the portion of the tea which will not get burnt up at very high temperatures (500° C). Under ISO 3720, it should not exceed 8% or be less than 4% and at least 45% of it should be water-soluble.

4. *Moisture content.* No limit is specified for this, though it can be a very critical factor, especially in respect of the storage life of the product. Manufactured tea is liable to 'pick up' moisture at all stages of its progress from the drier to the taster's cup. It has been found that moisture much above 6.5% and certainly at 8% can lead to undesirable chemical reactions, as well as to contamination with bacteria and moulds.[5]

So much for the technical background. But, ever since ISO 3720 was published, argument has continued. Is it adequate within its own terms? Does it provide the basis for a true and meaningful minimum International Standard for Black tea which might help to give the consumer a better product and the producer a better price?

On the first point, the question of revising ISO 3720 came under serious scrutiny at a meeting of the ISO's Subcommittee on Tea, convened at Balatonfüred, Hungary, in May 1983, with a British representative, Mr Derek Macauley, in the chair. A major amendment which had been much canvassed was the possible inclusion of *theoflavin* content as an additional parameter.[6] Theoflavin is an important chemical compound produced at the oxidisation phase of tea manufacture and is recognised as a factor in quality. Unfortunately, however, from the point of view of a valid Standard, the amount of theoflavin present depends largely on whether the leaf has been subjected to harsh maceration (for example, by the LTP or CTC processes) or has gone through Orthodox rollers. The latter may generate less theoflavin, but the resultant teas can in fact be some of the most valued in the market-place.

At Balatonfüred it was decided that more work needed to be done on theoflavin before its suitability for inclusion in ISO 3720 could be assessed; the Secretariat would also study other suggested modifications to the Standard.

On the question of whether the Standard, however revised or amplified, is capable of providing an adequate minimum International Standard, the current view among teamen would appear to be that while it could certainly contribute to this end, chemical parameters would always need to be supplemented by sensory tests; in other words, *tasting* in the countries of origin, which is where any future minimum Standard will have to be applied. The point was strongly emphasized in the draft revision of ISO 3720.

Grading

A major obstacle to any attempt to treat tea as a uniform product, whether under Standards legislation, buffer stocks proposals or for the purposes of a futures market, is its multifarious character. For a curious proof of this we may turn to another ISO Standard – 6078, 'Black Tea Vocabulary'. Here are to be found results of some nine years' work by the Subcommittee (Tea) of Technical Committee 34 (Agricultural Food Products), for which the United Kingdom provided the Secretariat. Lists of 'tea-tasters' terms' are a familiar feature of all the older manuals, but this is surely the ultimate. One hundred and ninety-eight terms are listed and defined, under the subheadings of *Dry Leaf* (appearance 47 definitions; colour 7; odour 7); *Liquor* (taste 96; appearance 25); *Methods of Manufacture* 6; *General* 8.

Appended to the vocabulary is an unusually comprehensive list of grades – 38, compared with 25 in Appendix 1 at the end of this book – ranging from Tippy Golden Flowery Orange Pekoe (TGFOP) down to Red Dust (RD). But serious questions do overhang the whole question of grading. With the rise of the teabag and its high-speed machinery, packers today need more scientifically accurate data on bulk density and particle size than present methods of grading afford. Accordingly, the Tropical Products Institute, London, with the help of a research officer sponsored by the tea trade, has carried out tests on some 800 samples drawn from the grades most relevant to teabag manufacture (for example, Pekoe Fannings, Fannings, Pekoe Dust). Even when the results of these tests have been evaluated by the trade, it is unlikely that traditional grading of this small-leaf material will be abandoned, but more meaningful symbols may eventually be attached to some grades.

Health issues

A rather different problem relating to ISO 3720 is whether it ought to take account of toleration levels for heavy metal and pesticide residues. The latter come partially within the purview of the *Codex Alimentarius* operated by the

FAO and covering, for example, the use of pesticides such as DDT. As to metals, lead levels in tea are already controlled, though under varying formulae, in many countries. Coming more into prominence recently is the fact that mechanical processes like CTC/LTP/Rotorvane manufacture may produce a higher incidence of minuscule metal fragments than Orthodox procedures.

Such issues are sensitive and, though there can be few food products 'cleaner' than tea, the consumerist lobby will no doubt continue to focus on it from time to time, both with regard to metals and pesticides and to its allegedly deleterious caffeine content, about which alarmist noises tend to emanate from the United States.[7]

Meanwhile, further data on residues, collated by the European Tea Committee, were due for presentation to the ISO in 1984. In the long run, detailed regulation is likely to be a matter between individual governments (some of which, such as that of West Germany, already have fairly stringent legislation) and the local distributive trade.

Aid and its problems

Any survey of the 'international framework' within which the tea industry operates today would not be complete without a reference to aid. It is a truism that tea is grown almost entirely in 'developing' or 'Third World' countries, while until recently its main customer was the comparatively wealthy West. This pattern of consumption has greatly changed; nevertheless, a certain 'East–West' (or 'North–South') dichotomy remains and gives rise to tensions from time to time. Thus, there is perhaps justice in the fact that tea-growers are now among the beneficiaries of so many loan or grant programmes by the 'developed' sector of the world.

It is impossible to give a comprehensive picture of such programmes. Their number and scope have been and remain impressive, with, of course, a good deal of shading off from those exclusively concerned with tea to those covering housing, welfare and infrastructural improvements, such as roads, drainage and public utilities in the plantation zones.

Examples have occurred in several of the earlier chapters of this book. The part played in establishing the Kenya Tea Development Authority (KTDA) has long been a plume in the cap of the UK's Commonwealth Development Corporation (CDC), though the West German government, the World Bank and OPEC countries also contributed finance. Now the CDC is helping to put the same message across in Malawi, via that country's Smallholder Tea Authority.

Elsewhere in Africa, we have seen the EEC, through its Development Fund (EDF), stimulating farmers in a whole series of Central and West African countries to move into tea, while the World Bank has recently added to its series of initiatives in Sri Lanka a US$20 million credit for the large-scale rehabilitation of tea estates and factories in the island. OPEC and the Asian

Development Fund are also involved in this scheme. In fact, there is hardly a tea-producing country, actual or potential, which has not received support from one development agency or another.

There is a paradox here, which perspicacious commentators have not overlooked.[8] We seem to be confronted by two groups of international agencies pulling in opposite directions: on the one hand, FAO/UNCTAD working towards an Agreement which might eventually limit exports; on the other, the aid organisations providing funds to increase production.

It is no doubt true that encouragement given to farmers to grow tea in Cameroon or Sudan is unlikely to upset the balance of the world's supplies, while doing a beneficent local service in terms of employment and cash flow. It can even be argued, on the precedent of the 1930s, that some of the smaller producers who would be exempted from an Agreement might find it working to their advantage — greater demand and better prices.

However, as long ago as 1973, the most powerful aid agency of all, the World Bank, showed itself sensitive to the problem when its board of directors laid down, as a general rule, that the Bank should not lend any more money for tea production, except in countries with no acceptable investment alternative or where rehabilitation could be carried out without increasing output. Diversification out of tea was actively to be encouraged.

Requests for help continued to come in from various countries, including Bangladesh, Kenya, Papua New Guinea, Rwanda, Sri Lanka and Tanzania. Two factory developments in Kenya and Rwanda were eventually authorised and a project in Papua New Guinea was given exemption because the area selected for tea planting had no viable crop alternative and 'the beneficiaries were very poor'.

The giant among these comparative 'small fry' is the Sri Lanka project. Here the World Bank has accepted the argument that the scheme will restore, but not expand, the productivity of the tea lands concerned, while allowing for further diversification.

Though it is recognised by the World Bank that it cannot control the actions of other lenders, it believes that its policy puts 'the welfare of the developing countries before that of the developed, or of the world as a whole'.[9]

How can the whole paradox be resolved? Aid is a vast and complex machine which is not easy to halt or divert and which more often than not has politics at the controls. But should a long-term Agreement ever appear to be in sight, common sense might force the aid-giving agencies to say to their major recipients, 'We will honour our existing commitments, but can give no further stimulus for the tea sector if supply looks like outstripping demand, or if it appears that food-growing ought to be given precedence over cash crops.' The last dozen words in this formula have of course been rendered poignantly relevant by events in Africa in 1984/85, though tea-growers have on the whole had the foresight to avoid the 'famine belt'.

17 Advertising and Promotion

To explore the field of tea promotion in its most dynamic days – the late nineteenth and early twentieth centuries – is a positively carefree exercise compared with trying to sort out what is happening today. This applies both to the campaigns of individual tea firms and those conducted by planters, exporters, governments or international agencies.

However, a pause can reasonably be made in those happy pastures before we are compelled to emerge into the roaring and confused traffic stream of competitive promotion in the 1980s.

Promotion in the past

The famous treatise *Cha' Ching*, commissioned by the tea merchants of China in about AD 780, can be classified as a public relations exercise, though it seems intended to enhance the dignity of the beverage and its producers rather than directly to promote sales.[1] Advertising as such was not one of those inventions in which China anticipated the West; in fact, the idea was only reluctantly borrowed from the latter many centuries later.

Hardly less famous in tea's annals than the *Cha' Ching* are the solitary press advertisement and the equally unique broadsheet[2] which proclaimed the arrival of the 'China drink' in Britain in the late 1650s. For over 150 years after that tea promotion was virtually confined to the following:

1. Neat little trade cards issued by individual dealers or coffee-house keepers.
2. Discreet press announcements, often alleging the arrival of some 'parcel' of specially choice leaf.
3. Books and pamphlets with an advertising slant.

Examples of all three can be traced in the principal importing countries.

Britain is perhaps the *locus classicus* of the trade card, many elegant eighteenth-century examples of which survive in the British Museum and elsewhere; colonial America foreshadowed the future by being quickly off the mark with press advertisements and handbills; while in the Netherlands and France promotional tea 'literature' began to appear as early as the 1670s. The good cause was particularly well served, it seems, by the *Tractat van Het Excellente Cruyt Thee*, published at The Hague in 1679 by a certain Dr Cornelius Decker, using the pseudonym of Bontekoe.

For long, the preaching of the tea gospel was bedevilled – and still is, for that matter – by the question of whether or not the beverage is 'good for you'. As with other innovatory foodstuffs, it went through a regular cycle: *promotion* (also known as 'puffing'), when still little known, as a health panacea; *denunciation*, when showing signs of popularity, as a health menace; *promotion* again, when universally accepted, on various hygienic or dietary grounds. The first two phases may be observed today in countries where tea is still relatively unfamiliar – Yugoslavs drinking it for 'strictly health reasons', as a prophylactic against flu, Mexicans suspicious of it as ruinous to the nerves. The third stage – active promotion as a health drink – has been somewhat intermittent, though the linking of tea with physical fitness in a generalised way is an integral part of most modern advertising and public relations schemes aimed at youth.

For the promotion of a particular blend on medical grounds, one has to go back to 'Typhoo Tips', as it used to be called – 'leaf-edge tea, free from injurious gallo-tannic acid' – which in its early days (as we saw in Chapter 10) was sold extensively by chemists' shops and earned a remarkable degree of support from doctors when claiming exemption from 'pooling' in World War I.

It must seem almost an affront to the contemporary adman that the tea-drinking habit managed to take root in the era of the various East India Companies with no artificial stimulus beyond trade cards, small advertisements and more or less erudite pamphlets. But we have to believe that the peoples of one country after another simply made up their minds that here was something which would enrich their lives and for which they were prepared to pay very good money. All that the Companies, their clients (the dealers) and *their* clients (the grocers and coffee-house keepers) had to do was to make sure they kept the clumsy wheels of the distributive system turning.

Two massive developments led eventually to the situation which now confronts us and they evolved more or less in parallel during the second half of the nineteenth century. One was the breakdown of the China monopoly, the other the emergence of tea as a branded and packeted article. The former has produced a whole array of tea-growing countries which are having to make a perplexing choice between promotional rivalry or co-operation; the latter catapulted the product into the very forefront of the consumer advertising battle.

Tea branded and packeted

Of these phenomena, the first is much the more intricate and it will be convenient to dispose of the second before settling down to discuss it. The modern promotion of tea under brand labels shows no great advance on the techniques which first turned names like 'Horniman', 'Mazawattee', 'Lipton' into household words. The repeated hammer-blows of press and poster advertising, the lure of price reductions and the 'special offer', gift schemes in a thousand more or less extravagant forms – they are still with us today. Even the portentous arrival of television has changed only the medium, not the basic methods.

The *impact* of tea advertising, everywhere, is less overwhelming than in the days of 'Tommy' Lipton. Margins on tea in most countries are too low, in relation to the cost of the popular media, for really hefty and sustained campaigns on a national scale to be viable. The United States, second among the world's importers and fifth (after China, India, the United Kingdom and Japan) as consumer, inevitably has a bigger advertising bill than any other country, though the graph seems to be sloping downwards. Figures published by UNCTAD showed expenditure on all media in the United States of US$34 million during 1979;[3] by 1981 this is believed to have declined by more than a third, with a further fall expected in 1982. As a percentage on retail sales, the 1979 total represented about 4%; the 1982 figure may have been no more than 2.25%.

The United Kingdom comes second. Packers spent £6 million on advertising in 1977 – quite 'big' money, but still only 2% of retail sales. By 1980 (partly due to inflation) expenditure had increased to about £12 million (including over £1 million added by the Tea Council) and it was £19 million in 1984. It is apparent that the greater part of this outlay went on television promotion of teabags by three of the leading packers.

In countries with lower consumption, the ratio of expenditure to sales is inevitably higher – UNCTAD quoted as much as 7% in Italy and 8% in Japan.

In competitive terms, the brand advertising of tea is modest compared with that of some other beverages – scarcely a seventh of what is put into coffee in the United States, and a twelfth of the boost given there to the various categories of soft drinks.

Nor is the *quality* of tea advertising, worldwide, exactly outstanding. The claims and slogans lack colour and audacity, as is perhaps inevitable in our time. Gone are the days when teamen could unblushingly depict the British Royal Family or Mr Gladstone's entire Cabinet enjoying their wares. However, there are still a few sprightly initiatives, with television as the obvious medium. If there were a first prize for originality and verve it would surely have to be awarded to the gang of 'chimps' who rampaged through the Brooke Bond television commercials in the UK from 1956 onwards. The linking of their screen antics with 'personal appearances' at point of sale promotions was an almost perfect example of maximum impact from a single advertising idea. The same firm, incidentally, was responsible for reviving the picture card, inserted into the packet and once a gigantic element in the promotion of cigarettes.

Prudence and financial restraints have toned down the gift schemes which in nineteenth-century Britain added the somewhat derogatory catch-phrase 'given away with a pound of tea' to the English language. Even at the time of their inauguration in the 1880s such methods were criticised as 'suicidal'. Yet they flourished in many countries and, in fact, the elaborate catalogues of domestic 'goodies', from baby carriages to antimacassars, which would be exchanged for quite modest numbers of labels, rather strikingly fore-shadowed the trading stamp furore of recent times.

The link between television and point of sale, referred to in connection with the 'chimps', reminds us that the main battle of modern tea promotion is fought in the self-service store and, in particular, in the comparatively modest footage of shelf-space which it is prepared to devote to tea. The 1982 UNCTAD paper already quoted rather naïvely suggested (paragraph 66) that chain-stores and catering organisations may be 'compelled to buy their processed tea from the companies which supply them with other goods'. This could conceivably happen in a few hole-and-corner instances, but such is the bargaining strength of the supermarkets that they are 'much more likely to dictate the terms on which they are prepared to take the goods'[4] rather than the other way around. Such 'dictation' comes in various forms, but it usually hinges on discounts, plus the promise of an advertising drive, preferably on television. In certain European countries shelf-space has actually to be bought, at so much a metre; elsewhere, as in Canada, the understanding is that, to get 'listed', compensatory payments must be guaranteed should sales fall below a pre-agreed level. Hence, of course, the apparition of the big, hard-selling teabag carton as described in Chapter 9.

Promotions by producers and governments

The advertising of tea, brand against brand, is at least a forthright commercial mêlée, not all that different from what goes on in other commodity fields; it is when producers and/or governments get into the act that complications sprout. But first, a definition of terms: *uninational* campaigns promote the teas of a single country; *multinational*, those of two or more countries working together; *generic*, 'tea as tea'. There is no convenient term for the frequent situation in which uninational, multinational or generic campaigns are financed jointly with the tea trade of a given consuming country, but the vehicle for such campaigns is usually a Tea Council.

Historians of the subject tend to lead off from the early 1880s, when

Ceylon tea was beginning seriously to compete with Indian in the world's mass markets. But, in fact, Japan launched out as early as 1876 with exhibits sent to the Centennial Exposition at Philadelphia, and from 1880 onwards the Japanese government subsidised propaganda by the industry's Central Tea Association at countless exhibitions all over the world.

When Ceylon and India entered the field, they did so from slightly different points of departure. It was the Planters' Association of Ceylon, eager to promote its members' teas, which vainly urged its government to send a commissioner to the Sydney (Australia) Exhibition of 1879, took part under its own steam at Melbourne (1880) and even Calcutta (1883) and finally extorted a government subsidy for the Colonial and Indian Exhibition in South Kensington in 1886,[5] and a long series of events thereafter. In India, on the other hand, the initiative came from the Indian Tea Association (power-fully supported by merchants) immediately upon its formation at Calcutta in 1881. The ITA got in the first blow in the United Kingdom with a stand at the London Health Exhibition and competed head-on with Ceylon planters at the great South Kensington show, two years later. The Indian government, pleading poverty, refused a grant, but coughed up Rs2,500 for Brussels 1888.

On the whole, the Ceylon planters showed the more imaginative approach. Breaking away from the exhibition treadmill, they launched into public relations ploys, such as well-organised presentations to crowned heads, and, by grants of cash or actual leaf 'subscribed' by individual planters, persuaded dealers all over the world to stock and promote Ceylon tea. Just as they participated in the Calcutta Exhibition, it is notable that among the cities included in this campaign were Bombay, Karachi and Ahmadabad, but there is nothing to show that they seriously entertained the idea of India as a market for Ceylon tea.

These simple beginnings are worth recalling because they show the concept of uninational promotion in its formative phase. There was no sign yet of generic campaigning – 'tea as tea' – but thoughts about the possibility of India and Ceylon working together were already astir. H. K. Rutherford, Ceylon's most energetic publicist, had breathed the word 'co-operation' as early as 1885 and there were behind-the-scenes talks at intervals during the next decade. From the Indian side, Sir John Muir, of Messrs James Finlay, took the lead and in January 1894 the editor of the *Ceylon Observer*, in a letter to Mr P. R. Buchanan, suggested that Sir John might be persuaded to invite Ceylon to join in a big campaign in the United States. He added this emphatic comment:

The danger is of India and Ceylon going on separately in a peddling way and creating suspicions of each other in place of uniting forces on behalf of pure clean teas against the 'faced', inferior Japan and China . . . in the former case, it means a slow advance over many years, in the latter, a big and rapidly progressive gain.[6]

Sentiments, the echoes of which have reverberated from that day to this.

The ITA was all in favour, but difficulties were raised from the Ceylon side and rivalry continued, notably at the Chicago World Fair of 1893, where each country had a magnificent stand. The first modest breakthrough did not come until three years later, when it was agreed that a series of advertisements placed by Ceylon in American magazines should be revamped to publicise Indian tea as well. Co-operation continued spasmodically and after another celebrated World's Fair, in St Louis (1904), where there were again separate exhibits, the ITA's Richard Blechynden became joint Commissioner for the St Louis district for a period of three years.

There were now real prospects for multinational promotion on a serious scale, but a financial problem – the first of many – loomed up. Tea promotion by both countries was carried on in the early days by committees under a variety of titles, financed partly by voluntary levies and partly by *ad hoc* government grants. But in 1893, with the Chicago World Fair on the horizon, the government of Ceylon was persuaded to impose the first compulsory propaganda levy or 'cess' – 10 cents per 100 lb of all tea exported, to be paid at Customs. India did not bring in a cess until 1903, but within five years Ceylon had ceased to levy hers! Feeling had grown in Ceylon that the cess was being used for the benefit of Planters' Association members rather than for the tea industry as a whole and when the government proposed to suspend it, opposition was mournful rather than outraged.[7]

As the above compressed narrative may suggest, expansionist hopes were mainly pinned on the United States – that opulent market which seemed to hold out such promise, never quite fulfilled.

It may be noted that India and Ceylon, whether separately or jointly, did not have the field quite to themselves. Japan continued to battle on, while before, during and after World War I, several *démarches* were made on behalf of tea from the Netherlands East Indies. There was even a small flurry of generic advertising by the American Tea Association in the 1920s and in 1929 the Association secured modest grants from Ceylon, India, Japan, Formosa and the Netherlands East Indies – some US$34,000 in all. By then, however, tea promotion in the United States and, indeed, worldwide was on the verge of a new era with the formation of the International Tea Market Expansion Board (ITMEB).

International Tea Market Expansion Board

In Chapter 16 details were given of how the slump of 1929–31 led to the International Tea Committee being charged with the double task of regulating exports and promoting sales. For the latter, ITMEB was the executive arm. The memorandum which created it (October 1934) conveniently summarises the then promotional picture:

Valuable as is the propaganda work being conducted by the Indian Tea Cess Committee, the Ceylon Tea Propaganda Board[8] and the Amsterdam Association in India, the UK, the USA, Canada, South Africa and Europe, they [the ITC] do not feel it is adequate to meet the urgent need not only to find new markets . . . but also of checking any decline of consumption in existing markets.

Accordingly, only nine months later, ITMEB came into being in London, with two representatives each from the three producer countries whose cesses were to provide its funds. The Organising Director was Mr Gervas Huxley, formerly Chief Commissioner of the Ceylon Tea Propaganda Board and a graduate of the Empire Marketing Board. Under his inspiration it set to work with great energy and during the late 1930s conducted campaigns in the United Kingdom, the United States, Canada, Australia, South Africa, Egypt, the Netherlands, Belgium, Sweden and Germany. ITMEB's brief was not wholly generic, since in the United Kingdom, for example, it began by pushing Indian and Ceylon tea only, through an organisation called the Empire Tea Growers, later the Empire Tea Bureau.

World War II diverted ITMEB's energies into other fields, but with the return of peace, New Zealand, Iraq, Denmark, Ireland and several African territories were added to the tally of campaigns; work in Sweden and Belgium, on the other hand, was not renewed.

Relevant to our present-day situation is the fact that ITMEB was a *tea-growers'* organisation, virtually independent of governments at first, even though the latter collected the propaganda cesses and gave benevolent support to the campaigns. It seemed quite natural in those simple days that ITMEB should be located in London, with an Anglo-Dutch Board and a mainly British headquarters staff.

Such halcyon conditions did not last. The first sign of impending change was when government representatives from the now-independent producing countries were added to the Board in 1949. Three years later, just when the ITMEB campaigns everywhere were getting into top gear, came the real trauma: Pakistan, which had made token contributions, decided not to join the Board and then, far more lethally, India expressed dissatisfaction with certain aspects of ITMEB's policy and withdrew. It is probably, however, that there was already a movement of opinion in favour of working uninationally for India's teas. Indonesia followed suit (she had previously suspended her contributions); the African producers, who had been associated with the Board's work since before World War II, stayed on a little longer.

By 1955, however, Sri Lanka was left as the sole remaining member of ITMEB, which became, for all practical purposes, part of the Ceylon Tea Propaganda Board. It has continued to function in the same way under the Tea Board of Sri Lanka.

So ended, for the time being, the concept of a single body drawing funds from the producing areas and dispensing them in campaigns under its own control. It is fair to say (though this varied from country to country) that the ITMEB operation was never quite accepted as an organic part of the machinery of tea-selling in most of the markets where it worked and a good deal of misconception reigned about its 'cost' to the industry and trade.

In hindsight, it was probably a weakness that packers and distributors could not be brought directly into the picture, though there was one exception to this which helped to point the way forward. In order to provide enough funds for meaningful promotion in the desperately expensive American market, a joint USA Tea Council had been set up in 1950 with ITMEB and the trade matching contributions. After the débâcle, it seemed logical to establish similar councils in Canada and West Germany (1954), Ireland (1955), Australia (1963), France (1964), the United Kingdom (1965) and New Zealand (1966).[9] In each case all or some of the main producing countries joined with the local trade to conduct generic campaigns.

A very different sequel to the events of 1954, which might have been foreseen, was the re-emergence of uninational promotion in some important markets. Sri Lanka, sole inheritor of ITMEB, did not hesitate to adapt the organisation centred on 22 Regent Street, London, so as to encourage a demand for pure Ceylon tea or, where this was not feasible, for blends with a high Ceylon content and to convince the trade that that demand was worth meeting. Soon the Lion sign began to appear on a wide range of packs, even though the promoters of the new initiative were aware that it was in a sense cutting across the prevalent pattern of big distributors working on a transnational basis.

The outcome of all this was and is a somewhat confused mosaic of uninational, multinational and generic campaigns, often coexisting in the same country. The fact, for example, that since 1965 the United Kingdom has had an extremely active Tea Council, backed by both the producing countries and the trade, has not inhibited India (as well as Sri Lanka) from spending considerable sums on pushing her individual wares.

International Tea Promotion Association (ITPA)

It is hardly surprising that by the mid-1970s the original ITMEB concept began to show signs of renewed life. Early in 1976, under the stimulus of a symposium which had been organised in December 1974 by the Commonwealth Secretariat, London, in conjunction with the FAO and the International Trade Centre, Geneva, the latter put out a memorandum entitled 'The Establishment of an International Tea Promotion Association' and invited the views of the trade and of exporting countries. The idea received a cautious welcome (not without murmurs about the danger of 'unproductive bureaucratic costs') and by September of 1976 it proved possible for an inter-governmental conference, meeting under the auspices of UNCTAD/GATT, to prepare a form of Agreement whereby the promotion of tea would be undertaken on a global scale. Signatures were obtained from nine countries responsible for nearly 90% of the world's export of Black tea – Bangladesh, India, Indonesia, Kenya, Malawi, Mauritius, Sri Lanka,

Tanzania, Uganda – and, on 23 February 1979, the Agreement came into force.

There was some idea of a London headquarters alongside that of the International Tea Committee, but in the end a generous invitation was accepted from the Netherlands government to set up shop in Rotterdam, where support facilities from the Dutch Centre for the Promotion of Imports from Developing Countries (CBI) would be available.

Under the leadership of Mr T. S. Broca (formerly Chairman of the Indian Tea Board) and his successor Mr Ngoima wa Mwaura, ITPA set to work with the same vigour which marked the launching of ITMEB some 45 years earlier. Worldwide market appraisals were assembled from a variety of sources and digests of many of them appeared in due course in ITPA's excellent *International Tea Journal* and in various publications abroad.

At the third session of the Governing Board (October 1980) it was possible to put forward generic programmes for three important markets – Egypt, Nigeria and the Netherlands – 'the first time in 16 years[10] that any new generic promotion programmes had been started anywhere in the world'. Only the Nigeria and Netherlands campaigns were actually launched. Plans were also considered for the reactivation of the Tea Councils in Australia and New Zealand and for a further ambitious series of studies in potential markets. Altogether some 30 surveys have been completed, six of them in conjunction with the Commonwealth Secretariat.

Funds were still comparatively modest, with an outlay of just over US$1 million envisaged for the 1981 administrative and promotional budgets. It was expected, however, that resources would be strengthened with contributions from the trade in the various countries where programmes were undertaken and there were hopes of additional support from UNCTAD's Common Fund of Commodities, whenever that might commence business.[11]

Alas, less than four years after the coming into force of the ITPA Agreement, a rift began to appear. Late in 1982, Sri Lanka, doubtful apparently about the benefits she had obtained while bearing 31% of ITPA's costs, announced that she would withdraw from membership as from January 1983. The result was a virtual 'freeze' at Coolsingel 58, Rotterdam, and it was no great surprise when India, which had already made warning sounds, gave notice of her withdrawal to the July 1984 session of the governing body. This might well have signalled the collapse of the whole organisation, but in the event the remaining signatories to the original Agreement (who had been joined by Mozambique) decided at a further meeting in November 1984 that it ought to be kept in being for at least another two years, while possible areas of co-operation among the governments could be explored. Unfortunately the publication of *International Tea Journal*, to which the present work owes so much, had to be suspended. A variety of factors were at work, most importantly perhaps the failure to progress towards an International Tea Agreement.

The reaction to these events of anyone who had been involved in the ITMEB break-up of 1954 was inevitably – 'here we go again'. The parallels are certainly close, with Sri Lanka playing almost exactly the same role as that of India 39 years before.

Both organisations had their constitutional weaknesses; the tea producers who created ITMEB never achieved a totally secure rapport with either governments or distributors, while ITPA's constitution kept it narrowly inter-governmental – more akin to the international civil service in Chapter 16 than anything else. Another handicap was that, unlike ITMEB, ITPA had to obtain funds for each campaign according to the subscribers' interests in that particular market, instead of drawing on a general pool.

Viability of co-operative promotion

So at last we arrive at the basic question: is the co-operative promotion of tea viable in itself and if not, why not? Some ten years ago the present writer, musing upon the vicissitudes of the UK Tea Council (much the same in kind as those of ITMEB and ITPA), remarked that they were strictly in line with the experience of three-quarters of a century: 'always an impulse – and sometimes an urgent need – to co-operate; never the total commitment to carrying co-operation through'.[12] That word 'commitment' is surely the ultimate clue to answering the question with which this paragraph began. There is no reason to suppose that teamen are more 'awkward' than other categories of traders or their governments uniquely incapable of working together. Unfortunately, what they lack is a forum in which all sections can sit down and consider, without haste or heat, exactly what needs to be done, and where, and by what means. At one time it was thought that something of the kind would evolve from the various branches of the United Nations centred in Rome or Geneva, but it now seems unlikely that they can ever provide the right governmental and commercial 'mix'.

A paper on this subject, presented by the Secretariat of UNCTAD to its Inter-governmental Group of Experts on Tea (Geneva, October 1983), envisaged control by a promotion committee as part of the machinery of any future International Tea Agreement. Again, the ITMEB pattern! This paper also explored the possible channels through which funds might be generated, including an export levy, supplemented by tea trade contributions in campaign areas.

Current cost of campaigns

At the time of writing, some US$2 million – much less than a few years ago – was being spent by governments and the trade on generic promotion in the four main 'Tea Council' countries (the United Kingdom, the United States, Canada and West Germany), plus US$300,000 in the Netherlands and Nigeria, where ITPA works with the local trade. To this, ITPA suggested, would have to be added not less than US$3.5 million to finance campaigns in the 15 additional countries[13] in which their surveys had uncovered 'promotion potential' – a total budget of about US$6 million per annum. When it is considered that the promotion fund for coffee (the export levy plus trade contributions) in 1976/77 and 1977/78 combined amounted to US$48 million, one may wonder what tea could hope to achieve with a quarter of that sum, especially since the generic funds being currently deployed by Tea Councils are manifestly too small to be effective.

It may well be that, as with the International Tea Agreement itself, it would be wise to let the whole problem simmer in everyone's mind until the supply/demand equation, particularly in respect of India and China, becomes much clearer, as it assuredly will in the next decade.

Meanwhile it would seem shortsighted totally to dismantle ITPA and any other existing means of co-operation, however limited their scope. It has never been a profitable exercise to attempt precise statistical analyses of Tea Council campaigns and their results and it must be admitted that from time to time claims of increased consumption, partly due, in fact, to other causes, have been abruptly invalidated as market conditions change. Tea does need good public relations, it does need a solid and sensible programme for schools and youth organisations and these activities in themselves go far to justify the modest financial burden which ITPA and most of the Tea Councils impose on their subscribers.

18 *The Prospect Before Us*

Or, 'It is all so Different Now' – to borrow the title of one of Mr van de Meeberg's thought-provoking newsletters,[1] in which he contrasted some aspects of the immediate past with the present world tea picture. Different indeed it is and the preceding chapters are an attempt to explain how and why in a larger perspective.

Recent price fluctuations

The forces for change which have been and are at work are broadly of two kinds – short term and long term. The former may be transitory, but they are often disconcerting. Prices are an example. Twice in recent years they have 'taken off' in a manner which to outside observers did not seem wholly rational.

The first instance, a classic 'boom and bust' situation, occurred in 1976/77. It stemmed from the interaction between a sharp rise in coffee prices, following the notorious 1975 frost in Brazil, and poor out-turns in the tea-producing territories up to August 1976. A switch in demand from coffee to tea was widely expected and supermarkets round the world hastened to build up their stocks. Using 'medium teas' in the London auctions as barometer, we can see the price rising by fairly easy stages from 98p per kilogram in August 1976 to 158p in February 1977. Then came panic. On 21 March medium teas fetched an average of 270p and for the whole month the figure was 235p. April showed little change, but by May sanity began to return and, though falls were irregular, the average for the year was no more than 129p. More significantly, the weight of tea attracted to London during 1977 was 97,000 tonnes, against only 89,000 tonnes the previous year. Auctions in the producing countries showed a similar pattern, as exemplified by the 'all teas' averages in Colombo: 1976 Rs9.63; 1977 Rs16.51; 1978 Rs14.09; 1979 Rs12.19.

Retail prices, of course, also swung upwards and in the United Kingdom drew the fire of the Price Commission when the auction fallback in the second half of 1977 was not immediately reflected at retail level. In February 1978 the Secretary of State concerned, Mr Roy Hattersley, announced that he intended to make an Order fixing maximum prices for half a dozen named blends. The trade, true to its independent character, made strong representations that the basis of the Order was quite inequitable, but, in the event, prices began to fall and the Order was never made.

Meanwhile plenty of bad blood had been vented in Parliament and the Press, and the producer countries were also upset by an unprecedented decision to suspend the London auctions for three weeks in the month of March 1978, pending a decision on the proposed maximum prices. This was regarded in Kenya, for example, as a 'boycott' of the auctions by the leading packers – a misunderstanding which was quickly put right.

The trauma of 1977/78 left the markets timorous and sluggish. By mid-September 1982, the price for 'all teas' in London remained only 111p per kilogram, a mere 17p up on the previous three years' average – hardly enough to take care of inflation – and many producers, especially in India, were selling their tea below cost. Although by November London prices had edged up to about 120p and showed every sign of going higher, the browser through planters' association reports continued to encounter the word 'crisis', followed as often as not by appeals to government to 'save our industry'.

The tea-drinking public was oblivious to all this. But the sequel once again made headlines. All through 1983 auction and private sales moved towards a boom,[2] with the inevitable reaction on retail prices, which up to the beginning of that year had remained astonishingly stable while all around them inflation surged on. Pressure continued right up to the end of the year. When the London auctions reopened after the Christmas break on 3 January 1984, medium teas at 308p per kilogram easily broke their March 1977 record and by the 16 January sale they were fetching 332p, against only 139p a year before. The Kenyas on offer averaged a remarkable 357.26p. Packers, in fact, were 'fighting' for tea and one may be permitted to suppose that some very experienced people had got their sums wrong months before.

The various explanations put forward this time bundled up 'short term' and 'long term' in a somewhat confusing package. The fact, for example, that 1982 had been a disappointing year climatically for Sri Lanka (and 1983 looked like being no better) and that this had contributed to a general 'tightness' in supplies was clearly a short-term factor, as was the inadequate carry-over of stocks from the previous two seasons, both in countries of origin and on the London spot market. In contrast, increased consumption in India belonged to the long-term category, though it was widely publicised as though it had taken the world by surprise!

The ITC prudently surrounds the figures in Table 18.1 with qualifications, but they do indicate that, since 1980 at least, world absorption has moved

Table 18.1   World supply and absorption of tea ('000 tonnes)

	1979	1980	1981	1982	1983
Supply					
Total production					
India, Bangladesh, Sri Lanka,					
Indonesia	858	881	896	868	905
East Africa	182	168	173	185	196
Exports only					
China	107	108	92	106	125
Rest of Eastern Asia	32	31	28	23	25
Rest of Africa	15	15	16	16	17
Other countries	52	57	49	52	56
Total supply	1,245	1,260	1,255	1,250	1,324
Absorption					
Importing countries					
United Kingdom	179	183	180	174	168
USSR	38	56	72	61	56
Rest of Europe	88	94	95	94	95
America	117	118	119	114	110
Asia	211	216	214	212	225
Africa	139	139	135	125	150
Oceania	32	30	31	29	29
Total	804	836	847	809	833
Exporting countries					
India, Bangladesh, Sri Lanka,					
Indonesia	381	403	425	447	477
East Africa	17	19	18	18	19
Other (imports only)	16	17	15	13	14
Total	414	439	458	478	510
Total absorption	1,218	1,275	1,305	1,287	1,343

Note: Estimated figures are in italics.

ahead of supply. Late in 1983, as we saw on page 36, India took corrective action in the export field; it remains to be seen whether and how soon producers can also respond to the situation. Apart from a resort to 'coarse plucking' (which nobody wants to see), it would normally be three to five years before any campaign of intensified in-filling or extension begins to show in yield. To prophesy about tea supplies and prices is to plunge into a minefield, but it does seem that the era of large export surpluses is over for the time being. Early in 1985 a modest 'shake-out' in prices was apparent.

Futures market

The vicissitudes described above again turned many people's thoughts to the pros and cons of a futures (or terminal) market for tea. The subject had been fairly thoroughly explored between 1971 and 1974 and even then it was not new; the London Produce Trading House had been dealing in Indian and Ceylon tea futures way back in the 1890s, although – for reasons now obscure – that market did not flourish. In modern times, futures of all kinds have become big business, with London taking the lead over New York in several important commodities, including sugar, coffee and cocoa.

So inevitably the question continues to be asked: if coffee and cocoa have benefited from a futures market, surely tea might also do the same? Consideration in depth was begun by a Tea Futures Study Group in London (1971), which in turn gave rise to two seminars the following year under Tea Trade Committee auspices. The response seemed sufficiently good to justify the setting up of a Formation Sub-committee, which, after some hard work on the possible machinery, unanimously recommended that 'the establishment of a Tea Futures Market is both practicable and desirable'.[3] Prolonged consultations with the various sections of the trade followed, but in the end the Tea Trade Committee somewhat reluctantly decided (April 1975) that no general agreement was possible and the Formation Sub-committee was disbanded. A frustrating exercise. Some vagueness remains as to just why certain of the interests involved could not bring themselves to endorse the plan.

Stated as summarily as possible, a futures market is distinguished from the 'forward trading' which has always been part of the tea market mechanism by the fact that, instead of a firm contract for the delivery of goods at an agreed date and price, the vast majority of futures contracts are not intended to reach delivery at all. Buyer and seller are given the option of meeting their obligations simply by selling out what they have already bought or buying back what they have previously sold. This is done with the help of a member of the appropriate clearing house through whose account the various purchases and sales are netted off. Parties with opposing interests are thus enabled to 'hedge', or cover themselves, against opposing price risks. Since the tea futures market is 'dead' (or dormant) for the time being, it is unnecessary to enter into the technical detail of how 'hedges' would work, but in addition to this basic function it is argued (in the words of the original study group) that such a market would do the following:

1. Provide a barometer of current and future values.
2. Make tea more acceptable as collateral.
3. Provide a forum for market information. (A floor member, immediately after making a sale, has to ensure that his transaction is chalked up for all to see.)

Some of the objections on which the proposal apparently foundered are as follows:

1. *Standards.* To make a futures market work, transactions would have to be in an agreed grade or grades of tea and, though the Formation Sub-committee went into considerable detail on how this could be done, some people felt that the product is too diverse for grading to be feasible.
2. *Continuous crop.* This is the point which has been made repeatedly –

that tea is not a commodity the out-turn of which can be estimated year by year, but is infinitely adjustable.

3. *Small compass of the trade.* It was argued that the number of people trading in tea under modern conditions is too limited to make a futures market worthwhile. An essential feature of such a market is the participation of outside speculators or 'risk-takers', to keep buying and selling on the move – perhaps to the unease of the more conservative elements in the tea trade.

4. *Present methods satisfactory.* The feeling that since 'forward buying' seems to work quite well, why change? The experiences of 1976/77 and of 1983 may have modified that view.

Distribution and the market-place

Given that there is no futures market and the International Agreement is always receding towards the horizon, fundamental changes hardly appear imminent in the way the world output and distribution of tea is (or is not) regulated or in the day-to-day mechanism of the market-place. At one time it seemed that an increased trend towards state trading might lead to a flood of 'government-to-government' transactions and the diversion of large quantities of tea out of the 'usual channels'. More than 200,000 tonnes of tea annually, or nearly a quarter of all exports, are, in fact, bought on behalf of state corporations, but virtually the whole of this represents auction bidding through agents (often local companies) operating in Calcutta, Colombo, Jakarta, Mombasa or elsewhere. And though, as we have seen, markets can be profoundly affected by governmental buying policies, the trade has learnt to 'roll with the punch' and to operate worldwide with undiminished dynamism.

If state trading has increased without undermining tea's unique selling apparatus – the auctions – the same cannot quite be said of the private sales and direct deals which, stimulated by the 'container revolution', represent the other conspicuous 'growth area' of the present day. No great harm has been done so far, but if they were to by-pass the auctions in a really big way, old suspicions of occult overseas influence might be reawakened. However, Sri Lanka already sees to it that virtually all its tea goes out through the Colombo auctions, while Kenya stipulates a 20% minimum (at present greatly exceeded) for Mombasa and, of course, it is well within the powers of any other government to tread the same path if it thinks necessary.

All this presupposes the continuance of something like the 'mixed economies' which prevail in all the great exporting countries other than China. And even there, though every contract must be with one branch or another of the Tea Corporation, the foreign buyer enjoys infinitely more freedom to shop around than in the days of the 'Co-Hong'.

Value-added exports

More difficult to assess is the likely long-term effect on the industry of the present drive in favour of 'value-added' teas – that is, those blended and packeted prior to export. This is in part a spin-off from a much more profound movement of opinion. It is now received doctrine in the Third World that its members must no longer be regarded simply as a source of raw materials for the industries of the developed countries, but should themselves profit from manufacturing the finished article. Teamen may not see their product in quite these terms, but today the argument comes from all sides – whether in the form of sometimes acrid propaganda about the richer countries ('North') exploiting the poorer ('South') or of more sober, but none the less insistent, voices heard in the corridors of the United Nations and its agencies.

To come down to the current facts, although China is sending increasing quantities of packeted tea abroad, the two countries mainly involved are India and Sri Lanka. Each has established over the past decade a fairly solid base for the export of foil-wrapped packets to West Asia, the Gulf and North Africa; both recognise that though this may continue slowly to expand, the only form of value-added export with a future worldwide is the teabag. It also presents the greatest challenge.

Statistically, Sri Lanka is well ahead of India in both departments – about a quarter of her exports are value-added, against less than 10% of India's. Sri Lanka's 1983 figures are shown in Table 18.2.

Table 18.2   Sri Lanka – value-added exports 1983

	Quantity (tonnes)	Value ('000 Rs)	Unit value f.o.b. (Rs)
Bulk	115,101	5,731,112	49.80
Packets	41,688	2,458,154	58.96
Bags	936	81,312	86.87

Packet exports showed, in fact, a 25% increase over the previous year and teabags, too, were doing well when one considers that as recently as 1978 the weight exported was a mere 36,000 kg.

The history of value-added exports from India has not been so buoyant. A peak was reached in the season 1978/79, when 38.5 million kg of packet tea went abroad, valued at Rs777 million (unit value Rs20.14), plus 238,167 kg of teabags, value Rs10.5 million (Rs44.38 per kilogram). These were abnormal figures; by 1981/82 packet tea was down to 20 million kg, though bags had risen to 690,000 kg.

In strict money terms, when the cost of packaging materials (higher in the East than in Europe) and freight charges have been taken into account, it does not appear that packet tea represents more than a marginal advantage over bulk for the exporters, though there is a modest gain in employment and perhaps a more substantial one in improved technology. India and Sri Lanka are not 'on all fours' in this sector, since India already has an internal market for packet tea six or seven times that of Sri Lanka's.

Teabags offer a livelier prospect, since the demand for them is increasing in many of the more sophisticated markets of West Asia and beyond and, of course, they have become dominant in Europe and North America. At one time, apprehension was caused among some European packers by the various forms of incentive, ranging from direct subsidy – for example India's 13% 'cash compensatory support' – to import duty concessions on machinery and raw materials, offered by producing countries to their exporters of teabags (and value-added teas generally, for that matter). However, the European Tea Committee has pointed out[4] that competition from India and Sri Lanka has so far been on a very minor scale and that by far the greater part of value-added imports recorded in the EEC represents trading among the European countries themselves. This situation may well change, since India in particular, with her rapidly advancing technology[5] and wide choice of teas on which to draw, will surely be able to compete on level terms, sooner or later, even with the ultra-efficient teabag industries of the West.[6]

Working conditions

A page or two ago the word 'exploiting' made a passing appearance. One cannot quit the subject of tea as a plantation crop without reference to its human dimension. The industry, and in particular one or two of its leading multinationals, has in recent years been the target of organisations which have come to believe that estate labour is indeed exploited.

In Chapter 1 something was said about how the pattern of this labour grew up. It is in a sense tea's misfortune that it is derived from countries where the standard of living is low and where, by reason of inadequate resources and the pressure of population, it is peculiarly difficult to raise it. Minimum wages and other benefits are everywhere fixed by governments (usually under trade union pressure), and British-owned companies still involved (as in India, Bangladesh and East and Central Africa) can fairly claim that working conditions on their estates are at least as good as on those in indigenous ownership. So they have some reason to feel aggrieved when they are singled out for obloquy, as they have been, for example, on British television programmes from time to time. The awkward fact is that improvements taking place everywhere in housing, health care and so on, were started in most cases from a fairly low base. In particular, one has long felt that a good deal of criticism might have been avoided if, in the past, the estate owners had been quicker off the mark in the reconstruction of 'workers' lines' or even their replacement by something more civilised, which could have been done at a fairly moderate cost over a period of years.[7]

The saving grace is that, at local level, attacks on British-owned tea enterprises by the British-based media appear to do little to undermine confidence between governments, planters and people. It may be that, in another generation or two, expatriate planting companies will have vanished from the scene; if so, they will have left behind something which, on balance, has been far more beneficial than otherwise to the people of the tea countries.

Future prospects

'*Mit Tee und Optimismus ins Neue Jahr*' was the message on the 1983 Christmas card of a famous West German company. How much *Optimismus* is justified for teamen (or indeed teapersons), looking further ahead than 1985? The favourable signs predominate.

As the producing countries develop their economies, land use will become more intensive and tea will feel the pressure; there is no foreseeable reason, however, why higher yields should not continue to be secured from a static or even a reduced hectarage. The best minds in the world of tea research believe that we have only just begun to focus science on *Camellia sinensis* itself and its potentialities. Even as and when labour become prohibitively scarce and dear (not so far a problem in the older producing areas), there will be plenty of scope for mechanisation to lend a hand.

As to demand, we need not rake over once again the questions raised by the growth of tea-drinking in countries of origin. The one certain thing is that, short of artificial restraints, it will continue to increase, and faster. At the importing end of the pipeline, the past half-century has, of course, seen a radical shift in the pattern of demand. Whereas before World War II the United Kingdom and the rest of Europe, plus North America, were absorbing over 60% of all production, by the mid-1950s this had shrunk to less than 50% and at the time of writing to 30% at most. Though earlier chapters have shown a certain *Pessimismus* about trends in some of the traditional 'white' markets on both sides of the Atlantic and in Australasia, the likelihood is that even there we have just about reached a plateau, and meanwhile the slack has been more than taken up by the tea-drinkers of West Asia, the Gulf and North Africa.

The price of tea will continue to rise, but no more quickly than that of competing beverages, and its age-old claim to be 'the cheapest drink in the world next to water' is likely to hold good as far as thought can reach. And, since population seems to be expanding fastest in those regions where tea is on the up-and-up, it looks as though the call will continue to echo round the world, '*lai pei cha ch'ing*' – 'bring more tea, please'!

Appendix 1 *The Grading of Black Tea*

There is neither an exact nor a uniform system of grading and it varies considerably from one country of origin to another. The broad division today is between the Orthodox and the CTC grades.

The grades shown below are, as a rule, an indication of *size of leaf* in descending order, though in some cases they indicate appearance – the long, wiry Orange Pekoes for example.

The whole leaf grades and the 'Tippy' and 'Golden' brokens meet a specialised demand in various markets and hardly form part of modern mainstream grading.

Orthodox grades

Whole leaf

TGFOP	Tippy Golden Flowery Orange Pekoe
GFOP	Golden Flowery Orange Pekoe
FOP1	Flowery Orange Pekoe One
FOP	Flowery Orange Pekoe
OP	Orange Pekoe

Brokens

TGBOP	Tippy Golden Broken Orange Pekoe
GBOP	Golden Broken Orange Pekoe
FBOP	Flowery Broken Orange Pekoe
BOP1	Broken Orange Pekoe One
BOP	Broken Orange Pekoe
BP	Broken Pekoe

Fannings

BOPF	Broken Orange Pekoe Fannings
GOF	Golden Orange Fannings

OF   Orange Fannings
PF   Pekoe Fannings

Dusts
PD   Pekoe Dust
D1   Dust One
D   Dust

CTC grades

Brokens
BP1   Broken Pekoe One
BP   Broken Pekoe

Fannings
PF1   Pekoe Fannings One
PF   Pekoe Fannings

Dusts
PD   Pekoe Dust
D1   Dust One
D   Dust

Appendix 2 *Tea Research Institutes*

The following representative list of Institutes is based on one annexed to a paper on 'Research and Development Activities' which Dr R. T. Ellis presented to the Inter-governmental Group of Experts on Tea meeting at Geneva on 3 October 1983.

It includes some general agricultural research institutes which make a study of tea.

Argentina
Estación Experimental Agropecuaria
Casilla de Correos 101
3315 L.N. Alem
Misiones
Argentina

Australia
Southedge Agricultural Research Station
PO Box 174
Mareeba 4880
Queensland
Australia

Bangladesh
Bangladesh Tea Research Station
Srimangal
Sylhet
Bangladesh

Burundi
Institut des Sciences Agronomiques du
    Burundi (ISABU)
BP 795
Bujumbura
Burundi

China
Tea Research Institute
Agr. Akadamy of China
Hangzhou
Zhejiang
People's Republic of China

India
Toklai Experimental Station
Jorhat 785 008
Assam
India

UPASI Tea Research Station
Cinchona 642 106
Coimbatore District
S. India

Indonesia
Research Institute for Tea/Cinchona
Gambung
Box 148
Bandung
Indonesia

Japan
National Research Institute of Tea
Kanaya – Chô
Shizuoka – Ken
Japan

Kenya
Tea Research Foundation of Kenya
PO Box 820
Kericho
Kenya

Malawi and Zimbabwe
Tea Research Foundation of Central
  Africa
PO Box 51
Mulanje
Malawi

Papua New Guinea
Mount Hagen Research Station
Mount Hagen
Papua New Guinea

Rwanda
Office des Cultures Industrielles du
  Rwanda (OCIR)
BP 104
Kigali
Rwanda

Sri Lanka
Tea Research Institute of Sri Lanka
St Coombs
Talawakele
Sri Lanka

Tanzania
Tea Research Station
Marikatanda
Box 93
Mufindi
Tanzania

Turkey
Cay Arastirma Enstitusu
Rize
Turkey

Uganda
Tea Research Station
Rwebitaba
Box 96
Fort Portal
Uganda

USSR
All Union Institute for Tea and other
  Subtropical Crops (tea in the field); All
  Union Institute for Tea Industry (tea
  manufacture)
Annaseuli
Georgia
USSR

Scientific Research Institute of Mountain
  Cultures, Horticulture and Agriculture
Sochi
Krasnador
USSR

Appendix 3 *Tea Councils*

Australia
Tea Council of Australia
38th Floor
50 Bridge Street
Australia
NSW 2000

Belgium
Comité Belge du Thé et des Infusions
Boulevard de L'Humanité
B-1190 Bruxelles
Belgium

Canada
Tea Council of Canada
701 Evans Avenue
Suite 501
Etobicoke
Ontario
Canada
M9C 1A3

France
Comité Francais du Thé
5 Rue de Stockholm
Paris 75008
France

Ireland
Tea Council of Ireland Ltd
85 Harcourt Street
Dublin 2
Ireland

New Zealand
Tea Council of New Zealand
PO Box 2172
Auckland C1
New Zealand

Sweden
Swedish Tea Council
Box 1542
111 85 Stockholm
Sweden

United Kingdom
Tea Council of the United Kingdom
Sir John Lyon House
High Timber Street
London
UK
EC4V 3NJ

United States
Tea Council of the USA Inc.
230 Park Avenue
New York City 10017
USA

West Germany
German Tea Council
Steindamm 9
9–2000 Hamburg
West Germany

Appendix 4 *Statistical Tables*

All the following tables are derived from the International Tea Committee's 1984 *Annual Bulletin of Statistics*.

Table A.1 Area under tea (hectares)

	1972	1982
India		
Assam, Bengal, Bihar, Tripura	280,078	299,891
Punjab, UP and HP	5,993	
South India	74,055	74,082
Total	360,126	373,973
Bangladesh	42,649	44,000
Sri Lanka		
Estates	198,287	189,010
Smallholdings	43,571	53,131
Total	241,858	242,141
Indonesia		
Estates (Java)	47,967	50,113
(Sumatra)	14,157	12,627
Smallholders (Java)	(34,700)	(45,234)
Total (estates only)	62,124	62,740
China (Mainland)	–	–
Taiwan	33,500	29,300
Iran	30,200	30,200
Japan	55,500	61,000
Malaysia	2,986	2,566
Turkey	28,782	64,499
Vietnam	7,960	49,600

Table A.1   cont.

	1972	1982
Burundi	1,660	4,700
Cameroon	747	1,880
Kenya	49,763	81,081
Malawi	15,842	18,985
Mauritius	4,841	3,799
Mozambique	15,605	15,935
Rwanda	3,657	9,507
South Africa	*2,856*	*5,500*
Tanzania	14,012	18,548
Uganda	19,085	20,905
Zaïre	10,052	10,300
Zimbabwe	4,221	4,989
USSR	74,700	78,700
Argentina	35,000	41,450
Brazil	4,450	*5,000*
Ecuador		*1,140*
Peru		*4,000*
Papua New Guinea	3,766	3,909

Note: Estimated figures are in italics.

Table A.2   Production (tonnes)

	1972		1982		1983	
	Quantity	% Share	Quantity	% Share	Quantity	% Share
India						
Assam, Bengal, Bihar, Tripura	350,816		*435,821*		*473,744*	
Punjab, UP and HP	1,871		*1,380*		*	
South India	103,309		*123,531*		*114,051*	
Total	455,996	37.9	560,732	29.3	587,795	29.7
Bangladesh	23,836	2.0	40,947	2.1	43,851	2.2
Sri Lanka						
High-grown	81,393		71,665		67,761	
Medium-grown	74,922		51,645		48,458	
Low-grown	57,160		64,506		63,068	
Total	213,475	17.7	187,816	9.8	179,287	9.1
Indonesia						
Estates (Java)	34,795		51,759		68,070	
(Sumatra)	13,479		21,888		24,454	
Smallholders (Java)	1,503		*		*	
Smallholders (Java and Sumatra)*			(16,511)		(25,348)	
Total	49,777	4.1	73,647	3.8	92,584	4.7

Table A.2   cont.

	1972		1982		1983	
	Quantity	% Share	Quantity	% Share	Quantity	% Share
China (Mainland)			397,000	20.7	400,500	20.2
Taiwan	26,229	2.2	24,051	1.3	24,308	1.2
Iran	22,000		23,500	1.2	23,500	1.2
Japan	94,832		98,503	5.2	102,700	5.2
Malaysia	3,364		3,188		3,348	
Turkey	46,500	3.9	68,038	3.6	70,000	3.5
Vietnam	5,100		22,000	1.2	22,500	1.1
Total Asia (Exc. China for 1972)	941,109	78.2	1,499,422	78.3	1,550,313	78.3
Burundi	485		2,164		2,293	
Cameroon	1,438		1,799		2,000	
Kenya	53,322	4.4	96,033	5.0	119,738	6.0
Malawi	20,682	1.7	38,482	2.0	32,010	1.6
Mauritius	4,678		5,354		6,142	
Mozambique	18,678	1.6	21,000	1.1	15,000	0.8
Rwanda	2,522		7,050		7,250	
South Africa	2,000		6,770		6,800	
Tanzania	12,706	1.1	16,230	0.8	15,620	0.8
Uganda	23,376	1.9	2,580	0.1	3,169	
Zaïre	7,000		5,500		5,000	
Zimbabwe	4,560	0.4	10,799	0.6	10,808	0.5
Total Africa	151,447	12.6	213,761	11.2	225,830	11.4
USSR	71,300	5.9	139,800	7.3	143,000	7.2
Argentina	27,010	2.3	36,855	2.0	37,065	1.8
Brazil	6,500	0.6	10,000	0.5	10,000	0.5
Ecuador	467		2,600		2,600	
Peru	2,500		3,000		3,000	
Total South America	36,477		52,455	2.7	52,665	2.6
Papua New Guinea	2,689		8,461		7,743	
Grand total (Exc. China for 1972)	1,119,534		1,913,899		1,979,551	

Production of Green tea (included in figures above)

	1972	1982	1983
India	8,772	6,000	6,000
Indonesia – Smallholders		16,511	25,348
China		327,950	332,500
Taiwan	Not available		
Japan	94,816	98,500	100,000
Vietnam	5,100	22,000	22,000

Notes: *Mainly Green tea, not included in the totals. Estimated figures are in italics.

Table A.3   Sales by auction

	Quantity sold (tonnes)			Average price			
	1972	1982	1983	1972	1982	1983	
London	112,676	59,398	53,654	42.20	110.50	149.60	Pence/kg
Calcutta	169,603	119,676	112,130	6.99	16.82	26.15	Ind. Rs/kg
Gauhati	18,866	75,342	74,612	5.65	15.00	23.48	Ind. Rs/kg
Siliguri		79,945	64,071		14.53	21.89	Ind. Rs/kg
Cochin	58,580	50,201	46,774	6.29	15.12	22.66	Ind. Rs/kg
Coimbatore		13,896	15,932		15.36	24.17	Ind. Rs/kg
Coonoor	9,652	13,809	18,082	5.24	14.00	20.37	Ind. Rs/kg
Chittagong	19,960	35,519	38,258	3.18	32.53	49.99	Taka/kg
Colombo	177,315	180,637	166,856	4.39	23.43	43.24	SL. Rs/kg
Jakarta		29,367	34,543		151.85	196.83	US$ cents/kg
Singapore		1,739	476		174.14	231.16	US$ cents/kg
Mombasa	13,598	36,638	48,572	5.79	17.87	25.46	K. shs/kg
Limbe		10,516	9,504		137.80	259.07	Tamb/kg*

Note: *There are 100 tambalas to the Malawi kwacha.

Table A.4   Exchange rates – selected end-of-year rates (per US dollar)

	1972	1982	1983
India (rupee)	7.5940	9.4550	10.0990
Bangladesh (taka)	7.5950	22.1180	24.6150
Sri Lanka (rupee)	6.0010	20.8300	23.5290
Indonesia (rupiah)	415.0000	661.4200	909.600
Kenya (shilling)	7.1429	10.9220	13.3120
Malawi (kwacha)	.8016	1.0543	1.1748
Tanzania (shilling)	7.1429	9.3340	11.7150
France (franc)	5.0443	6.5724	7.6213
West Germany (DM)	3.1886	2.4266	2.5533
Netherlands (guilder)	3.2095	2.6702	2.8541
United Kingdom (sterling)*	2.5018	1.7505	1.5170
Canada (dollar)	.9908	1.2337	1.2324
Japan (yen)	303.1100	249.0500	237.5200
Pakistan (rupee)	8.9410	11.8590	13.1170
Australia (dollar)	1.1923	1.0174	0.9025

Note: *US dollar per £1 sterling.

Table A.5 Exports (tonnes)

	1972 Quantity	1972 % Share	1982 Quantity	1982 % Share	1983 Quantity	1983 % Share
India	209,814	30.0	*189,895*	23.1	*209,140*	24.1
Bangladesh	13,186	1.9	34,415	4.2	29.989	3.5
Sri Lanka	190,088	27.1	181,140	22.0	157,938	18.2
Indonesia	38,529	5.5	63,660	7.7	68,583	7.9
China (Mainland)	48,128	6.9	105,818	12.9	125,062	14.4
Taiwan	21,301	3.0	9,961	1.2	11,572	1.3
Iran	507		*1,200*	0.1	*2,000*	0.2
Japan	1,883	0.3	2,475	0.3	2,124	0.2
Malaysia	766		*600*		*1,000*	0.1
Turkey	14,881	2.1	380		*500*	
Vietnam	*2,351*	0.3	*9,500*	1.2	*10,000*	1.2
Total Asia	541,434	77.1	*599,044*	72.7	612,908	71.1
Burundi	486		*1,702*	0.2	*2,178*	0.2
Kenya	47,297	6.8	79,798	9.7	100.645	11.6
Malawi	19,855	2.8	37,082	4.5	36,090	4.2
Mauritius	3,931	0.6	4,590	0.5	4,935	0.6
Mozambique	18,351	2.6	*18,500*	2.2	*14,000*	1.6
Rwanda	2,319	0.3	5,416	0.6	*6,000*	0.6
Tanzania	9,203	1.3	13,622	1.7	*14,000*	1.6
Uganda	20,678	3.0	1,198	0.1	1,333	0.1
Zaïre	7,061	1.0	*3,500*	0.4	*3,000*	0.4
Zimbabwe	2,782	0.4	7,178	0.9	7,600	0.9
Total Africa	131,963	18.8	*172,586*	20.8	*189,781*	21.8
Argentina	18,894	2.7	33,083	4.0	44,733	5.2
Brazil	4,247	0.5	8,969	1.1	7,798	0.9
Ecuador	442		*1,000*	0.1	*1,000*	0.1
Peru	*50*		*100*		*100*	
Total South America	23,633	3.2	43,152	5.2	53,631	5.2
Papua New Guinea	2,792	0.4	6,475	0.8	7,234	
Other countries	382		*300*		*300*	
Total	700,204		*821,557*		*868,854*	

Exports of Green tea (included in figures above)

	1972	1982	1983
India	2,792	*3,000*	*3,000*
Indonesia		192	104
China	27,000	53,591	57,613
Taiwan	11,207	3,289	*5,000*
Japan	1,846	2,443	*1,800*
Vietnam	2,351	*9,500*	*10,000*
Total	45,196	*72,015*	*77,517*

Note: Estimated figures are in italics.

Table A.6   Selected export values ('000 US dollars)

	1972	1982	1983
India	212,500	*375,921*	*518,566*
Bangladesh	7,672	46,966	56,674
Sri Lanka	187,900	304,266	351,369
Indonesia	29,763	89,493	120,423
Japan	1,234	2,751	2,354
Turkey	3,805	1,215	–
Kenya	46,230	144,816	185,427
Malawi	15,148	42,834	48,089
Mauritius	3,921	6,316	8,245
Mozambique	11,610	–	–
Rwanda	–	8,695	–
Tanzania	7,544	21,550	–
Uganda	17,635	877	–
Zimbabwe	–	7,997	–
Argentina	11,219	29,077	–
Brazil	3,325	11,913	11,765
Papua New Guinea	2,406	9,061	12,458

Note: Estimated figures are in italics.

Table A.7   Imports for consumption, adjusted for re-exports (tonnes)

	1972	1982	1983
Western Europe			
United Kingdom	192,109	183,587	155,183
Austria	719	1,213	1,196
Belgium and Luxembourg	683	1,379	*1,200*
Denmark	1,998	2,292	2,410
Faeroe Islands	96	*120*	*130*
Finland	557	1,007	915
France	4,104	7,579	*8,800*
West Germany	9,952	*15,500*	*15,000*
Gibraltar	60	*80*	*80*
Greece	232	320	*370*
Iceland	44	47	*50*
Ireland	12,735	8,808	10,865
Italy	2,587	3,415	3,212
Malta	461	240	530
Netherlands	8,465	9,598	9,438
Norway	711	846	822
Portugal	246	225	*250*
Spain	608	892	*850*
Sweden	1,986	2,859	2,856
Switzerland	1,597	1,996	1,761
Yugoslavia	1,809	*1,500*	*2,000*
Total W. Europe (Exc. UK)	49,650	59,916	62,735

Table A.7 cont.

	1972	1982	1983
Eastern Europe			
Bulgaria	76	550	550
Czechoslovakia	1,303	2,544	2,600
German Dem. Rep.	1,961	2,500	2,500
Hungary	964	1,312	1,300
Poland	12,035	26,764	25,908
Romania	200	300	300
USSR	39,900	61,000	55,800
Total E. Europe	56,439	94,970	88,958
North America/West Indies			
Canada	21,205	17,695	17,467
USA	68,676	82,706	77,140
Bahamas	55	80	80
Barbados	105	130	130
Bermuda	53	66	60
British Honduras and Belize	62	50	50
Jamaica	160	129	130
Trinidad and Tobago	244	192	200
Netherlands Antilles	90	105	100
Other countries	370	450	500
Total	91,020	101,603	95,857
Latin America			
Mexico	19	100	130
Central America	140	160	180
Argentina	14	43	50
Bolivia	400	187	300
Brazil	10	5	5
Chile	9,196	10,462	12,215
Peru	8	10	5
Uruguay	422	605	700
Other countries	500	600	650
Total	10,709	12,172	14,235
Asia			
Abu Dhabi	–	1,460	1,700
Bahrain	533	586	476
Dubai	4,205	12,500	13,000
Kuwait	1,976	6,000	6,500
Oman	–	1,431	1,500
Qatar	527	623	800
Saudi Arabia	7,117	15,060	15,500
Other Arabian states	3,323	8,000	8,500
Afghanistan	14,352	10,730	11,000
Hong Kong	6,264	8,752	8,820
Iran	8,967	11,800	22,300
Iraq	21,980	36,500	37,500
Israel	2,409	1,846	2,000
Jordan	2,444	3,227	3,500

Table A.7 cont.

	1972	1982	1983
Lebanon	3,576	2,500	2,600
Malaysia	2,079	4,000	4,000
Nepal	620	700	800
Pakistan	39,387	72,459	86,654
Philippines	298	278	350
Sabah	158	200	220
Sarawak	227	300	330
Singapore	–	500	600
Syria	4,161	11,034	10,000
Thailand	1,151	650	600
Other countries	1,400	1,000	1,100
Total	127,154	212,136	240,350
Africa			
Algeria	3,383	8,000	9,000
Benin	2	2	2
Cameroon	2	3	3
Canary Islands	76	400	450
Central African Republic	16	1	1
Ceuta	27	20	30
Chad	847	800	825
Congo	2	10	10
Egypt	27,300	57,300	65,000
Ethiopia	1,021	1,000	1,000
Gabon	3	10	10
Ghana	93	170	170
Guinea	–	3	3
Ivory Coast	80	200	200
Kenya	24	−2,765	2,520
Libya	12,784	6,500	7,300
Mali	1,150	850	900
Mauritania	500	1,200	1,200
Mauritius	6	10	10
Melilla	47	79	220
Morocco	12,367	13,866	20,000
Niger	486	1,200	1,200
Nigeria	878	2,000	2,200
Senegal	1,287	1,000	1,000
Somalia	3,627	2,800	2,800
South Africa	19,343	12,923	15,252
Sudan	18,033	8,000	8,500
Tanzania	156	–	–
Togo		15	20
Tunisia	5,972	7,425	8,000
Uganda	38	–	–
Upper Volta	16	400	400
Zaïre	3	10	10
Zambia	979	300	300
Zimbabwe	652	37	100
Other countries	560	1,000	1,200
Total	112,760	124,769	149,836

Table A.7 cont.

	1972	1982	1983
Oceania			
Australia	26,266	21,647	21,767
Fiji	548	709	*700*
New Zealand	8,090	*6,239*	*6,244*
Papua New Guinea	374	*350*	*350*
Other countries	*280*	*330*	*300*
Total	35,558	29,275	29,361
Major producing countries in Asia			
India	–	–	
Sri Lanka	–	–	–
China	–	–	–
Japan	18,930	11,536	11,984
Total	20,500	*13,100*	*13,500*
Summary			
UK and Ireland	204,800	192,400	166,000
Rest of Western Europe	37,000	*51,100*	*51,900*
USSR and Eastern Europe	56,400	95,000	*89,000*
North America and West Indies	91,000	101,600	95,900
Latin America	10,700	12,200	14,200
Asia	127,200	212,100	*240,300*
Africa	*112,800*	124,800	*149,800*
Oceania	35,600	29,300	*29,400*
Major producing countries	20,500	*3,100*	*13,500*
Grand total	*696,000*	*831,600*	*849,400*

Note: Estimated figures are in italics.

Table A.8   Apparent consumption per head (total triennial average in '000 tonnes, per head in kilograms)

	1974–76		1978–80		1980–82	
	Total	Per head	Total	Per head	Total	Per head
United Kingdom	199.16	*3.55*	175.92	*3.14*	179.02	*3.19*
Austria	0.80	*0.11*	1.03	*0.14*	1.20	*0.16*
Belgium and Luxembourg	0.91	*0.09*	1.10	*0.11*	1.23	*0.12*
Czechoslovakia	2.67	*0.18*	2.17	*0.14*	2.47	*0.16*
Denmark	2.15	*0.42*	2.17	*0.43*	2.35	*0.46*
Finland	0.76	*0.16*	0.78	*0.16*	0.92	*0.19*
France	5.49	*0.10*	7.32	*0.14*	8.20	*0.15*

Table A.8   cont.

	1974–76		1978–80		1980–82	
	Total	Per head	Total	Per head	Total	Per head
West Germany	10.82	*0.17*	13.50	*0.22*	15.23	*0.25*
East Germany	1.72	*0.10*	2.00	*0.12*	2.51	*0.15*
Ireland	11.62	*3.65*	11.60	*3.44*	11.41	*3.32*
Italy	3.20	*0.06*	3.36	*0.06*	3.39	*0.06*
Netherlands	9.01	*0.66*	8.96	*0.64*	9.43	*0.66*
Norway	0.79	*0.20*	0.70	*0.17*	0.80	*0.19*
Poland	15.09	*0.44*	21.79	*0.62*	24.44	*0.68*
Sweden	2.70	*0.33*	2.80	*0.34*	2.84	*0.34*
Switzerland	1.60	*0.25*	1.55	*0.24*	1.86	*0.29*
USSR	130.03	*0.51*	157.13	*0.60*	193.96	*0.72*
Canada	21.40	*0.94*	19.71	*0.83*	18.96	*0.78*
United States	78.22	*0.37*	77.10	*0.35*	84.10	*0.37*
Chile	11.07	*1.10*	12.73	*1.17*	10.81	*0.96*
Afghanistan	14.89	*1.26*	15.10	*0.97*	13.99	*0.86*
Bahrain	0.67	*2.58*	0.74	*2.37*	0.51	*1.60*
Hong Kong	6.63	*1.51*	7.91	*1.61*	8.24	*1.60*
India	272.67	*0.46*	337.75	*0.52*	375.35	*0.56*
Iran	34.61	*1.05*	40.04	*1.08*	N.A.	N.A.
Iraq	25.84	*2.32*	32.56	*2.55*	N.A.	N.A.
Japan	113.70	*1.02*	112.86	*0.97*	112.29	*0.96*
Jordan	2.71	*1.00*	3.11	*0.99*	3.23	*0.96*
Kuwait	3.68	*3.68*	6.98	*5.40*	6.29	*4.31*
Pakistan	48.63	*0.69*	62.53	*0.78*	70.99	*0.84*
Qatar	0.70	*4.12*	1.37	*5.95*	1.11	*4.46*
Saudi Arabia	6.30	*0.88*	15.38	*1.79*	15.54	*1.67*
Sri Lanka	20.90	*1.55*	21.27	*1.47*	21.07	*1.41*
Syria	5.14	*0.70*	10.56	*1.22*	8.71	*0.94*
Thailand	0.85	*0.02*	0.72	*0.02*	0.62	*0.01*
Turkey	51.91	*1.29*	90.31	*2.04*	65.39	*1.44*
Algeria	4.92	*0.29*	7.56	*0.42*	8.66	*0.44*
Egypt	20.99	*0.56*	29.90	*0.73*	N.A.	N.A.
Kenya	7.53	*0.56*	12.33	*0.81*	14.14	*0.82*
Morocco	13.62	*0.79*	20.31	*1.04*	21.22	*1.03*
South Africa	24.12	*0.87*	22.04	*0.74*	21.80	*0.66*
Sudan	12.96	*0.82*	12.74	*0.71*	8.38	*0.44*
Tanzania	2.59	*0.17*	3.42	*0.19*	3.49	*0.19*
Tunisia	7.19	*1.28*	8.89	*1.42*	8.08	*1.23*
Uganda	1.61	*0.14*	0.78	*0.06*	0.69	*0.05*
Australia	26.18	*1.90*	22.68	*1.57*	22.31	*1.50*
New Zealand	7.30	*2.38*	6.61	*2.13*	6.47	*2.07*

Note: Estimated figures are in italics.

Notes and References

Prologue

1. W. H. Ukers, *All About Tea* (New York, Tea and Coffee Trade Journal, 1935).
2. W. H. Ukers, *All About Coffee* (New York, Tea and Coffee Trade Journal, 1900).
3. D. M. Forrest, *A Hundred Years of Ceylon Tea* (London, Chatto and Windus, 1967); *Tea for the British* (London, Chatto and Windus, 1973).
4. Linnaeus was, of course, the great Swedish botanist who classified tea in 1723; O. Kuntze was the German scientist who first published the words *Camellia* and *sinensis* in association.
5. Forrest, *Tea for the British*, p. 43. Other continental merchants went further – they bought tea in the London auctions, obtained a rebate of the import duty by re-exporting it to Europe and then smuggled it back across the Channel.
6. The unwritten rule that brokers only, and not principals, should bid seems to have come in very early – certainly before 1720.
7. For the natural history of the tea plant and its varieties, or *jats*, see Chapter 1. The later evolution of the trade in the United Kingdom is traced in Chapter 10.

Chapter 1

1. C. F. Marshall, *The World Coffee Trade* (Cambridge, Woodhead-Faulkner, 1983), Table 5.2.
2. K. P. Chowkhani, 'Low Yield of Tea in Nazira Circle, Assam', *TAI Newsletter* (May 1982), p. 7.
3. The fact that *Camellia sinensis* is naturally out-pollinating and has mechanisms which protect it from self-pollination is partly responsible for what Dr R. T. Ellis (Tea Research Foundation of Central Africa) calls 'this hybrid swarm'.
4. T. Eden, *Tea*, revised edition (London, Longmans, 1958), p. 54.
5. Mention should be made here of a plucking system (sometimes called 'scheme plucking') which has been adopted with good results in China and on some of the Brooke Bond African estates. By this, instead of the traditional 'gang' labour, the individual plucker is given responsibility for a group of bushes, the number of which is worked out according to the pruning and plucking cycle of that particular field. This is said to give him or her a sense of 'belonging' and leads, in fact, to higher productivity and improved earnings.
6. Eden, *Tea*, p. 68.
7. *Xyleborus fornicatus*, which, as Dr Ellis has remarked, 'surely bears one of the most splendidly descriptive names in biology'. (From R. T. Ellis, 'Tea', 30, 5, *Biologist* (1983), pp. 247–55.)

8. International Tea Committee, *Annual Bulletin* (1982).
9. See Ukers, *All About Tea*, Vol. I, p. 463, for an illustration of the machine.
10. Tea Research Foundation of Central Africa, *Quarterly Newsletter* (October 1983), p. 19.

Chapter 2

1. Appointed in 1977 to consider a wide range of problems relating to the financing, selling and promotion of Indian tea. Its recommendations (some of which will be referred to later) were on the whole conservative; for example, it appreciated the role of the London auctions and recommended that it should be 'left to the buyers' choice to buy in London or abroad'.
2. The situation is not new. As early as 1900 the government put a ban on further extensions in the Anamallais in South India, in the interests of timber conservation. This was not lifted for more than a decade.
3. Mr S. K. Mehera (Chairman) at the Indian Tea Association's Annual General Meeting, 1982.
4. A much higher figure was expected as a result of the tea price boom of 1983/84.
5. C. R. Harler, *Culture and Marketing of Tea*, 3rd edition (Oxford, OUP, 1964), p. 7.
6. *Ibid.*, pp. 38–39.
7. Sir Percival Griffiths, *History of the Indian Tea Industry* (London, Weidenfeld & Nicolson 1967), p. 160.
8. *Ibid.* Chapter 4.
9. The founding date of this firm, leaders among Calcutta commodity brokers, does not seem to be known, but they were dealing with spices, indigo, shellac and jute, as well as tea, for some time before that 1861 auction. Generally speaking, the various auction centres are serviced by some or all of the established Calcutta brokers, with a few local specialists. Apart from Messrs Thomas, they include Carritt Moran and Contemporary Tea; Forbes Ewart & Figgis are important in Cochin.
10. For the removal of the London auctions from Plantation House, Mincing Lane, to Sir John Lyon House beside the Pool, see page 123.
11. David Wainwright, *Brooke Bond – a Hundred Years* (Brooke Bond Group, 1970).
12. Loose tea has, in fact, gained on packet during the past decade, mainly through the attraction of price. The current proportion is about one-third packet to two-thirds loose.
13. Griffiths, *History*, p. 127.
14. UNCTAD Secretariat, *The Marketing and Processing of Tea* (UNCTAD paper, 1982), para. 54 and Table 4. For the involvement in tea policy of the United Nations Conference of Trade and Development, see Chapter 16.
15. Argentina, inconspicuous up to 1983, came well into the picture in that year, and seemed likely to take the lead in 1984. But Pakistan may well have become overstocked with low-priced tea.

Chapter 3

1. Loolecondera is in Hewaweta District, just south of Kandy – a stony and discouraging environment, though it eventually became part of a big, well-found group under Anglo-Ceylon and General Estates.
2. Eden, *Tea*, p. 249.
3. Forrest, *A Hundred Years*, p. 249.
4. The understanding reached after prolonged negotiations is that India would accept 600,000 repatriated Tamils and Sri Lanka would grant citizenship to the remaining 400,000. But by the end of 1981, only about half of this programme had been completed. For resettlement in South India see page 28.
5. Forrest, *A Hundred Years*, Chapter 8.
6. A new system of incentives for estate staffs, including superintendents (or managers, as they are now usually called), was due for implementation in 1984.
7. An all-Sri Lanka estimate for 1983 was 179,289 tonnes and for 1984 208,058 tonnes, against 187,816 in 1982 and 210,148 in 1981. Out-turns of over 200,000 tonnes were of regular occurrence in the 1960s and 1970s.
8. Forrest, *A Hundred Years*, pp. 149–50.
9. Fortunately, the tea trade, its premises and stocks, escaped extensive damage or disruption

and this applied also to the estates, then and much later, in spite of their large work-force of Indian Tamils.

10. Forrest, *A Hundred Years*, p. 358.
11. A typical instance was in April 1983, when Iraq withdrew temporarily from the Colombo auctions. This was popularly associated with an unfavourable balance of payments; a large oil purchase agreement was then signed, and by mid-May the tea began to flow again.
12. For details see p. 166.
13. Ukers, *All About Tea*, Vol II, p. 11.
14. For an Uva Broken Orange Pekoe Fannings on 26 August 1980. It has been exceeded since.
15. The Centre was closed in 1984 for reconstruction and the offices were temporarily moved elsewhere.

Chapter 4

1. Edward Bramah, *Tea and Coffee* (London, Hutchinson, 1972), pp. 97–104.
2. *Ibid.*, p. 102.
3. *Ibid.*, p. 103.
4. Spellings are the latest official transliterations, with the previous spellings in brackets.
5. T. R. Tregear, *China: A Geographical Survey* (London, Hodder and Stoughton, 1980).
6. For a similar deal with Tunisia (but for Black tea) see page 162.
7. Chinese officials, recently visiting the West, admitted that their per hectare figures are still very low and giving cause for anxiety.
8. James Norwood Pratt, *Tea Lover's Treasury* (San Francisco, 101 Productions, 1982), p. 141.
9. *Ibid.*, p. 140.
10. *Ibid.*, p. 152.
11. More recently, mechanical devices have been used (see page 17–19).
12. The International Tea Promotion Association, *The Japanese Market for Black Tea* (a study furnished to the Commonwealth Secretariat, 1979).

Chapter 5

1. 'Spotlight on Producers: Indonesia', *International Tea Journal* (August 1983).
2. They had been nationalised some years after the Dutch, but were soon returned to their owners. British investors still have a modest stake.
3. R. L. S. Stone-Wegg, 'A Visit to the Malaysian Tea Plantations', *Finlay's Magazine* (Winter 1982), p. 2.
4. Ukers, *All About Tea*, Vol. II, pp. 452–54. Ukers gives a remarkably detailed account of both estate and smallholding tea production in Indo-China in the 1930s. He makes the interesting comment that the pioneer planters assumed, quite wrongly, that the climate of Tonkin would approximate to that of Java, but, in fact, the winter is severe and dry, with cold winds blowing in from North Asia.
5. Nevertheless, this area suffered from drought conditions in 1982.

Chapter 6

1. The situation up to 1969 is set out in admirable detail in *Tea Production in Africa*, 2nd edn (London, Wilson, Smithett & Co., 1969). A third edition is a great desideratum, but costs today would no doubt be daunting.
2. In the month of October 1983, with somewhat abnormal conditions beginning to prevail, the demand for the comparatively heavy amounts of Indian tea coming forward showed signs of pushing its price above the Kenyas. For the whole year, in fact, India obtained an average of 162.46p per kilogram, against Kenya's 148.03. Sri Lanka was also above Kenya. Comparative figures for 1984 were: India 286.84p, Kenya 271.70p, Sri Lanka 247.41p. Rwanda (see page 88) attained 274.09p.
3. Except perhaps in Indonesia, where the ancient system of tea smallholdings is being extensively modernised.
4. Drought conditions in 1984 do not seem to have inhibited production in the main estate areas, but some KTDA smallholders were hard hit.

5. P. D. C. Jayatunga and C. Ramanden, 'Tea in Kenya', *Journal of the National Institute of Plant Management*, vol. 1, no. 2 (1981).
6. The border was reopened in November 1983.
7. There was also for many years a single estate at Chombe, in the Nkhata Bay district of Northern Malawi, but a further one has recently been set out under the auspices of the government agency the ADMARC. First plantings were in January 1978; yields already 'exceed all expectations' and it is hoped gradually to increase the area under tea from 400 to 1,000 ha.
8. Some chests are containerised at Johannesburg *en route* and, in a recent development, many containers are now being 'stuffed' on the estates in Malawi itself. This route in turn became subject to congestion from heavy movements of other crops towards the end of 1983, with a consequent build-up of containers at Blantyre.
9. *Economic Times* (India, 14 October 1982).
10. Large quantities of Mozambique tea are consigned to Rotterdam, for subsequent trans-shipment to the United Kingdom, the United States and other destinations.
11. Tea is also to be found much further to the north-west in the Hoima and Bunyoro districts, not far from Lake Albert.
12. *Tea Production in Africa*, pp. 48–50.
13. For example, Kenya 1,295–1,905 mm (51–75 in.); Malawi 1,270–2,108 mm (50–83 in.); Mozambique 1,955–2,210 mm (77–87 in.).
14. There is believed to be a certain amount of smuggling into Nigeria from Central African territories.
15. To the tune of ECUs 3,048,000 – 50% of it in grants, 50% in loans. Recently the EDF emphasis has been on the latter.
16. *Tea Production in Africa*, p. 68.
17. The value of the rand at the time was US$0.97.
18. Leading brand names include Five Roses (Beckett & Co.) and Joko and Pitco (Lipton).
19. On 21 December of that year, a broker called George Townend rashly offered a parcel of Bush tea at the London Commercial Salerooms, and in spite of yells of protest from all sides, tried to obtain bids. None was forthcoming, and what the *Grocer* described as 'a monstrous bale of rubbish' was withdrawn. (See Forrest, *Tea for the British*, pp. 149–50).

Chapter 7

1. Quoted in Ukers, *All About Tea*, Vol. I, p. 206.
2. C. R. Harler, 'The Tea Industry in Iran,' *Tea and Rubber Mail* (8 September 1960), p. 7.
3. International Tea Promotion Association, *Tea in Chile* (a survey carried out by the United Nations Development Project in 1982).
4. Harler, *Culture and Marketing*, p. 41.
5. The 'Legg Cutter', adapted from tobacco processing, was a predecessor of CTC/LTP, but is in little use today.
6. International Tea Promotion Association, *Market Survey for Tea in Mexico* (survey sponsored by the Commonwealth Secretariat for ITPA, London, 1980).

Chapter 8

1. Tea Trade Committee (UK), *Annual Report* (1978), para. 94.
2. The advantages – and the snags – of factory door containerisation were well set out in 'Tea by Container', *Finlay's Magazine* (Winter 1983), p. 8. Other sources suggest that keeping the flow of tea and containers in balance remains a headache.
3. Set up in 1953 as a consultative body with every section of the trade represented. The name changed to the United Kingdom Tea Association in 1981. Eight sub-committees cover the whole spectrum of current topics, from shipping to minimum standards and the Association's records have been of the greatest value in the preparation of this book.
4. Less in the UK, where a tea chest may cost £2.50, against 75p for a sack.
5. One of the biggest US importers, who had pioneered the material, issued something of an ultimatum on this point in 1982.

Chapter 9

1. Forrest, *Tea for the British*, p. 198.
2. In a few countries, however, notably West Germany and Scandinavia, it has made a comeback in a new form – the 'pouch'.
3. Pratt, *Tea Lover's Treasury*, p. 168. Pratt pinpoints the year as 1944 and the firm as Messrs Bigelow, for the first experimental introduction.
4. The essential ingredient in the now proliferating Earl Grey blends is discussed in Chapter 10.
5. A partial exception is 'batch marking' with a maximum durability date. This is already insisted on in certain countries, for example, in the Middle East, but in Europe the EEC has accepted that tea is a 'long life' product with a durability of at least 18 months and should therefore be exempted.
6. For example, the dilution of genuine Black tea with ash and sloe leaves and the 'facing' of Green with such lethal substances as verdigris and Prussian Blue to improve its colour. See Forrest, *Tea for the British*, pp. 71–72, 130–31.
7. Ukers, *All About Tea*, Vol. II, p. 81.
8. UNCTAD, *Marketing and Processing* (using various surveys).
9. H. H. Godecaux, 'Tea Bag Usage and Tea Promotion', *International Tea Journal* (October 1982), pp. 8–9.
10. *Ibid.*, p. 9.
11. Most teabag machinery manufacturers tend to specialise; for example, the West German Constanta firm makes only string-and tag, the British Rose Foregrove and the Swiss Sig only heat-sealed. The Italian IMA, however, offers both.
12. Green leaf instant should be superior to black leaf in that the original leaf only has to be dried once. But there does not appear to be all that much difference in quality, which in the case of green leaf is subject to the local seasonal variations. Both hot-water and cold-water instants are produced in countries of origin.

Chapter 10

1. There had been auctions briefly at Garraway's Coffee House and then at an adjacent dancing academy. The London Commercial Salerooms were on the opposite side of Mincing Lane from Plantation House. The auctions were transferred to the latter in January 1937.
2. Reference books consulted by the 'Mastermind' team, though published in 1978, 1981 and 1982, had not been brought up to date in this respect. In addition to the trade, Sir John Lyon House accommodates such bodies as the Tea Brokers' Association, Tea Clearing House, Tea Council of the UK and International Tea Committee.
3. Forrest, *Tea for the British*, pp. 130–31.
4. Just as examples, Tetley sends out teabags to far-flung destinations from Eaglescliffe, Co. Durham; Brooke Bond packs at Redbourn, Hertfordshire and elsewhere; Twinings is located at Andover, Hampshire; and the Co-operative Wholesale Society has an ultra-modern installation at Crewe, Cheshire.
5. Forrest, *Tea for the British*, p. 258.
6. Involved with tea by a side wind, though being the Scottish port of entry for Indian and Bangladesh jute. Conversely, Swansea, exporting steel to the East, may periodically receive containers of tea as 'return loads'.
7. Before World War II, sales were spread over four days, Thursday being allotted to Javas and Sumatras, with occasional Chinas thrown in.
8. Including a drastic reduction in the 'prompt' period (see Chapter 8).
9. Forrest, *Tea for the British*. pp. 264–65.
10. See P. J. Banyard, *A History of the Tea Trade* (Thompson Lloyd & Ewart, 1981).
11. Buying brokers work on a commission of 0.5%; selling brokers on 1.25%, plus a sale charge of £7.50 per lot for teas catalogued for auction.
12. Forrest, *Tea for the British*, p. 235.
13. *Ibid.*, pp. 246–48.
14. Horse-drawn in the 'old days' and not completely mechanised until 1954. Ringtons even design and build their own electric vehicles and sell them through a subsidiary.
15. Tea is normally shipped from countries of origin on f.o.b. (free on board) terms – that is, with

the seller paying expenses only up to the point of loading; for re-exports, c.i.f. (costs, insurance, freight) terms are usual, with the seller responsible for all these charges up to the specified destination.
16. Meaningful comparisons between tea and coffee consumption can only be made on a cuppage basis. In these terms, tea, in spite of the ground it has lost, still leads coffee in a ratio of two and a half to one. British tea drinkers (over ten years of age) average close on four cups a day.

Chapter 11

1. Conspicuous in this type of business are companies like the international firm of van Rees, which also participates in import/re-export and in trans-shipment. Another is Vriesthee.
2. For a detailed survey of export and import duties on tea worldwide (a complex web indeed), see *ITC Annual Bulletin 1984*, pp. 114–22. Changes in duties are recorded in the *Monthly Statistical Summaries*.
3. 'On-going Tea Promotion Programmes: France', *International Tea Journal* (June 1982), pp. 24–25.
4. The conversion of youth still has some way to go, since it appears that French students conform closely to the national pattern in their beverage habits: 48% of a recent sample said that their usual drink at breakfast was coffee and 34% said 'other hot beverages' (milk, chocolate, etc.). Only 15% spoke up for tea.
5. International Tea Promotion Association.
6. Marshall, *World Coffee Trade*, p. 137.

Chapter 12

1. Ukers, *All About Tea*, Vol. I, p. 207.
2. Much of the information in the rest of this chapter is derived from a study, *Tea in the USSR*, made by Messrs J. Thomas, of Calcutta, in 1980.
3. Forrest, *A Hundred Years*, p. 206.
4. The other members of the East European bloc – East Germany, Hungary, Bulgaria, Romania – import only about 4,500 tonnes between them. Lipton, however, reports an increasing market for its teabags over the past decade in coffee-conscious Hungary.
5. See the excellent *Tea Promotion Survey of Poland* (United Nations Development Programme, for International Tea Promotion Association, October 1980).

Chapter 13

1. The source for some of the facts in this chapter is the International Tea Promotion Association, *West Asia Survey* (United Nations Development Programme, 1980).
2. International Tea Promotion Association, *Tea Promotion Survey: Selected Arab-speaking Markets in West Asia* (International Trade Centre/UNCTAD/GATT, August 1982).
3. International Tea Promotion Association, *Market Survey of Tea in Egypt* (International Trade Council/UNCTAD/GATT, 1981).
4. E. A. Weiss, 'Morocco Tea', *World Coffee and Tea* (January 1983).

Chapter 14

1. The surplus was estimated at no less than 21 million lb, largely because of the competition from smugglers. Ironically, this 'tea mountain' melted harmlessly away within a couple of years.
2. Under the Tea Act of 1897 (the oldest consumer-protection law on the US Statute Book) all teas entering the country are tested for purity and quality by examiners in New York and New Orleans, against standards set by the trade's own Board of Tea Experts.
3. The Association's 19 committees cover an impressive range. They include arbitration, armed forces, tea procurement, brewing, consumer affairs, food service, foreign affairs, substitute tea chests, tasting panel, tea acts, technical standards and traffic.
4. Pratt, *Tea Lover's Treasury*, pp. 195–96.

5. *Cost Benefit Study of Tea Promotion* (presented to the International Tea Promotion Association by the Commonwealth Secretariat, October 1981).
6. Gordon F. Reynolds, 'On-going Programmes: Canada', *International Tea Journal* (October 1982), pp. 10–12.
7. About 2,000 tonnes per annum. In 1982 only 611 tonnes of Green were imported, though this was well up on the previous year. The figure for 1983 was 443 tonnes.
8. *Cost Benefit Study of Tea Promotion in Canada* (Peat, Marwick, Mitchell, 1981).

Chapter 15

1. Since about 1977 the position had, in fact, been fairly stable; the 1981/82 figure quoted was almost identical with that for 1977/79.
2. Much earlier, exhibitions at Melbourne and Sydney had been the scene of the Ceylon planters' first essays in publicity (see Forrest, *A Hundred Years*, pp. 193, 199). So it was something of a throwback when in 1959–66, Ceylon tea centres were opened in the same two cities and in Brisbane.
3. Letter to the author from F. R. Hobman, agronomist at Southedge Research Station. The Department of Primary Industries has published an excellent monograph, *Tea in Queensland*, reprinted from the *Queensland Agricultural Journal* (September–October 1980).
4. Ukers, *All About Tea*, Vol. II, p. 353.

Chapter 16

1. In this chapter, the contemporary weights and measures and nomenclature have been retained.
2. The average price in world markets had fallen to the same level, in dollar terms, as it was in 1946. For 25 years, increasing production costs had been absorbed by the growers.
3. See *Parliamentary Report* (Hansard) (14 May 1975).
4. Further discussions held in October 1983 did, in fact, come close to agreement on quotas and it was hoped that the exporting countries would clinch these in time for a fourth preparatory meeting in March 1984, at which the framework for an International Tea Agreement would be formally considered with a view to action. But the price 'explosion' of 1983/84 put the whole timetable back and even a meeting on quotas alone, held in July 1984, reached no conclusions. The machinery for operating an Agreement was well set out in four UNCTAD papers (TD/B/IPC/TEA/AC/16–19) prepared for the October 1983 meetings.
5. This summary owes much to Godwin Roberts, 'World Trade in Tea and Minimum Standards', *International Tea Journal*, October 1982.
6. This was one of the recommendations of Dr R. T. Ellis, director of the Tea Research Foundation of Central Africa and tea adviser to UNCTAD.
7. The average cup of tea contains a little under a grain of caffeine. As the infusion is drunk, the caffeine is released gradually and there is no solid evidence that it does more than provide a mild and benignant stimulus to the central nervous system, particularly in combating fatigue.
8. See, for example, A. G. Davies, 'History Reviewed – the International Tea Agreement', *Tea and Coffee Trade Journal* (January 1982), p. 44.
9. Letter to the author from Ron Duncan, Chief of Commodities Studies and Projections Division, World Bank (23 November 1983).

Chapter 17

1. For an excellent digest of the *Cha' Ching* ('Tea Classic'), compiled with the help of the late Sir Dennison Ross, see Ukers, *All About Tea*, Vol. I, pp. 11–22.
2. The advertisement, by the Sultaness Head Coffee House, appeared in *Mercurius Politicus* (23–30 September 1658). Robert Garraway, or Garway, issued his broadsheet a little later. For the full story, see Forrest, *Tea for the British*, pp. 22–26.
3. *Marketing and Processing of Tea*, Table 35.
4. UK statement to the UNCTAD Permanent Sub-committee on Commodities (17–21 January 1983).
5. Samples from no fewer than 167 estates were on show – quite an organisational feat at such an early stage by the commissioner, J. L. Loudon-Shand.

6. Griffiths, *History*, p. 588.
7. In the interim there had been complete India–Ceylon co-operation in trying to get the UK tea duties abolished or reduced. Partial success was achieved (1905–06).
8. This body had been created in July 1932. It still exists as part of the Sri Lanka Tea Board, though with the word 'Promotion' substituted for 'Propaganda'.
9. All these tea councils are still in existence. There is also a council in Japan, but it is supported only by the distributors.
10. Reckoning from the UK Tea Council's foundation in 1964, though it did not take formal shape until 1965.
11. The origins of this fund go back to UNCTAD's fourth session (Nairobi, 1976) and the agreement to set it up dates from 1980. It was to consist of two accounts (or 'windows', in Geneva jargon), the first mainly to finance buffer stocks, the second to help with marketing and promotion. If all 163 states listed in the Agreement were to pay their contributions, the second account would have US$35 million at its disposal. But ratification was still not complete by 30 September 1983, to which the dateline had been extended.
12. Forrest, *Tea for the British*, p. 275.
13. Australia, Bahrain, Denmark, Egypt, Iraq, Jordan, Kuwait, Oman, Poland, Portugal, Qatar, Saudi Arabia, Sweden, the United Arab Emirates and Yugoslavia.

Chapter 18

1. Circulated 30 December 1982. Mr van de Meeberg was reflecting in particular on the problems arising when the pound is weak, from the fact that in many contexts tea is treated as a sterling commodity, whereas in its countries of origin auctions are conducted in local currency or (at Jakarta) in US dollars.
2. For the period January–August 1983, average prices were higher than 1982, by 41% in Calcutta, 39% in Cochin, 78% in Colombo, 54% in Chittagong, 32% in Mombasa, 31% in Limbe and 23% in London (FAO, *Tea, Current Situation*, November 1983). Later in the year London drew ahead. Taking 1983 as a whole, the average price of tea in Colombo almost exactly doubled betwen 11 January (Rs28.64) and 21 December (Rs58.67).
3. Tea Futures Study Group (formation sub-committee), *Report to the Tea Trade Committee* (December 1973).
4. Letter from Mr van de Meeburg to Mr M. Viby, of the Danish Tea Association (February 1983).
5. One of the most serious overheads of teabag production in Asia is the cost of imported filter papers. It has been estimated that a turnover of 74,000 tonnes is required to make the manufacture of such papers viable.
6. For a careful analysis of the economics of value-added tea, see R. C. Wanigatunga, 'The Packaging of Tea into Bags and the Manufacture of Instant Tea for Export in India and Sri Lanka', in *Case Studies on Industrial Processing of Primary Products* (Washington, World Bank and Commonwealth Secretariat, 1983), Vol. 2, pp. 217–90. Dr Wanigatunga clearly believes that in spite of all handicaps the producer countries have much to gain by pressing forward in this field.
7. In India, a combined loan and subsidy scheme for improved housing has been in operation during the past two decades. More recent rehousing schemes in Bangladesh, Sri Lanka and Indonesia have been mentioned in the text.

Sources

As earlier bibliographies have shown, there is no lack of historical material about tea, but remarkably little bearing on the contemporary trade has appeared in book form during the past ten years. The main written sources for the present work have therefore been the reports and newsletters of tea companies, research institutes, trade and planters' associations and government departments in many lands, together with the output (often very copious) of the various international organisations currently concerning themselves with tea.

For statistics, we have always been well served, not only by the comprehensive *Annual Bulletins* and *Monthly Summaries* of the International Tea Committee, but also by the contributions of individual firms, such as the *Tea Market Annual Reports* and *Tea Statistics* of Messrs J. Thomas of Calcutta and the *Ceylon Tea Reviews* of Messrs Forbes & Walker.

Among periodicals, the *Tea and Coffee Trade Journal* and *World Coffee and Tea* are both valuable, though because of their US origin, tea inevitably plays 'second fiddle'. A welcome newcomer in the spring of 1981 was the *International Tea Journal* (organ of the International Tea Promotion Association), with its thoughtful economic analyses and surveys of markets worldwide; unfortunately publication was suspended in 1985.

Indian periodicals include *Tea Today*, published by the Calcutta Tea Traders' Association, *Planters' Chronicle*, the long-established organ of the United Planters' Association of South India (UPASI), and *Cha-ke-Bat*.

Printed works which have been consulted include:
Antobus H. A., *History of the Assam Company* (London, 1957).
Banyard, P. J., *A History of the Tea Trade* (London, 1981).
Bramah, Edward, *Tea and Coffee* (London, 1972).

Case Studies on Industrial Processing of Primary Products (Washington, World Bank and Commonwealth Secretariat, 1983).

Eden, T., *Tea* (London, 1958).

Forrest, Denys, *A Hundred Years of Ceylon Tea* (London, 1967).
                    Tea for the British (London, 1973).

Griffiths, Sir Percival, *History of the Indian Tea Industry* (London, 1967).

Growth and Potential for Indian Tea (Economic and Scientific Research Association of India, 1983).

Hardy, Serena, *The Tea Book* (Weybridge, England, 1979).

Harler, C. R., *Culture and Marketing of Tea* (Oxford, 1984).

Marshall, C. F., *The World Coffee Trade* (Cambridge, 1983).

Pratt, J. N., *The Tea Lover's Treasury* (San Francisco, 1982).

Tregear, T. R., *China: A Geographical Survey* (London, 1980).

Ukers, W. H., *All About Tea* (New York, 1935).

Wilson, Smithett & Co., *Tea Production in Africa* (London, 1969).

Woodward, N. H., *Teas of the World* (New York, 1980).

Index